FIQH us-SUNNAH

at-Tahara and as-Salah

Muhammad Sa'eed Dabas
Jamal al-Din M. Zarabozo
(Translators)

American Trust Publications
721 Enterprise Drive
Oak Brook, IL 60523

© American Trust Publications 1405/1985
Makatabat al-Khadamat-e al-Hadithah, P.O. Box 720, Jeddah,
Saudi Arabia

American Trust Publications
721 Enterprise Drive
Oak Brook, IL 60523

Phone: (630) 789-9191
Fax: (630) 789-9455

First Published 1985
Reprinted 1989, 1990, 1994, 2012

Library of Congress cataloging in publication data
A catalog record for this book is available from the
Library of Congress

ISBN 0-89259-060-2

Printed in the United States of America

فَلَا وَرَبِّكَ لَا يُؤْمِنُونَ حَتَّىٰ يُحَكِّمُوكَ
فِيمَا شَجَرَ بَيْنَهُمْ ثُمَّ لَا يَجِدُواْ
فِى أَنفُسِهِمْ حَرَجًا مِّمَّا قَضَيْتَ وَيُسَلِّمُواْ تَسْلِيمًا .

But no, by your Lord!
They do not really believe
unless they make you
(O Prophet) a judge
of all on which they disagree
among themselves,
and then find in their hearts
no bar to an acceptance
of your decision
and give themselves up to it
in utter self-surrender (an-Nisa' 4:65).

ACKNOWLEDGMENTS

This work has many debts. First, to the family of as-Sayyid Sabiq, who bore with us for bringing the English edition so late; second, to Maktabat al-Khadamat-e al-Hadithah, *Fiqh us-Sunnah's* publishers, for their support and understanding; third, to Kamal al-Shaarawy and 'Atif Ibrahim of NAIT for their enthusiasm and help; and last but not least, to our translators Muhammad Sa'eed Dabas and Jamal al-Din M. Zarabozo (his associates Muhammad, Bashir, Fawzi, Jamal, Farage, Mustafa and Taha) who worked hard like *mujahideen* and helped us beat the deadline. To all of them, we are grateful. The reward is only with Allah the Magnificent.

CONTENTS

FROM THE PUBLISHERS OF
THE ENGLISH EDITION

With the publication of *Fiqh us-Sunnah* Volume 1 (*at-Taharah* and *as-Salah*), a process started four years ago has come to a successful culmination.

In all, we will be publishing 12 volumes.

Fiqh us-Sunnah, though the simplest in fiqh literature, is still not the easiest to translate. Fiqh content aside, Arabic diction is very different from that of Aryan languages. Translating into English is like putting the Arabic soul into Anglo-Saxon body. This is why, despite the good work done by our translators Muhammad Sa'eed Dabas and Jamal Zarabozo, and the editorial manipulation of the English language by our editors, we cannot claim that it is a literal translation or that the work is free from any problem.

Besides, Sabiq's style can easily lead a translator into a problem of a serious nature if he resorts to literal translation. For instance, page 67 of the original says:

وحرمتها متفق عليها بين الأئمة ولم يخالف فى ذلك أحد من الصحابة وجوز داود ابن حزم ...

The translators rendered it into English in the following way:

"The companions were all agreed that it is forbidden to touch or carry the Qur'an while one is in the state of impurity. Among the jurists, only Dawud Ibn Hazm allows the physically unclean person, whether because of sex or menstruation, to touch or carry the Qur'an and they see nothing wrong with this."

This translation, as pointed out by one of the members of our Editorial Board, had two problems:

> First, Dawud Ibn Hazm is not one person but two persons, that is, Dawud and Ibn Hazm.
> Second, there are also other jurists who hold the same position as that of Dawud and Ibn Hazm.

The validity of these objections notwithstanding, the text shows Dawud and Ibn Hazm as one person because there is no punctuation nor a conjunction such as 'and,' even though Br. Jamal Zarabozo, one of our translators, had corrected this problem in his footnote to the text.

Second, the text does not allow a construction other than: " Among the jurists, only Dawud Ibn Hazm allows the physically unclean person to touch or carry the Qur'an..." The member of our Editorial Board could point to a factual position because he knew the opinion of other jurists on the subjuect. Nevertheless, the fact remains that this was a case of extrapolation – reading into the text something which was not there, even though it would be correct to say that Dawud and Ibn Hazm are not the only one with their opinion.

In *fiqh* works of this nature, any claim to infallibility will be, therefore, sheer insanity. However, we can say with *some* confidence that in its present form, it is a very readable work, with an unencumbered narrative flow. This is a very important aspect of this work because, in our view, no matter how sound technically a translation may be, it serves no purpose if its contents remain elusive to the reader. Elusiveness or being abstruse may be an asset to philosophy but not to a living faith like Islam, which meant to be conveyed and understood.

In transliteration, we have kept the Arabic words and terminology free from the cumbersome use of symbols and diacritical marks. This does not mean that we have failed to distinguish between the Arabic consonants *'ayn* (') and *hamzah* ('). To us, differentiation between velarized and non-velarized consonants and long from short vowels may be important in correct pronunciation and meaning of a word but not very helpful to non-Arabic speaking readers who need more than such symbols to understand and pronounce the Arabic words correctly.

Besides, such an exercise may be important to an academic's ego, but it certainly mars the text.

As to the selection of *Fiqh us-Sunnah* for translation, we may say that the present schismatic differences among the Muslims call for a book which, in its approach toward *fiqh* issues, could go to the main sources of Islam, the Qur'an and *Sunnah* and help one find out how different interpretations can be made from the same source of information. At the same time, such an approach may help one examine the *fiqh* position of his *madhhab* to see if it is grounded in the Qur'an or *sunnah*, or just a practice without a proof from the *shari'ah*. Viewed as such, this work should encourage more tolerant *fiqhi* attitude among the four schools of *fiqh* rather than enhance their prevalent divide. The work has, however, some limitations, which are more of a juristic nature than of anything else. If Sayyid Sabiq had tried to overcome them, perhaps his work would have changed its nature, that is, it would have turned into a more complex presentation.

At least at three places in this volume, he leaves an average reader confused:

√ Loosing one's ablution on touching one's private parts;

√ Loosing one's ablution on eating camel meat; and

√ The obligatory nature of Jumu'ah's *ghusl*.

He quotes authentic *hadith* for the issues under reference, but the *hadith* in their contents are contradictory and may leave the reader guessing about the issue and the import of *hadith* itself. For instance, on loosing one's ablution on eating camel meat, he says, "That this does not nullify the ablution, was the opinion of the four rightly-guided caliphs, the companions and the following generation, although there is an authentic *hadith* that states one should make ablution after it" (p.38).

Three serious objections can be raised to it:

√ First, it gives the impression as if the rightly-guided caliphs, the companions and the following generation did not care for the saying of the Prophet, upon whom be peace.

√ Second, the statement is incorrect because the caliphs and the companions could not have gone against the saying of the Prophet. The companions were the best followers of Allah and His Messenger and such a conclusion will be contrary to their character and therefore not logical.

√ Third, if that is the case, then what is the truth? Is

there a problem with the criterion of the *muhaddathin* that the *hadith* is graded as *sahih,* its subject matter notwithstanding.

Any such implication is of a serious nature, but Sabiq would gloss over it without resolving the issue. This, however, does not belittle his work which remains peerless — yet to be surpassed in its scope, clarity, and sincerity.

What is Fiqh

Ibn Khaldun in his *Muqaddamah* reckons two kinds of sciences: Rational or ones which have been generated by our (human) intellect; and revelational, received through *wahy* and transmitted as such from the Prophet, upon whom be peace, to his contemporaries and to later generations. The latter kind of knowledge *('ilm)* excludes the use of intellect as far as its reception, reporting, and transmission are concerned. This relates to injunctions of fundamental import *(usul).* However, when it comes to injunctions of secondary import, which are derived from *usul,* it calls into play one's intellect and ability to exercise analogical reasoning. The *fiqh* falls into this category.

The *fiqh,* in general, is a product of later generations. The companions (sahabah) did not need its formulation into a new branch of knowledge because the law-giver (the Prophet, upon whom be peace) was still among them, their linguistic abilities were unsurpassed and those who narrated *hadith* were alive. Checking and cross-checking of a report was therefore not much of a problem. But the Madini society was not a fossilized society: it was an ever-expanding society, with new situations demanding exercise of one's mind as to the application of the revelational injunctions and the Prophet's commandments to them. In fact, one *may* say that the Prophet himself was the founder of *fiqh.* When he sent Mu'adh ibn Jabal to Yemen he asked him a few questions as to the resolution of issues in the light of the *shari'ah.* Mu'adh's response was that first he would look into the Qur'an; second, he would look into the sunnah; and third, if he didn't find anything in these two, he would exercise his judgement. The Prophet, upon whom be peace, is reported to have been pleased with his three-step approach and supplicated for him. Mu'adh's reply, in a way, provided the paradigm for the *fiqh* which later saw its formulation upon it. But how one can have two different opinions on an injunction and still be right is evident from the following incident:

When the Prophet, upon whom be peace, sent an expedition to punish Banu Quraizah for their infraction of the agreement with him, he instructed them as under:

> Those of you who believe in Allah and the Day Hereafter they should offer *salat al-'Asr* after reaching Banu Quraizah.

While still on their way to Banu Quraizah the time for '*asr* fell. Some companions offered '*asr* during their ride to their destination, while others offered it late after reaching Banu Quraizah. The first group thought that the Prophet's intention was to make them reach the place in the shortest possible time; the second group thought that they were expressly told not to offer '*asr* on the way to the place of conflict. The issue was brought to the Prophet's attention and he ruled both of them right in their execution of his commandment. The reason was that the first group reflected on the intention of the Prophet's commandment, while the second group took it literally. These kind of divergent positions are always possible and cannot be avoided. What can be avoided, as the companions did, is the alignments along the *fiqhi* divide to the deteriment of Muslim unity. One can hold a different *fiqhi* point of view and yet not create a sect out of it, or turn it into an issue of life and death, or of faith and disbelief *(kufr)*. According to the Qur'an, this will be the negation of Islam:

> And do not be like those who separated and disputed after the clear proofs had come to them. For such, there is an awful doom (*āl-'Imran 105*).

M. Tariq Quraishi
Plainfield, Indiana.
Rab'i al-Awwal 5, 1406

PREFACE TO THE ARABIC EDITION

Praise be to Allah, the Lord of the Worlds. Blessings and peace be upon our leader Muhammad, his family, his companions, and those who follow his guidance until the day of judgement.

This book deals with the *fiqh* questions and provides supporting evidence to them from the clear Book (of Allah), the authentic *sunnah* of the Prophet, upon whom be peace, and what this *ummah* has agreed upon.

In dealing with the subject, I have recorded what is basic, to the point, and what a Muslim is supposed to know. I have kept myself away from controversial points except where differences are permissible. I have referred to the varying opinions among the scholars. I say with confidence that I have presented the authentic *fiqh* which Allah has sent the Prophet with. At the same time, I have tried to make it easier for the people to understand and to bring them together upon the Book and the *sunnah*. I have avoided the differences and the wrong practice of blindly sticking to one school of thought. I have also desisted from following the nonsensical statement that the door to *ijtihad* is closed.

And by doing so, I had only the desire to serve our faith and to benefit our brothers. I ask Allah to make this work beneficial for the Muslims, and make our deeds solely for His pleasure. He is sufficient for us and the best Guardian.

as-Sayyid Sabiq

SAYYID SABIQ'S INTRODUCTION

The Message of Islam and its Universality and Purpose

Allah sent Muhammad, upon whom be peace, with the true way of worship of Allah and the complete code of law which provides mankind with the most honorable life and takes them to the highest degree a human being can attain.

In a period of about twenty-three years, the Prophet, upon whom be peace, completed his mission of inviting people to Allah and preaching His religion and gathering people into its fold.

The Universality of the Message

Islam was not meant for a certain time or a certain generation or a certain people; in fact, it was a message for all of mankind for all time. Says Allah in the Qur'an, "Blessed is He who has revealed to His slave the Criterion (of right and wrong), that he may be a warner to all of the peoples" *(al-Furqan: 1)*. He also said, "And We have not sent you (O Muhammad) save as a bringer of good tidings and a warner to all mankind; but most of mankind knows not" *(Saba': 28)*. And, "Say (O Muhammad): O mankind, Lo! I am the messenger of Allah to you all (the messenger of) Him unto whom belongs the Sovereignty of the heavens and the earth. There is no God save Him. He qives life and He gives death. So believe in Allah and His Messenger, the Prophet who can neither read nor write, who believes in Allah and in His words and follow him that haply, you may be led aright" *(al-A'raf: 158)*. In an authentic *hadith*, the Prophet, upon whom be peace, said, "Every Prophet was sent only to his people, but I have been sent to every 'red' and 'black' human" (i.e., to all of humanity).

That this message is universal can be illustrated by the following:

1) There is nothing difficult in this religion for any person to believe or act upon. Says Allah in the Qur'an, "Allah does not burden a soul beyond what it can bear... Also, Allah desires ease for you, and He does not desire hardship for you" *(al-Baqarah: 286, 185).* And, "He has not laid upon you any hardship in religion" *(al-Hajj: 78).* In *Sahih al-Bukhari,* it is recorded from Abu Sa'eed al-Muqbiri that the Messenger of Allah, upon whom be peace, said, "This religion is easy. If anyone tries to make this religion difficult (upon himself), then it will overcome him." In *Sahih Muslim,* a *hadith* says: "The most beloved religion in the sight of Allah is the pure and tolerant worship of Allah."[1]

2) Those aspects that are eternal regardless of time or place, for example, matters of belief and worship, have been thoroughly explained in clear texts that encompass every aspect. No one can add or delete anything from them. Those aspects that are subject to change due to time or place, for example, affairs related to politics or war, and so on, have been explained with general guidelines useful for mankind in every age. These guidelines are to be used by national leaders to establish truth and justice in their lands regardless of time or location.

3) The teachings of this religion aim at preserving faith, life, intellect, procreations, and legitimate earnings. These goals are definitely in harmony with the nature of mankind, easy for one to accept, and fit for every time, and place. Says Allah in the Qur'an, "Say: (O Muhammad) Who has forbidden the adornment of Allah which He has brought forth for His bondmen, and the good things of His providing? Say: Such, on the Day of Resurrection, will be only for those who believed during the life of the world. Thus, do We detail Our revelations for people who have knowledge. Say: My Lord forbids only indecencies which are apparent and falls under sin and wrongful oppression, and that you associate with Allah that for which no warrant has been revealed and that you tell concerning Allah that which you know not" *(al-A'raf: 156-157).* He also says, "My Mercy embraces all things; therefore, I shall ordain it for those who ward off (evil) and pay the *zakah,* and those who believe in our revelations, and those who follow the messenger, the Prophet who can neither read nor write, whom they will find described in the Torah and the Gospel (which are) with them. He will enjoin on them that which is right and forbid them from doing that which is wrong.

He will make lawful for them all good things and prohibit for them only the foul; he will relieve them of their burdens and the fetters that they used to wear. Then those who believe in him, honor him, help him, and follow the light which is sent down with him: they are the successful" *(al-A'raf: 156-157).*

The Goal of the Message

Islam seeks to purify the souls through the recognition of Allah and His worship and to reinforce the ties of mankind and to establish them on the basis of love, mercy, brotherhood, equality and justice. This will bring happiness to mankind in both this life and the Hereafter. Says Allah in the Qur'an, "He it is Who has sent among the unlettered ones a messenger of their own, to recite unto them His revelations and to make them grow, and to teach them the Scripture and Wisdom, though before they were indeed in manifest error" *(al-Jumu'ah: 2).* Allah also says, "We sent you not (O Muhammad) but as a mercy for mankind" *(al-Anbiya': 107).* In a *hadith* the Prophet, upon whom be peace, says, "I am a merciful guide."

The *Shari'ah* of Islam Or *Fiqh*

The *shari'ah* is the most important aspects of Islam; it is the practical aspect of this message.

But genuine laws, such as those related to worship, can only be a revelation from Allah to His Prophet, upon whom be peace, that is from the Qur'an or the *sunnah.* Needless to say, the Prophet, upon whom be peace, did not go beyond conveying and explaining the message. Says Allah concerning him, "Your companions (i.e., Muhammad) errs not, nor is he deceived, nor does he speak of (his own) desire. It is nothing but a revelation that is revealed to him" *(al-Najm).*

There are some general principles that Islam lays down which the Muslims are expected to follow. These are:

1) It is not allowed to speculate about events that have not happened until they actually occur. Says Allah in the Qur'an, "O you who believe! Ask not of things which, if they were made known to you, would trouble you; but if you ask of them when the Qur'an is being revealed, they will be made known to you. Allah pardons this, for Allah is Forgiving, Clement" *(al-Ma'idah: 101).* There is a *hadith* in which the Prophet, upon whom be peace, prohibited the discussion of events that have not yet occurred.

2) One should avoid asking too many questions which lead to speculation. A *hadith* says, "Verily Allah dislikes vain talk, asking

too many questions, and wasting wealth." The Prophet also stated, "Allah has made certain things obligatory, so do not cause them to be lost. He has fixed certain limits, so do not transgress them. And He, without being forgetful, has been silent about certain things as a mercy, so do not search into them." He also said, "The person who has the greatest sin is one who asked about something that was not forbidden, and that thing was made forbidden due to his questions."

3) One should avoid creating differences, splits or sects within Islam. Says Allah in the Qur'an, "And lo! This nation of Yours is one nation and I am your Lord, so keep your duty to Me *(al-Mu'minun: 52)*... And hold fast, all of you together, to the cable of Allah, and do not separate *(al-'Imran: 103)*... And do not dispute with each other lest you should falter *(al-Anfal: 46)*... Lo! As for those who sunder their religion and become schismatics *(al-An'am: 159)*... Of those who split up their religion and became schismatics, each sect exulting in its tenets *(ar-Rum: 32)* and Be not as those who separated and disputed after the clear proofs had come unto them. For such there is an awful doom" *(al-'Imran: 105)*.

4) Any disputed issue is to be referred to the Qur'an and the *sunnah*. This is in accordance with Allah's words, "And if you have a dispute in any matter, refer it to Allah and the Messenger if you are (in truth) believers in Allah and the Last Day *(an-Nisa': 54)*... And in whatever you differ, the verdict therein belongs to Allah" *(ash-Shura: 100)*. This is because the religion has been explained in the Book. Says Allah, "And We reveal the Scripture to you as an exposition of all things *(an-Nahl: 89)*... and We have neglected nothing in the Book" *(al-An'am: 38)*.

The *sunnah* explains how the Book is to be applied. Says Allah, "And We have revealed to you the Remembrance that you may explain to mankind that which has been revealed to them *(an-Nahl: 44)*... and, Lo! We reveal to you the Scripture with the truth, that you may judge between mankind by that which Allah shows you" *(an-Nisa': 105)*. The injunctions were completed and the teachings were made clear. Thus says Allah, "This day have I perfected your religion for you and completed My favor to you and have chosen Islam for you as religion" *(al-Ma'idah: 3)*.

As such, there is no need for any differences. Says Allah in the Qur'an, "Lo! Those who find (a cause of) disagreement in the Scripture are in open schism *(al-Baqarah: 176)*... But no, by you Lord, they will not believe (in truth) until they make you adjudicate between them and find themselves in agreement with what you have decided, and submit with full submission" *(an-Nisa': 66)*.

The companions and those who followed them in the early pious generations followed the preceding principles. They did not differ among themselves save in a few questions, primarly because some of them had a better understanding of some verses or *hadith* than the others.

When the founding *imams* of the four legal schools appeared, they followed the same way as the people before them, except that some of them were closer to the *sunnah*, such as those in the Hejaz, because of their familiarity with a large number of *hadith* and reports from the earlier generations. Others were more familiar with juristic reasoning, such as those in Iraq, who did not have access to as many *hadith* as the others.

These scholars did their best to teach the people their religion and offer them proper guidance, but they forbade people from following them blindly and told them, "It is not allowed for anyone to say what we have said without knowing the evidence for our position." They made it clear that their school of thought was whatever the authentic *hadith* stated. They did not have the intention of having the people follow them like they should follow the Prophet Muhammad, upon whom be peace, who was protected from sin or mistake by Allah. All of them just intended to aid the people in understanding the commands of Allah.

But the people after them exaggerated their importance and began to follow them more and more blindly. Every group thought it sufficient just to follow what was found in their school of thought and to strictly adhere to it. They put the statements of their *imam* on the same level as that of the *shari'ah*. They went to such an extreme in their trust of their *imam* that al-Karkhi ventured as far as to say, "Every verse or *hadith* that differs from what the people of our school of thought follow either has a non-obvious explanation or it is abrogated."

This blind observance of one *madhhab* caused the Muslim nation to lose the guidance of the Qur'an and the *sunnah*. The door to juristic reasoning was closed. The *shari'ah* became the statement of the jurists, and the statement of the jurists became the *shari'ah*. Anyone who differed from what they said was regarded as an innovator, whose words were neither to be trusted nor followed.

What deteriorated the situation further was the attitude of the rulers and wealthy who supported the institutes of learning. They limited themselves to one *madhhab* or to certain *madhhabs* only. This was one of the reason why certain *madhhabs* were accepted at the expense of others, and why people turned away from independent juristic reasoning. In this way, they protected their wages and sustenance. Abu Zar'ah asked his teacher al-Balqeeni, "Why doesn't shaikh Taqiyyudin as-Subki exercise juristic reasoning *(ijtihad)* when he is qualified to do so?" Al-Balqeeni had no response. Said Abu Zar'ah, "As far as I can see, there is nothing to keep him from doing so except jobs and positions, that are available to jurists of the four *madhhabs*, for such jobs are not available to those who depart (from the four *madhhabs*). They are not allowed to become judges, and people are discouraged from following their rulings by accusing them of innovations." Al-Balqeeni agreed with his opinion.

By blindly following the *madhhabs* and losing the guidance of the Qur'an and *sunnah* and by closing the door to juristic reasoning *(ijtihad)*, this nation lost its unity and entered into the den of the lizard, which the Messenger of Allah, upon whom be peace, had warned it about.

As a result, the Muslim nation broke into different groups and sects to such an extent that they differed over whether or not it was permissible for a follower of the Hanafi *madhhab* to marry a woman of the Shafi *madhhab*. Some said that such a marriage would not be valid because the Shafi woman's faith was in doubt.* Others said that such a marriage is valid by analogy to marriage with the "people of the book."** Other effects were: the spreading of innovations, the loss of the *sunnah's* teachings, a decay in intellectual thought, and reasoning, and so on. This led to the weakening of the nation's integrity. They lost the purposeful life and hense progress and growth. With cracks inside, the outsiders were able to strike at the core of Islam.

Generations passed; and in every period, Allah would raise some-one to renew His religion and guide His people. But whenever Muslims awoke, they would remain so only for a short while, for they would soon return to their previous state of existence or to something even worse.!

Finally, the implementing of the *shari'ah*, by which Allah guides mankind, had reached a stage never reached before. Learning it was tantamount to ruining one's intellect and thus a waste of time. This kind of attitude was of no benefit to Islam or to the life of the Muslims.

We can give an example from one of the later jurists. Ibn 'Arafah defined rent as, "...dealing in what can be exchanged, save ships or animals, but does not include what can be distinguished from it, but the parts of it are considered parts of the whole." One of his students responded to him by saying that the inclusion of the word "parts" was redundant and not necessary. The teacher thought about it for two days and then he gave him a reply, which is not worth due to its useless content*.

The scholars, oblivious of the changes around them, kept themselves occupied with the texts, commentaries, debates and discussions until Europe triumphed over the East. Muslims were shaken; they woke up to find themselves facing a new world. Astonished and amazed by what they saw, they began to reject their history, disrespect their forefathers and forget their religion. They followed Europe in its good as well as harmful aspects, in its beliefs and disbeliefs. Those who were ignorant took a negative attitude. They equated the *shari'ah* with decadence rather than progress. Europeanization ruled every aspect of life; the ties with the past were severed. Yet the earth is never void of a proof from Allah. The calls to Islam appeared harking people back to their roots. They warned them that the evil way of the West could only have an evil result, that they were not following the true faith, and that they should follow the best example available, that of the Prophet. Soon, their sciences would lead the West to destruction, and they would face the final judgement. "Do you not consider how your Lord dealt with the people of 'Aad? With many-columned Iram, the like of which was not created in the lands; and with the people of Thamud, who clove the rocks in the valley; and with Pharoah, firm of might, who (all) were rebellious (to Allah) in their lands and multiplied iniquity therein? Therefore, the Lord poured on them the disaster of His punishment. Lo! the Lord is ever watchful" (*al-Fajr: 6-14*).

And the callers called the people back to the guidance of the Qur'an and *sunnah*, and challenged them to take their religion from these sources and spread this religion to others. By that, they will achieve the liberated life, and they will become truly happy. "Verily, in the Messenger of Allah you have a good example for him who looks unto Allah and the Last Day" (*al-Ahzab: 21*).

It is by the blessing of Allah that pious people responded to this call, and that hearts became pure. The youth embraced this religion, and they used their wealth and energies to revive it.

Would Allah permit light to spread over this world again? Does He desire for man a beautiful life full of faith, love, goodness, and justice? This is what the verses bear witness to: "He it is Who has sent His Messenger with the guidance and the religion of truth, that He may (use it to prevail) over all religions. And Allah suffices as a witness *(al-Fath: 28)*... We shall show them Our portents on the horizons and within themselves until it will be manifest unto them that it is the truth. Does not your Lord suffice, since He is witness over all things?" (*Fussalat: 53*).

REVIEWER'S NOTE

It was a privilege for me, among many others, to have had the opportunity to study with the author of *Fiqh us-Sunnah*, our Shaykh Sayyid Sabiq. The call to review this English translation immediately brought to my mind fond and special memories going back nearly two decades when I cosely witnessed the author completing the final volumes and discussed with him the background and circumstances that originally led to the emergence of this important work. I believe sharing some of this information, along with comments about the work and its translation, will be helpful to our readers.

In the 1940s, when the modern Islamic movement in Egypt was approaching its zenith, a new breed of Muslims emerged, shedding their fears, and yearning to understand Islam and enjoy living it as their way of life. Hassan al-Banna, who ignited the movement, was fully aware of a major obstacle preventing this understanding of Islam – blind, rigid adherence and unqualified allegiance to different juristic schools, a growing phenomenon that gained prevalence throughout the Muslim world in the later centuries. It was exactly for this reason that Hassan al-Banna summonded his brilliant student and associate, Shaykh Sabiq, to introduce *fiqh* through a new approach aiming to mirror the model performance of the Prophet, peace and blessings of Allah be upon him, and treating *fiqhi* opinions of our great imams, especially Abu Hanifah, Malik, ash-Shaf'i and Ibn Hanbal, in a light that does not dramatize their differences nor overlook them. The choice of the title *Fiqh us-Sunnah* instead of *Fiqh al-Madhahib* illustrates the spirit of that approach which runs through the entire work. Moreover, the author relied on many of the great comparative *fiqhi* works, such as, Ibn al-Qayam's *Zad al-M'ad*, Shaukani's *Nayl al-Awtar, al-Durar al-Bahiyah* and *al-Sayl al-Jarar*, Ibn Rushd's masterpiece *Bidayat al-Mujtahid*, Ibn Qudamah's *al-Mughni*, and San'ani's *Subul as-Salam.*

However, as a pioneer effort to facilitate fair and easy access to diverse opinions of the *fiqhi* schools, *Fiqh us-Sunnah* is not immune from problems. Introducing conflicting opinions without reasonable analysis or explication is one example.

Before going further, it should be noted that although diverse *fiqhi* opinions may create confusion in some minds, they reflect the accomodating nature of *fiqh*. After all, *fiqhi* opinions are not mere mind games of scholars but are viable and equally acceptable options, meeting the demands of a perpetually changing world.

The term *fiqh* is derived from the root word *faqiha* which means to understand. In its technical usage, it stands for the science of Islamic jurisprudence. However, *fiqh's* root meanings are not at all divorced from its technical sense. Doesn't it require comprehensive knowledge and understanding to master the *fiqh* (laws) that govern and regulate all aspects of public private, business, social and spiritual concerns of the Muslim ummah? Finally, Islamic jurisprudence has as its primary function the necessary task of reaching an understanding *(fiqh)* of the *shari'ah*, the whole of Islamic life, completely in the light of the original source of our laws, the revelation from Allah the exalted.

In an attempt to facilitate maximum benefit from this translation, a summary of the factors that results in diverse *fiqhi* positions will be helpful.

1) The nature of the Arabic language may allow more than one and sometimes opposite meanings of the same word. For example: *As asa* may mean to advance or to retreat (see Surah *at-Takwir: 17*). The word *mahid* may mean the period of a woman's menstruation or the actual body region where menses occurs.

Abu Hanifah, Malik and a good number of other jurists accept the first interpretation and hold that it is forbidden for a man to sexually approach his wife (except for what has been allowed in *hadith*) during menstruation. Ash-Shaf'i and the Zahiri jurists hold that *mahid* means the area of the body where menses occurs. Therefore, they forbid only sexual intercourse during the menstruation period.

This difference pivots on the two meanings that the term *mahid* takes. This is indicative of the Arabic language to a certain degree.

2) *Fuqaha'* differ on their approaches toward the sources of *fiqh*, namely the Qur'an, Sunnah, *Ijma'* and *Qiyas*. The Zahiris, for example, do not regard *qiyas* (analogical reasoning) as a source of law. Other schools which regard *qiyas* as a source accept rulings and judgments based on *qiyas* which may lead, therefore, to different conclusions than that of the Zahiris.

3) The Qur'an, being the first source of law is well-known to all legists, especially those verses which directly treat *fiqhi* aspects. The situation, however, is different with *hadith*. Some *fuqaha'* suspect the authenticity of some particular *hadith* or are not aware of them, which obviously lead to different *fiqhi* conclusions.

4) Apparent conflicts between proofs *(adilla)* also lead to different rulings. For example, the Prophet, upon whom be peace, said whoever touches his genital needs to make *wudhu*. In another *hadith* the Prophet, upon whom be peace, was asked about this touching, and he said it is like touching any other part of the body. Now, Imam Ahmad, ash-Shaf'i and others are of the opinion that the first *hadith* abrogates the second; therefore, touching the genital does not break one's ablution. On the other hand, Abu Hanifah regards the first *hadith* to be authentic and rules that ablution is required after touching.

5) In a constantly evolving world, the arrival of new occurences requiring rulings which are not directly specified in the Qur'an and Sunnah is imminent. With these circumstances, it should not be surprising that today's *fuqaha'* will differ on some issues, such as economic and sociological concerns, and so on.

Regardless of the reasons that lead to diverse *fiqhi* opinions, the differences themselves should not be looked upon as being inherently evil; on the contrary, they can be a great help in learning as well as guarding us from the unyielding rigidity that has stunted the growth and the contribution of the Muslim Ummah in recent times. Reading this book will perhaps give you a feel of this fresh spirit.

As for the translation, it is never easy to translate from one language to another, especially an Arabic work on *fiqh* into English. The work of the translators was a high-spirited and gallant one and is to be appreciated and respected. Muhammad Sa'eed Dabas, with his training in the Arabic language and literature, was neatly complemented by Jamal Zarabozo's native feel for English. However, the *fiqhi* terms and style are in some need of standardization and overall tightening. American Trust Publication should be congratulated for its pioneer effort to provide English readers access to this unique *fiqhi* work.

Finally, we would like to caution that reading this book will introduce the reader to *fiqh* and its related issues, but it will not make any one a *faqih*. This certainly is the function of our future institutions to train eager North American young men and women and interested elders in Arabic, the sciences of the Qur'an, Sunnah, *Usul*, the development of Islamic jurisprudence, and so on. Until then, we will have to depend on our scholars in the East who are not exposed to contemporary challenges of North America.

Ahmad Zaki Hammad

PURIFICATION (AT-TAHARAH)

The *shari'ah* has divided water into four kinds: (a) *mutlaq* water, (b) used water (for purification), (c) water mixed with pure elements and (d) water mixed with impure elements. We shall discuss each of them separately.

Mutlaq Water

This kind of water is considered pure because of its inherent purity and as such, it can be used by an individual to purify him or herself. It consists of the following categories:

(i) Rain water, snow and hail. These substances are pure because Allah says so: "And sent down water from the sky upon you, that thereby He might purify you..." *(al-Anfal: 1)*, and "We send down purifying water from the sky" *(al-Furqan: 48)*. This is also supported by the following *hadith:* Abu Hurairah reported that the Messenger of Allah, upon whom be peace, used to be silent between the (opening) *takbir* of the prayer and the verbal Qur'anic recitation. Abu Hurairah asked him, "O Messenger of Allah, may my father and mother be sacrificed for you, why do you remain silent between the *takbir* and the recital? What do you say (silently during that time)?" He said, "I say, 'O Allah, make a distance between me and my sins similar to the distance you have made between the East and the West. O Allah, cleanse me of my sins in the manner that a white garment (is cleansed) from dirt. O Allah, wash my sins from me with snow, water, and hail.'" This *hadith* is related by the "group", except for at-Tirmidhi.

(ii) Sea water. Sea water's purity is based on the following *hadith*: Abu Hurairah related that a man asked the Messenger of Allah, upon whom be peace, "O Messenger of Allah, we sail on the ocean and we carry only a little water. If we use it for ablution, we will have to go thirsty. May we use sea water for ablution?" Said the Messenger of Allah, upon whom be peace, "Its (the sea) water is pure and its dead (animals) are lawful (i.e., they can be eaten without any prescribed slaughtering)." This *hadith* is related by "the five." At-Tirmidhi calls it *hassan sahih,* and al-Bukhari says it is *sahih.*

(iii) Water from the Zamzam Well. 'Ali narrated that the Messenger of Allah, upon whom be peace, called for a bucket that contained water from the well of Zamzam. He drank from the bucket, then made ablution (with its water). This *hadith* is related by Ahmad.

(iv) Altered Water. This involves water whose form has been altered because of its being in a place for a long period of time, or because of the place in which it is located, or because of its being mixed with a substance that cannot be completely removed from it (i.e., water mixed with algae, tree leaves, and so on).[1] The scholars agree that this type of water falls under the heading of *mutlaq* water.

The rationale is simple: everything that falls under the general term of water, without any further qualifications, is considered pure, for the Qur'an says, "...and if you find not water, then go to clean, high ground..." *(al-Ma'idah: 6).*

Used Water

This category refers to water which drips from the person after he performs ablution or *ghusl.* It is considered pure because it was pure before its use for ablution, and there is no basis to think that it has lost its purity. This statement is supported by the *hadith* of Rab'i bint Mu'wadh which describes the ablution of the Messenger of Allah. She states, "He wiped his head with (the water) remaining on his hands from his ablution." This *hadith* is related by Ahmad and Abu Dawud. Abu Dawud's version is, "The Messenger of Allah, upon whom be peace, wiped his head with the extra water that was in his hand." Abu Hurairah also reported that the Messenger of Allah met him alone in the streets of Madinah while he was in post-sex impurity. He therefore slipped away, made *ghusl* and returned. The Messenger of Allah, upon whom be peace, asked him

"Where have you been, Abu Hurairah?" He answered, "I was in post-sex impurity and did not want to sit with you while I was in that condition." The Prophet replied, "Glory be to Allah. The believer does not become impure." This is related by "the group."

This is based on the rationale that since a believer never becomes impure, the water he uses for purification also does not become impure. Thus, a pure object touching a pure object cannot result in one's becoming impure. Ibn al-Mundhir said that it is related that 'Ali, Ibn 'Umar, Abu Umamah, 'Ata, al-Hassan, Makhul and an-Nakha'i said that if a person forgot to wipe his head while making ablution, it is sufficient for him to wipe his head with any water remaining in his beard. Ibn al-Mundhir stated that this proves that they took "used water" as pure. This opinion comes from one of the narrations attributed to Malik and ash-Shaf'i. Ibn Hazm ascribes it to Sufyan al-Thauri, Abu Thaur, and all scholars of the Dhahiri school of thought.

Water Mixed With Pure Elements

This category includes water that has been mixed with substances like soap, saffron, flowers, and so on, that is, objects considered pure by the *shari'ah*. Such water is considered pure as long as it has not been so mixed with other substances that one can no longer call it water. If this is the case, the water is still considered pure, but it cannot be used for purification. Umm 'Atiyah narrated that the Messenger of Allah, upon whom be peace, entered her house after the death of his daughter Zainab and said, "Wash her three or five or more times — if you see fit to do so — with water and dry tree leaves. For the final washing, use some *kafoor* or something from *kafoor*. When you are finished, inform me." She did so, after which he gave the women his outer garment and told them to wrap Zainab in it. This was related by "the group."

The deceased should be washed with something that may purify a live person. Ahmad, an-Nasa'i and Ibn Khuzaimah record from Umm Hani that the Messenager of Allah and Maimunah washed themselves from one (water) container that had a trace of dough in it. In both of these *hadith*, we find that the water was mixed with another substance, but since the other substance was not substantial enough to alter its nature, it remained fit for consumption.

Water Mixed With Impure Elements.

We can divide this category into two sub-categories:

(i) The impure substance alters the taste, color or odor of the water. In this case, it can not be used for purification. According to Ibn al-Mundhir and Ibn al-Mulaqqin, there is a consensus on this point.

(ii) The liquid is still considered water, meaning that the impure substance has not altered its taste, color or odor. Such water is considered pure and may be used for purification. This is based upon the following *hadith*: Abu Hurairah reported that a bedouin urinated in the mosque. The people stood to get him (and stop him). The Prophet said, "Leave him and pour a bucket of water or a container of water over his urine. You have been raised to be easy on the people, not to be hard on them."

This *hadith* is narrated by "the group," except for Muslim.

Abu Sa'eed al-Khudri asked the Prophet, "Can we make ablution from the well of Buda'ah (i.e., a well in Madinah)?" The Prophet, upon whom be peace, told him, "Water is pure and nothing makes it impure."

This *hadith* is related by Ahmad, ash-Shaf'i, Abu Dawud, an-Nasa'i and at-Tirmidhi, who classified it as *hassan*. Ahmad said, "This *hadith* is *sahih* and Yahya ibn Ma'een and Muhammad ibn Hazm classified it as such." This is also the opinion of Ibn 'Abbas, Abu Hurairah, al-Hassan al-Basri, Ibn al-Musayyab, 'Ikrimah, Ibn Abu Laila, al-Thauri, Dawud adh-Dhahiri, an-Nakha'i, Malik and others. Says al-Ghazzali, "I wish ash-Shaf'i's opinion was like Malik's."

There is also a *hadith* from 'Abdullah ibn 'Umar in which the Messenger of Allah is reported to have said, "If there are at least two buckets of water, it will not carry any impurity." This *hadith* is related by the "five." However, this *hadith* is *mudhtarab* in its chain of narrators and text. Ibn 'Abdul-Barr said in *at-Tamheed*, "As to the opinion of ash-Shaf'i which is based on this *hadith*, it is weak on scrutiny and is not confirmed by historical reports."

LEFTOVER WATER

"Leftover water" is what remains in a pot after some has been drunk. There are five different types of leftover water. They are:

Water leftover after people have drunk from the pot. According to the *shari'ah,* such water is considered pure regardless of whether the one who drank from the pot was a Muslim, an unbeliever, a person in post-sex impurity or a menstruating woman.

Although Allah says in the Qur'an, "Verily, the idol worshippers are impure" *(at-Taubah),* this is a reference not to their physical state, but to their false beliefs and creed. They may come into contact with dirt or impurities, but this does not mean that their possessions or bodies are impure. In fact, they used to mix with the Muslims. Their emmissaries and delegations used to visit the Messenger of Allah and enter his mosque. The Prophet, upon whom be peace, did not order that the objects they touched be cleansed. As for mensturating women, 'Aishah said, "I used to drink (from a container) while I was menstruating. I would then pass it to the Messenger of Allah and he would drink from the same spot where I had put my lips." (Related by Muslim.)

Water left in a container after an "allowable" animal (i.e., an animal whose meat is permissible to eat) has drunk from it. Such water is considered pure. Since the animal qualifies for consumption, its saliva is also pure. Abu Bakr ibn al-Mundhir said, "The scholars are agreed that such water is permissible to drink or use for ablution."

Water remaining in a pot after it has been drunk from by a donkey, mule, beasts or birds of prey. Such water is also considered pure, based on the *hadith* of Jabir in which the Messenger of Allah was asked about making ablution with drinking water left by donkeys. The Prophet, upon whom be peace, answered, "Yes, and from the drinking water left by any of the beasts of prey." This *hadith* was related by ash-Shaf'i, ad-Daraqutni and al-Baihaqi who said, "When its different chains are put together they become strong." It has also been related from Ibn 'Umar that the Messenger of Allah went out at night while he was on a journey. He passed by a man who was sitting by a pond. Said 'Umar, "Did a beast of prey drink from your pond tonight?" The Messenger of Allah told him, "O owner of the pond, do not inform him. It is not necessary, for him (the beast of prey) is what he carried in his stomach and for us is what he left, water to be used for drinking and purifying." This is related by ad-Daraqutni. Yahya ibn Sa'eed reported that once 'Umar was among a group that included 'Amr ibn al-'Aas and, when they came upon a pond, 'Amr said, "O owner of the pond, have the beasts of prey discovered your pond?" 'Umar said, "Do not inform us, since the people drink after the wild beasts and the wild beasts after the people." This is related by Malik in *al-Muwatta*.

Water remaining in a pot after a cat has drunk from it. Such water is also considered pure. This is proven by the *hadith* of Kabshah bint Ka'b who, when she was under the care of Abu Qatadah, entered the room to pour some water for him. A cat came, drank some of the water, and Qatadah proceeded to tilt the container so the cat could drink more. Kabshah said, "He noticed that I was watching him." He asked, "Are you surprised, O niece?" I answered, "Yes." He said, "The Messenger of Allah, upon whom be peace, said, 'It (the cat) is not impure. They intermingle with you.'"[1]

Water left in a pot after a pig or dog has drunk from it. Such water is considered impure and must be avoided. Al-Bukhari and Muslim have recorded, on the authority of Abu Hurairah, that the messenger of Allah said, "If a dog drinks from one of your containers, wash it seven times." Ahmad and Muslim also have this addition, "Cleanse one of your containers if a dog licks it by washing it seven times, the first washing being with dirt." As for the leftover water of a pig, it is clearly considered filth and impure.

IMPURITIES (*Najasah*)

Najasah refers to impure substances that the Muslim must avoid and wash off if they should happen to contaminate his clothes, body and so on. Says Allah in the Qur'an, "Purify your raiment" *(al-Mudathar: 4);* and, "Allah loves those who repent and who purify themselves" *(al-Baqarah: 222).* The Messenger of Allah also said, "Purity is half of the faith."

Types of Impurities

Dead animals. This refers to animals which die from "natural causes," that is, without the proper Islamic way of slaughtering. It also includes anything that is cut off of a live animal. Abu Waqid al-Laithy reported that the Prophet, upon whom be peace, said, "What is cut off of a live animal is considered dead," i.e., it is considered like an animal that has not been properly slaughtered. This is related by Abu Dawud and by at-Tirmidhi, who classifies it

---

[1]This *hadith* was narrated by "the five." At-Tirmidhi called it *hassan sahih*. Al-Bukhari and others graded it as *sahih*.

as *hassan* and says that the scholars act according to this *hadith*.

The following are exceptions to this rule:

Dead animals of the sea and dead locusts. Ibn 'Umar reported that the Messenger of Allah said, "Two types of dead animals and two types of blood have been made lawful for us. The types of dead animals are seafood and locusts. The two types of blood are the (blood of the) liver and the spleen."

This is related by Ahmad, ash-Shaf'i, al-Baihaqi and ad-Daraqutni. The *hadith* is weak, but Imam Ahmad says that it is authentic in *mauqoof* form.[2] Abu Zar'ah and Abu Hatim have said the same. Such a report has the implication of a *marfu' hadith*[3] because a companion saying, "This was allowed for us" or "This was forbidden for us" is like one of them saying, "We were ordered to do this," or "We were forbidden to do this," and so on. (Such statements are considered *marfu'* with respect to their regulations). And we have already mentioned the Prophet's statement concerning the ocean, "Its water is pure and its 'dead animals' are allowable (to eat.)."

Dead animals that have no running blood, (that is) bees, ants, and so on. They are considered pure. If they fall into some substance and die, the substance will not become impure. Ibn al-Mundhir said, "I do not know of any disagreement concerning the purity of such water save what has been related from ash-Shaf'i. It is well-known that he views them as being impure. Nevertheless, it does not bother him if the object falling into a substance does not alter it (in any way)."

The bones, horns, claws, fur, feathers, skin and so on of dead animals. All of these are considered pure. Concerning the bones of dead animals, az-Zuhri said, "I have met some scholars of the preceeding generations who used such objects for combs and pots for oil, and they did not see anything wrong in that." This is related by al-Bukhari. Said Ibn 'Abbas, "The client of Maimunah was given a

---

[2]*Mauqoof* means it is traced back to a companion and not all the way back to the Prophet. *Marfu'* means it is traced back to the Prophet, upon whom be peace.

[3]Although it has only been traced back to a companion, the source of the companion's statement is considered to have been the Prophet, upon whom be peace, himself.

sheep as charity, and it died. The Messenger of Allah, upon whom be peace, passed by it and said, 'Why do you not remove its skin, treat it and put it to use?' She said, 'It is dead' (i.e., it has not been slaughtered properly). He said to her, 'Only eating it is forbidden.'" This is related by the group. Ibn Majah attributes the incident to Maimunah and her client. Al-Bukhari and an-Nasa'i do not mention treating the skin. It is reported from Ibn 'Abbas that he recited: "Say (O Muhammad): "In all that has been revealed to me, I do not find anything forbidden to eat; if one wants to eat thereof, unless it be carrion, or blood poured forth, or swine flesh..." *(al-An'am: 145)*. Then he said, "What is forbidden is its meat. As for its skin, skin used for waterskins, teeth, bones, fur and wool, they are permissible." This is narrated by Ibn Mundhir and Ibn Hatim.[4] Similarly, its rennet and milk are considered pure. This is supported by the fact that when the companions conquered Iraq, they ate the cheese of the Magians which was made from rennet, although their slaughtered animals were considered the same as 'dead animals.' It is confirmed from Salman al-Farsi that when he was asked about cheese, clarified butter and pelts, he said, "What is permissible is what Allah made permissible in His book. What is forbidden is what Allah made forbidden in His book. What he omits, He has pardoned for you." It is well-known that he was being asked about the cheese of the Magians, as Salman was 'Umar's deputy in Mada'in, Iraq.

Blood. This includes blood that pours forth from an animal's body, such as blood from a slaughtered animal, or from menstruation, except for what small amounts are overlooked. Ibn Juraij said about the Qur'anic verse "...or blood poured forth..." / *al-An'am*: 145 /, that this is the blood that flows out. The blood that does not flow out, but remains in the veins, is permissible. This is related by Ibn al-Mundhir. And it is also related from Abu Majlizn in his discourse on blood that he was asked, "What about the blood that remains in the slaughtered sheep or at the top of the cooking pot?" He answered, "There is no problem with it. What is forbidden is the blood that flows out (of the animal at the time of slaughtering)." This was recorded by 'Abd ibn Hameed and by Abu ash-Shaikh. It is also related from 'Aishah that she said, "We used to eat the meat when the blood was streaking the pot." Al-Hassan said, "The Muslims always prayed, even while they were bleeding." This was mentioned

---

[4]This is what it says in the text, but it should be Ibn Abu Hatim.

by al-Bukhari. It is confirmed that 'Umar prayed while his wound was bleeding. Elucidating the point, Ibn Hajr says in *Fath al-Bari* (a commentary on *Sahih al-Bukhari*): "Abu Hurairah did not see anything wrong in a drop or two of blood during the prayers. Based on this report from Abu Hurairah, the blood of a flee or the blood that comes from a pimple are to be overlooked. Abu Majlizn was asked about pus that gets on the body or the clothes. He said, 'There is nothing wrong with them. Allah mentions only the blood, not the pus.'"

Commenting on the subject, Ibn Taimiyyah says, "It is obligatory to clean the clothes from pus, purulent matter or similar fluids." He also says, "There is no proof concerning its impurity." It is preferred for the person to avoid contact as much as possible with these substances.

Pig's Meat. According to the verse *(al-An'am: 145)* quoted earlier, items mentioned therein are impure. The pronoun 'they' refers to all three of the mentioned items. It is, however, allowed to knit with the hair of a pig according to most of the scholars.

Vomiting of a person, urine and excrement. There is agreement among the scholars that these objects are impure. But, a slight amount of vomit (commonly understood as a small amount of liquid) and the urine of an unweaned male baby are overlooked and pardoned. It is sufficient just to sprinkle water over the urine of an unweaned male baby. This is based on the *hadith* of Umm Qais. She came to the Messenger of Allah with her unweaned son. After a while, the baby urinated in the Prophet's lap. The Prophet, upon whom be peace, called for some water, which he sprinkled over his clothes, and did not give them a complete washing.

This is related by al-Bukhari and Muslim.

'Ali narrated that the Messenger of Allah said, "The urine of a baby boy should have water sprinkled upon it. The urine of a baby girl is to be washed off." Says Qatadah, "This refers to a male baby that has not yet begun to eat. If he already eats, then the garment is to be washed."

This *hadith* is related by Ahmad, Abu Dawud, at-Tirmidhi and Ibn Majah. In *al-Fath*, Ibn Hajr says its chain is *sahih*.

Sprinkling is sufficient as long as the boy is still nursing. If he eats solid food, his urine must be washed from the clothes and body. There is no disagreement on this latter point. Perhaps the reason for this exemption to the male baby's urine is that people have a tendency to carry their male babies around, and it would have been difficult to clean the clothes after their frequent urinations.[5]

Al-Wadi. Wadi is a thick white secretion discharged (by some people) after urination. It is considered impure. 'Aishah said, "*Wadi* comes out after urination. The person should wash the private parts and perform ablution. It is not necessary to perform *ghusl*. This is related by Ibn al-Mundhir. Ibn 'Abbas related that "*mani* **(sperm)** requires *ghusl*. As for *madhi* (semen) and *wadi* they require a complete purification." This is related by al-Athram. Al-Baihaqi has it with the wording, "Concerning *madhi* (prostatic fluid) and *wadi*, he said, 'Wash your sexual organs and perform the same type of ablution as you perform for prayer.'"

Al-Madhi or **Prostatic Fluid.** This is a white sticky fluid that flows from the sexual organs because of thinking about sexual intercourse or foreplay, and so on. The person is usually not aware of when exactly it is secreted. It comes from both the male and the female sexual organs, although the amount from the latter is usually more than the former's. Scholars are agreed that it is impure. If it gets on the body, it is obligatory to wash it off. If it gets on the clothes, it suffices to sprinkle the area with water, as it is very hard to be completely protected from this impurity, especially for the young, single person. 'Ali said, "I used to excrete *madhi,* so I asked a man to ask the Messenger of Allah, upon whom be peace, about it. I was shy to do so because of my position with respect to his daughter ('Ali was the Prophet's son-in-law). He said, 'Make ablution and wash your penis." This is related by al-Bukhari and others. Sahl ibn Hanif said, "I used to suffer from excessive amounts of *madhi.* I used to make lots of *ghusl* because of it. So I mentioned this to the Messenger of Allah, upon whom be peace, and he said, 'It is sufficient to take a handful of water and sprinkle it over your clothes wherever the fluid appears."

The *hadith* is related by Abu Dawud, Ibn Majah, and at-Tirmidhi. The latter says, "The *hadith* is *hassan sahih*. In the chain is Muhammad ibn Ishaq, who is considered weak when he relates in *mu'an'an* (handed-down) form because of his reputation as one who committed

---

[5]Ibn al-Qayyim has a good discussion of this point in his *I'lam al-Muwaqieen*, volume 2.

tadlis.[6] But in this narration, he makes it clear that he heard the *hadith* directly." Al-Athram narrated the same *hadith* with the wording, "I was bothered by a great deal of *madhi,* so I went to the Prophet, upon whom be peace, and informed him of this. He said 'It is sufficient for you to take a handful of water and sprinkle it over (the *madhi*).'"

Al-Mani or Sperm. Some scholars say that sperm is impure, but apparently it is pure, for it is only recommended to wash it off if it is still wet, and to scratch it off if it is dry. Said 'Aishah, "I used to scratch the sperm off the Messenger of Allah's clothes if it was dry, and wash it off if it was still wet." (This is related by ad-Daraqutni, Abu 'Awanah and al-Bazzar). It is also related that Ibn 'Abbas said, "I asked the Messenger of Allah about sperm on clothes. He said, 'It is the same as mucus and spittle. It is sufficient to rub the area with a rag or cloth.'"

The *hadith* was related by ad-Daraqutni, al-Baihaqi and at-Tahawi. There is a difference in the narration over whether it should be in *marfu'* or *mauqoof* form.

The status of the urine and stools of animals that are permissible to eat. Both of these are considered impure. Ibn Mas'ud related that the Messenger of Allah, upon whom be peace, went to answer the call of nature. He asked 'Abdullah ibn Mas'ud to bring three stones. 'Abdullah said, "I could not find three stones, so I found two stones and animal dung and brought them to him. He took the two stones and threw away the dung saying, 'It is impure.'"

The *hadith* is related by al-Bukhari, Ibn Majah, and Ibn Khuzaimah. In one narration it states, "It is impure. It is the stool of a donkey." A little amount of it is pardoned though, as it is very difficult to completely protect one's self from it. Al-Waleed ibn Mus-

---

[6]This statement of at-Tirmidhi is somewhat difficult to translate into English. *Tadlis* refers to the case where the narrator uses an ambiguous term which does not tell us if he heard the *hadith* directly from the one on whose authority he has narrated it. For example, a *mu'an'an hadith* is one in which the narrator has used the term *'an,* e.g., *'an* Muhammad meaning "on the authority of Muhammad." He could have heard the *hadith* directly from Muhammad or from someone else, possibly a fabricator of *hadith.* In both cases, it is permissible to use the term *'an.* Muhammad ibn Ishaq is one such narrator, who used to commit *tadlis.* If he narrated the *hadith* in such a way that it is clear that he heard it directly from the one on whose authority he is relating it, then his *hadith* is acceptable. Such is the case with the *hadith* in question.

lim says, "I said to al-Auza'i, 'What about the urine of animals whose meat is not eaten, like the mule, donkey and horse?' He said that they used to come into contact with these during their battles, and that they did not wash it off their bodies or clothes. As for the urine and stools of animals whose meat is permissible, Malik, Ahmad and a group of the Shaf'iyyah says that it is pure. Commenting on the subject, Ibn Taimiyyah says, "None of the companions held that it is impure. In fact, the statement that it is impure is of recent origin and not from the early generations of the companions."

Said Anas, "A group of people from the tribes of Ukul or 'Uraina came to Madinah and became ill in their stomach. The Prophet ordered them to get a milking she-camel and drink a mixture of its milk and urine." This *hadith* is related by Ahmad, al-Bukhari and Muslim and points to a camel's urine as being pure. Therefore, by analogy, other permissible animals' urine may also be considered pure. Says Ibn al-Mundhir, "Those who claim that that was permissible only for those people are incorrect. Specification is only confirmed by some specific proof." He also says, "The scholars permit, without any objection, the sale of sheep's stools and the use of camel's urine in their medicine, both in the past and in the present, again without any objection. This shows that they are considered pure." Says ash-Shaukani, *"Apparently,* the urine and stools of every living animal permissible to eat is pure." There is nothing to prove otherwise.

Al-Jallalah. *Jallalah* refers to an animal that eats the waste or flesh of other animals, such as camels, cows, sheep, chickens, geese, and so on. Ibn 'Abbas reported that the Messenger of Allah forbade the drinking of such animals' milk.

This *hadith* is related by "the five," except for Ibn Majah. At-Tirmidhi grades it as *sahih.* In one narration it states, "It is also prohibited to ride upon a *jallalah.* (Related by Abu Dawud.) 'Amr ibn Shu'aib related on the authority of his father, from his grandfather, that the Messenger of Allah prohibited the meat of domestic donkeys. As for the *jallalah,* he prohibited riding or eating them." (Related by Ahamad, an-Nasa'i and Abu Dawud.) If the *jallalah* animal is kept away from the other animals for some time and is given clean food to eat, then it becomes pure and is no longer called *jallalah.* If this is the case, it becomes permissible to eat, as the reason for its prohibition was the change it underwent due to eating filth, a state which would no longer be present.

Alcohol. According to most scholars, alcohol is impure. Says Allah in the Qur'an, "Alcohol, games of chance, idols and divining arrows are only an infamy of Satan's handiwork." Some scholars say that it is pure, for they take the meaning of *rajis* in its abstract sense as describing alcohol and whatever is related to it. This is not labeled as impure in a definite, sensory way. Says Allah, "Stay away from the impurities of idols." Idols are impure in the abstract sense, and they are considered impure if one touches them. The explanation of the preceding verse is that they are a tool of Satan, for they cause enmity and hatred and keep people away from the remembrance of Allah and prayer. In *Subul as-Salaam* it says, "Their origin is pure, and their being prohibited does not mean that the object itself is impure. For example, hashish is prohibited but it is pure. But, something impure is not necessarily prohibited. Every impure thing is prohibited, but not vice-versa. That is because of the ruling that something impure can not be touched under any circumstances. If a ruling says that something is impure, it is also prohibited. This differs from a ruling that something is prohibited. For example, it is forbidden to wear silk and gold, but they are absolutely pure by consensus." If one understands that, then the prohibition of alcohol does not necessarily entail its also being considered impure: it needs some other evidence to prove that it is impure. If not, then we are left with the original position that it is pure. If one claims other than that, he must substantiate it.

Dogs. Dogs are considered impure. Any container that a dog has licked must be washed seven times, the first time with dirt. Abu Hurairah reported that the Messenager of Allah, upon whom be peace, said, "Purifying a container that a dog has licked is done by washing it seven times, the first washing being with dirt (that is, water mixed with dirt until it becomes muddy)." This was related by Muslim, Ahmad, Abu Dawud, and al-Baihaqi. If a dog licks a pot that has dry food in it, what it touched and what surrounds it must be thrown away. The remainder may be kept, as it is still pure. As for a dog's fur, it is considered pure.

PURIFYING THE BODY AND CLOTHES

If the clothes or body are contaminated with impurities, it is obligatory to wash them with water until they are cleansed of the impurities. This is especially the case if the impurity is visible, such as blood. If there are some stains that remain after washing which would be extremely difficult to remove, they can be overlooked. If the impurity is not visible, such as urine, it is sufficient to wash it one time. 'Asma bint Abu Bakr related that a woman came to the Prophet, upon whom be peace, and said, "Our clothes are contaminated with menstrual blood. What should we do about this?" He said, "Scrape it, rub it with water, pour water over it and then pray in it." (This is related by al-Bukhari and Muslim) If impurities get on the lower portion of a woman's dress, it is purified by dust as she trails along. A woman said to Umm Salamah, "I have a long dress that drags on the ground, even when I walk through places that contain filth. What should I do about it?" Umm Salamah answered her, "The Messenger of Allah said, 'What comes after it purifies it.'" This is related by Ahmad and Abu Dawud.

PURIFYING THE GROUND

If there are impurities on the ground, it is purified by pouring water over it. This is proven by Abu Hurairah's *hadith*, mentioned earlier, about the bedouin who urinated in the mosque. The Prophet, upon whom be peace, said all that needed to be done for purification was to pour water over it. Said Abu Qulabah, "The drying of the ground is its purification." 'Aishah said, "The purification of the ground is its becoming dry." (Related by Ibn Abi Shaibah.) This, of course, refers to the case where the impurity is a liquid. If the impurity is a solid, the ground will only become pure by its removal or decay.

PURIFYING CLARIFIED BUTTER AND OTHER SIMILAR SUBSTANCES

Ibn 'Abbas relates from Maimunah that the Prophet, upon whom be peace, was asked about a mouse that fell into a pot of clarified butter. He said, "Take (the mouse) and what is around it out, and throw it away. Then eat (the rest of) your clarified butter." This is related by al-Bukhari.

Commenting on the subject, al-Hafedh Ibn Hajr says, "Ibn 'Abdul Barr reported that there is agreement that if a dead animal falls into a solid matter, what the dead animal touches and what is around it must be thrown away, provided that one can make sure that the animal did not touch the remainder. As for a liquid substance, there is some difference of opinion. The majority say that the entire liquid becomes impure; az-Zuhri, al-Auza'i, and some others disagree with that opinion.

PURIFYING THE SKIN OF A DEAD ANIMAL

Tanning purifies the skin and the fur of a dead animal. This is based on the *hadith* of Ibn 'Abbas, in which the Prophet said, "If the animal's skin is tanned, it is purified." (Related by al-Bukhari and Muslim.)

PURIFYING MIRRORS AND SIMILAR OBJECTS

Mirrors, knives, swords, nails, bones, glass, painted pots and other smooth surfaces that have no pores are purified by simply wiping them and removing any impure remains. The companions of the Prophet used to pray while wearing swords smeared with blood, and they used to just wipe the swords to purify them.

PURIFYING SHOES

Shoes may be purified by rubbing them against the ground, as long as the remains of the impurity are removed. Abu Hurairah narrated that the Messenger of Allah, upon whom be peace, said, "If one of you stepped in some filth, the dirt will purify his shoes." Related by Abu Dawud. In another narration it states, "If one of you steps in some filth with his shoes on, the dirt will purify them." Abu Sa'eed reported the Prophet, upon whom be peace, saying, "When a person comes to the mosque, he should look at his shoes. If he finds any filth on them, he should wipe them against the ground and pray in them." (Related by Ahmad and Abu Dawud.) Since shoes are repeatedly exposed to filth, it is sufficient just to wipe them against the ground. This is similar to the case of defecation. In fact, it is stronger than that case, as defecation usually occurs only two or three times a day.

USEFUL POINTS THAT ARE GREATLY NEEDED

Rope used for hanging clothes with impurities on them may afterwards be used for hanging pure clothes.

If a liquid falls on a person and he does not know if it was water or urine, he need not inquire about it. If he does inquire, the one who is asked need not answer him even if he knows that the liquid is impure. In that case, the person need not wash his clothes.

If a person finds something moist on his body or clothes at night, and he does not know what it is, he need not smell it to discover what it might be. It is related that 'Umar passed by a gutter (and got wet). 'Umar's companion asked the owner of the gutter if the water was pure or impure. 'Umar told the owner not to answer the question, and went on his way.

Clothes that have street mud on them need not be washed. Reported Kamyal ibn Ziyad, "I saw 'Ali wading through the mud, after which he entered the mosque and prayed without washing his legs."

If a person finishes his prayer and sees some impurities on his clothes or body of which he was not previously aware, or he was aware of them but forgot about them, or he did not forget about them but he was not able to remove them, then his prayer is still valid and he need not repeat it. This opinion is supported by Allah's statement, "And there is no sin for you in the mistakes you make unintentionally." / *al-Ahzab*: 5 /. Many of the companions and those of the following generation gave this legal verdict.

If a person can not determine what part of his clothes contain the impurity, he should wash the whole garment. This is based on the axiom, "If an obligation cannot be fulfilled except by performing another related act, then that act also becomes obligatory."

If a person mixes his pure clothes with his impure clothes (and gets confused between them), he should investigate the matter and pray once in one of the clothes. This is similar to the question of the exact direction of the *qiblah*. It does not matter if the proportion of pure clothes was large or small.

GOING TO THE BATHROOM

In Islam, going to the bathroom involves the following etiquette:

It is not proper for one to carry something that has Allah's name upon it (unless he is afraid of losing it or having it stolen), while he is going to the bathrom. Anas related that the Messenger of Allah, upon whom be peace, had a ring engraved with *Muhammad Rasool-ullah*, (Muhammad the Messenger of Allah), which he would remove when he went to the bathroom. Ibn Hajr says that this *hadith* is *malul* (a type of weak *hadith* having a defect) and Abu Dawud says it is *munkar*, (singularly related by people who are not trustworthy). The first portion of the *hadith* is authentic, however.[7]

He should move and hide himself from others. This is espe-cially true in the case of defecation, so others can not hear noxious sounds or smell bad odors. Said Jabir, "We were journeying with the Messenger of Allah, upon whom be peace, and he would only relieve himself when he was out of sight." (This is related by Ibn Majah.) Abu Dawud records that, "When he wanted to relieve him-self, he would go where no one could see him." He also related, "When the Messenger of Allah, upon whom be peace, went out he would go very far away."

One should mention the name of Allah and seek refuge in Him when entering the privy or removing his clothes to relieve himself. Anas reported that when the Messenger of Allah, upon whom be peace, entered the privy he would say, "In the name of Allah. O Allah! I seek refuge in you from male and female noxious beings (devils)." This is related by "the group."

One should not talk. One should not respond to a greeting or repeat what the caller to prayer is saying. He may speak if there is some necessity (i.e., to guide a blind man who fears he may be harmed). If he sneezes, he should praise Allah to himself and simply move his lips (without making a sound). Ibn 'Umar related that a man passed by the Prophet, upon whom be peace, and greeted him while he (the Prophet) was urinating. The Prophet did not return his greeting. (This is related by "the group," except for al-Bukhari.) Abu Sa'eed reported that he heard the Messenger of Allah, upon whom be peace, say, "Isn't it true that Allah detests those who converse while they relieve themselves?" This was related by Ahmad, Abu Dawud and Ibn Majah.

This *hadith* seems to support the position that it is forbidden to talk. Many scholars, however, say that it is only disliked, not forbid-den.[8]

---

[7]This is a very strange statement from Shaikh Sabiq (may Allah have mercy on him). The first part of the *hadith* only states that the Prophet, upon whom be peace, had a ring with an engravement on it. The latter part, which is weak and, therefore, cannot be used as a proof, is the only part that is relevant to what he is trying to prove. - J.Z.

[8]This is one of the strange aspects of the American culture where many men go to urinate together and continue talking while urinating. -J.Z.

One should neither face nor turn his back on the *qiblah* while relieving himself. Abu Hurairah reported that the Messenger of Allah, upon whom be peace, said, "When one of you relieves himself, he should neither face the *qiblah* nor turn his back on it." This was related by Ahmad and Muslim.

The prohibition implies that it is only disliked. As Ibn 'Umar related that he once went to Hafsah's home, where he saw the Messenger of Allah relieving himself while facing Syria with his back to the *Ka'bah*. This is related by "the group." Some reconciliate these *hadith* by saying that in the desert it is forbidden to face or turn one's back on the *Ka'bah*, while it is permitted in buildings. Said Marwan al-Asghar, "I saw 'Umar sitting on his she-camel and facing the *qiblah* while urinating. I said, 'O father of 'Abdurahman ... is this not forbidden?' He said, 'Certainly not ... This has been prohibited only in open areas. If there is a barricade (or separator) between you and the *qiblah*, there is nothing wrong with it."

This is related by Abu Dawud, Ibn Khuzaimah and al-Hakim. Its chain is *hassan* as Ibn Hajr said in *Fath al-Bari*.

One should seek a soft and low piece of ground to protect himself from impurities. Abu Musa related that the Messenger of Allah came to a low and soft part of the ground and urinated. He then said, "When one of you urinates, he should choose the proper place to do so."

This is related by Ahmad and Abu Dawud. One of its narrators is unknown, but its meaning is sound.

One should not use a hole in the ground. Qatadah related from 'Abdullah ibn Sarjas who said, "The Messenger of Allah forbade urination into a hole." Said Qatadah, "What is disliked about urinating into a hole?" Said he, "It is the residence of the *jinn*."

This *hadith* is related by Ahmad, an-Nasa'i, Abu Dawud, al-Hakim and al-Baihaqi. Ibn Khuzaimah and Ibn as-Sakin classified it as *sahih*.

One should avoid shaded places and those places where people walk and gather. Abu Hurairah reported that the Messenger of Allah, upon whom be peace, said, "Beware of those acts which cause others to curse." They asked, "What are those acts?" He said, "Relieving yourself in the people's walkways or in their shade."

This *hadith* is related by Ahmad, Muslim and Abu Dawud.

One should not urinate in bathing places or in still or running water. 'Abdullah ibn Mughaffal narrated that the Prophet said, "None of you should urinate in a bathing place and then make ablution in the water. The majority of *waswas* comes from that." This is related by "the five," but the statement, "and then make ablution in it" was only related by Ahmad and Abu Dawud. Jabir said the Prophet forbade urinating in still as well as running water. (Related by Ahmad, an-Nasa'i and Ibn Majah.) In *Majma az-Zuwaid* it states, "This was related by at-Tabarani, and its narrators are trustworthy."

If there is a drain in the bathing place, it is permissible to urinate into it.

One may not urinate while standing. If a person can guarantee that no impurities will touch his clothes, it is permissible to urinate while standing. Said 'Aishah, "If someone relates to you that the Messenger of Allah urinated while standing, do not believe him. He only urinated while sitting." This *hadith* is related by "the five," except for Abu Dawud. At-Tirmidhi's comment is, "It is the best thing related on this point, and it is the most authentic."

One should not forget that what 'Aishah said is based on the knowledge that she had. Hudhaifah relates that the Messenger of Allah, upon whom be peace, went to a public garbage dump and urinated while standing. Hudhaifah went away, and the Prophet then called him over. The Prophet made ablution and wiped over his shoes. This is related by "the group."

Commenting upon the issue, an-Nawawi says, "To urinate while sitting is most desirable in my opinion, but to do so standing is permissible. Both acts are confirmed by the Messenger of Allah, upon whom be peace.

One must remove any impurities from his clothes and body. To do so, he can use a rock, stone or any other pure matter. One may use only water to clean the area, or any combinations of purifying agents. 'Aishah reported that the Messenger of Allah, upon whom be peace, said, "When one of you goes to relieve himself, he should clean himself with three stones." (Related by Ahmad, an-Nasa'i, Abu Dawud and ad-Daraqutni).

Anas related that the Messenger of Allah would enter the privy, and that Anas and another boy would carry the water container and spear for him. The Prophet would clean himself with water." (Related by al-Bukhari and Muslim.)

Ibn 'Abbas related that the Messenger of Allah, upon whom be peace, passed by two graves and said, "They are being punished. But they are not being punished for a great matter (on their part). One of them did not clean himself from urine and the other used to spread slander." (Related by "the group.")

Anas also related the Prophet as saying, "Purify yourselves from urine, as most punishment in the grave is due to it."

One should not clean himself with his right hand. 'Abdurahman ibn Zaid related that Salman was asked, "Your Prophet teaches you everything, even how to relieve yourselves?" Salman said, "Certainly ... He forbade us from facing the *qiblah* while doing so, from cleaning ourselves with our right hand, and from cleaning ourselves with less than three stones. We also should not use an impure substance or a bone to clean ourselves." (Related by Muslim, Abu Dawud, and at-Tirmidhi.)

Hafsah reported, "The Messenger of Allah, upon whom be peace, reserved his right hand for eating, drinking, putting on his clothes, taking and giving. He used his left hand for other actions." (Related by Ahmad, Abu Dawud, Ibn Majah, Ibn Hibban, al-Hakim and al-Baihaqi).

One should remove any bad smell from his hands after cleaning himself. Abu Hurairah said, "When the Messenger of Allah upon whom be peace, relieved himself, I used to bring him a container of water. He would cleanse himself, then rub his hands against the soil." (Related by Abu Dawud, an-Nasa'i, al-Baihaqi, and Ibn Majah.)

One should sprinkle his penis and underwear with water after urination to make sure that he has cleansed himself. If one finds some dampness in his clothes after so doing, he can content himself by saying, "That is just water." This is based on the *hadith* related by al-Hakim ibn Sufyan or Sufyan ibn al-Hakim who said, "When the Messenger of Allah, upon whom be peace, urinated, he would wash and sprinkle (his penis)." In another narration it states, "I saw the Messenger of Allah urinate, after which he sprinkled water over his penis." Ibn 'Umar used to sprinkle his penis until his underwear became wet.

Entering the bathroom. One should enter the bathroom or a privy with his left foot, and exit with his right foot, saying: "O Allah! I seek your forgiveness." 'Aishah related that when the Messenger of Allah left the bathroom, he would say this supplication. (Related by "the five," except for an-Nasa'i.) What 'Aishah stated is the soundest statement on this topic. It is related through a number of weak chains that the Prophet, upon whom be peace, used to say, "Praise be to Allah who made the filth leave me and who has given me health," and "Praise be to Allah who let me enjoy it, kept for me its energy and relieved me of its harm."

ACTS THAT CORRESPOND
TO THE NATURE OF MANKIND

Allah has chosen certain acts for all of His prophets and their followers to perform. These acts distinguish them from the rest of mankind, and are known as *sunan al-fitra*, (the acts that correspond to the nature of mankind). They are:

Circumcision. This prevents dirt from getting on one's penis, and also makes it easy to keep it clean. For women, it involves cutting the outer portion of the clitoris.[9] Abu Hurairah reported that the Messenger of Allah said, "Ibrahim circumcised himself after he was eighty years old." (Related by al-Bukhari.) Many scholars say that it is obligatory.[10] The Shafiyyah maintain that it should be done on the seventh day. Says ash-Shaukani, "There is nothing that states explicitly its time or indicates that it is obligatory."

Shaving pubic hairs and pulling out underarm hairs. They are two *sunan* acts. If the hair is only trimmed or pulled out, it will suffice.

Clipping one's fingernails, trimming and shaving his moustache. Ibn 'Umar related that the Messenger of Allah said, "Differ from the polytheists: let your beards (grow)[11] and shave your moustache." (Related by al-Bukhari and Muslim). Abu Hurairah reported that the Messenger of Allah, upon whom be peace, said, "Five things

---

[9]It is not, as is done in some Muslim countries, the cutting off of the entire clitoris (which Gloria Steinem and others call "female genital mutilation"). -J.Z.

[10]Although he doesn't state it explicitly, he is referring to male circumcision. J.Z.

[11]The jurists take this order to imply obligation and, based upon that, say it is forbidden to shave one's beard. S. Sabiq's footnote.

are part of one's *fitra*: Shaving the pubic hairs, circumcision, trimming the moustache, removing the hair under the arms and trimming the nails." (Related by "the group.") It does not mention which
one would specifically fulfill the *sunnah*. One should make sure that
his moustache is not so long that food particles, drink and dirt
accumulate in it. Zaid ibn Arqam related that the Prophet, upon
whom be peace, said "Whoever does not take (off) some of his moustache is not one of us." (Related by Ahmad, an-Nasa'i and at-Tirmidhi, who classified it as *sahih*.) It is preferred to cut the pubic
hairs, pluck out the underarm hairs, cut the nails and trim the
moustache on a weekly basis, a practice which is most hygenic. If
some unnecessary hair is left on the body for a longer period of time,
it may disturb the person. One may leave this action for forty days,
but no longer. Said Anas, "The time period for us to trim the moustache, cut the nails, pluck out the underarm hairs and cut the pubic
hairs was forty nights." (Related by Ahmad, Abu Dawud and others).

Letting one's beard grow and become thick. This is a feature
of dignity. It should not be cut so short that it appears like a shaved
beard, nor should it be left so long that it becomes untidy. It is also
a sign of manhood. Says al-Bukhari, "Whenever Ibn 'Umar made
the *hajj* or *'umrah*, he would hold his beard in his fist and, whatever
exceeded his fist, he would cut off."

Oiling and combing one's hair. Abu Hurairah reported the
Prophet, upon whom be peace, as saying, "Whoever has hair should
honor it." (Related by Abu Dawud.)

Said 'Ata ibn Yasar, "A man came to the Prophet with unkempt
hair and an untidy beard. The Prophet pointed to him, as if ordering
him to straighten his hair and beard. He did so and returned.
Thereupon the Prophet observed, 'Is that not better than one of you
coming with his hair unkempt, as if he were a devil?'" (Related by
Malik.)

Abu Qatadah related that he had a great amount of hair. He asked
the Prophet, "O Messenger of Allah, I have lots of hair. Should I
comb it?" He answered, "Yes ... and honor it." Abu Qatadah used to
oil it twice a day due to the Prophet's words, "... and honor it."

Cutting one's hair off is permissible, and so is letting it grow if
one honors it. Ibn 'Umar narrated that the Prophet, upon whom be
peace, said, "Shave it all or leave it all." (Related by Ahmad, Muslim,
Abu Dawud and an-Nasa'i). To shave part of it and leave part of it
is greatly disliked. Nafa' related from Ibn 'Umar that the Messenger

of Allah prohibited *qiza'*. Nafa' asked, "What is *qiza'*?" He said, "It is to shave off part of the hair of a youth and to leave part." (Al-Bukhari and Muslim.)

Leaving grey hairs in place. This applies to both men and women. 'Amr ibn Shu'aib related on the authority of his father from his grandfather that the Prophet said, "Do not pluck the grey hairs as they are a Muslim's light. Never a Muslim grows grey in Islam except that Allah writes for him, due to that, a good deed. And he raises him a degree. And he erases for him, due to that, one of his sins." (Related by Ahmad, Abu Dawud, at-Tirmidhi, an-Nasa'i and Ibn Majah.) And Anas said, "We used to hate that a man should pluck out his white hairs from his head or beard." (Related by Muslim.)

Changing the color of grey hair by using henna, red dye, yellow dye, and so on. Abu Hurairah reported that the Prophet, upon whom be peace, said, "The Jews and Christians do not dye, so differ from them." (Related by "the group.") Abu Dharr reported that the Messenger of Allah said, "The best thing that one can use to change the color of grey hairs is henna and *katm* (a reddish dye)." (Related by "the five.")

There are some narrations that state that dying is disliked, but it is obvious that these narrations conflict with the *sunnah* and custom. It is related from some of the companions that it is better not to dye, while others say it is better to do it. Some used a yellow dye, while others used henna or *katm*. Others used saffron, and a group of them used a black dye. Ibn Hajr mentioned in *Fath al-Bari* that az-Zuhri said, "We used black dye if our face was youthful, but if wrinkles were present and the teeth were gone we would not use it." Said Jabir, "Abu Quhafah (Abu Bakr's father) was brought to the Prophet during the conquest of Makkah while his head was "white." The Prophet, upon whom be peace, said, "Take him to one of his wives and let her change the color of his hair with something, but she should avoid (making his hair) black." (Related by "the group," except for al-Bukhari and at-Tirmidhi). This dealt with a certain incident, and cannot be generalized. Furthermore, black would not be proper for someone as old as Abu Quhafah.[12]

---

[12]This is a strange statement from Shaikh Sabiq (may Allah have mercy on him). First, according to the rules of *fiqh*, there must be some evidence that an action or order is to be taken as specific (*khass*) instead of general (*'aam*). His evidence is not

To use musk and other types of perfume. These are pleasing to the soul and beautify the atmosphere. Anas reported the Messenger of Allah as saying, "Among the things of this world, I love women and perfume, and the coolness of my eyes is prayer." (Related by Ahmad and an-Nasa'i.) Abu Hurairah reported that the Messenger of Allah said, "If someone offers perfume, do not reject it, for it is light to carry and has a sweet scent." (Related by Muslim, an-Nasa'i and Abu Dawud.) Abu Sa'eed reported that the Prophet said about musk, "It is the best of perfumes." (Related by "the group," except for al-Bukhari and Ibn Majah).

Nafa' narrated that Ibn 'Umar used to burn and inhale a branch called *aluwah* that has a nice smell. He also used camphor. He used to say, "This is the way the Messenger of Allah inhaled such scents (that is, by burning them.)" (Related by Muslim and an-Nasa'i.)

---

conclusive. Second, he quotes Ibn Hajr quoting az-Zuhri and he makes it appear that Ibn Hajr is also of the same opinion. But actually, Ibn Hajr also wrote, "Some scholars make exception (for the black dye to be used) in the case of *jihad* (i.e., to make themselves look younger and stronger in front of the enemy) while others allow it without any restriction. But the stronger (opinion) is that it is disliked. An-Nawawi says that this is a dislike of the forbidding type (i.e., *kiraha tahreem*) ..." etc., Ibn Hajr, *Fath al-Bari* (Ministry of Da'wah, Riyadh, no date), volume 10, p. 354. - J.Z.

ABLUTION (WUDHU)

Ablution means to wash one's face, hands, arms, head and feet with water. Further points are given below:

Part of Islamic law. This is proven from the three major sources of Islamic law:

(i). The Qur'an. Says Allah in the Qur'an, "O you who believe, when you rise for prayer, wash your faces and your hands up to the elbows and lightly rub your heads and (wash) your feet up to the ankles *(al-Mai'dah: 6)*.

(ii). The Sunnah. Abu Hurairah reported that the Messenger of Allah said, "Allah does not accept the prayer of one who nullified his ablution until he performs it again." (Related by al-Bukhari, Muslim, Abu Dawud and at-Tirmidhi.)

(iii). The Consensus. There is a consensus of scholarly opinion that ablution is part of Islamic law. Therefore, it is a recognized fact of the religion.

Its virtues. Many *hadith* state the virtues of ablution. We shall mention just a few:

(i) 'Abdullah ibn as-Sunnabiji stated that the Messenger of Allah said, "When a slave makes ablution and rinses his mouth, his wrong deeds fall from it. As he rinses his nose, his wrong deeds fall from it. When he washes his face, his wrong deeds fall from it until they fall from beneath his eyelashes. When he washes his hands, his wrong deeds fall from them until they fall from beneath his finger-nails. When he wipes his head, his wrong deeds fall from it until they fall from his ears. When he washes his feet, his wrong deeds fall from them until they fall from beneath his toenails. Then his walking to the mosque and his prayer give him extra reward." (Related by Malik, an-Nasa'i, Ibn Majah and al-Hakim.)

(ii) Anas reported that the Messenger of Allah said, "If good characteristics exist in a person, Allah makes all of his acts good. If a person purifies himself for prayer, he expiates all of his sins and his prayer is considered an extra reward for him." (Related by Abu Ya'la, al-Bazzar and at-Tabarani in *al-Ausat*.)

(iii) Abu Hurairah reported that the Messenger of Allah said, "'Shall I inform you (of an act) by which Allah erases sins and raises degrees?" They said, "Certainly, O Messenger of Allah." He said, "Perfecting the ablution under difficult circumstances, taking many steps to the mosque, and waiting for the (next) prayer after the (last) prayer has been performed. That is *ribat*.[13] (Related by Malik, Muslim, at-Tirmidhi and an-Nasa'i.)

(iv) Abu Hurairah also reported that the Messenger of Allah, upon whom be peace, passed by a grave site and said, "Peace be upon you, O home of believing people. Allah willing, we shall meet you soon, although I wish I could see my brothers." They asked, "Are we not your brothers, O Messenger of Allah?" He said, "You are my companions. My brothers are the ones who will come after (us)." They said, "How will you know the people of our nation who will come after you, O Messenger of Allah?" He said, "If a man has a group of horses with white forelocks amidst a group of horses with black forelocks, will he recognize his horses?" They said, "Certainly, O Messenger of Allah." He said, "They (my brothers) will come with white streaks

---

[13] *Ar-Ribat* literally stands for the tying down of the horses in the face of the enemy to prevent anyone from fleeing. Here the Prophet, upon whom be peace, has likened the waiting for the coming prayer to *ribat*. - J.Z.

from their ablutions, and I will receive them at my cistern. But there will be some who will be driven away from my cistern as a stray camel is driven away. I will call them to come. It will be said, 'They changed matters after you,' then I will say, 'Be off, be off.'" (Related by Muslim.)

The obligatory parts of the ablution. Ablution has certain components which, if not fulfilled according to the correct Islamic procedures, make one's ablution void. These are:

(i) Intention. This is the desire to do the action and to please Allah by following His command. It is purely an act of the heart, for the tongue (verbal pronouncement, and so on) has nothing to do with it. To pronounce it is not part of the Islamic law. That the intention is obligatory is shown in the following: 'Umar related that the Prophet, upon whom be peace, said, "Every action is based on the intention (behind it), and everyone shall have what he intended..." (Related by "the group.")

(ii) Washing the face. This involves "pouring" or "running" water from the top of the forehead to the bottom of the jaws, and from one ear to the other.

(iii) Washing the arms to the elbow. The elbows must be washed, for the Prophet, upon whom be peace, did so.

(iv) Wiping the head. This means to wipe one's head with his hand. It is not sufficient just to place the hand on the head or to touch the head with a wet finger. The apparent meaning of the Qur'anic words, "...and wipe over your heads..." does not imply that all of the head needs to be wiped. It has been recorded that the Prophet used to wipe his head three different ways:

(a) Wiping all of his head. 'Abdullah ibn Zaid reported that the Prophet, upon whom be peace, wiped his entire head with his hands. He started with the front of his head, then moved to the back, and then returned his hands to the front. (Related by "the group.").

(b) Wiping over the turban only. Said 'Amru ibn Umayyah, "I saw the Messenger of Allah, upon whom be peace, wipe over his turban and shoes." (Related by Ahmad, al-Bukhari and Ibn Majah). Bilal reported that the Prophet, upon whom be peace, said, "Wipe over your shoes and headcovering." (Related by Ahmad.) 'Umar once said, "May Allah not purify the one who does not consider wiping over the turban to be purifying." Many *hadith* have been related on this topic by al-Bukhari, Muslim and others. Most of the scholars agree with them.

Wiping over the front portion of the scalp and the turban.
Al-Mughirah ibn Shu'bah said that the Messenger of Allah, upon whom be peace, made ablution and wiped over the front portion of his scalp, his turban and his socks. (Related by Muslim.) There is, however, no strong *hadith* that he wiped over part of his head, even though *al-Ma'idah*: 6 apparently implies it. It is also not sufficient just to wipe over locks of hair that proceed from the head or along the sides of the head.

Washing the feet and the heels. This has been confirmed in *mutawatir* (continuous) reports from the Prophet, upon whom be peace, concerning his actions and statements. Ibn 'Umar said, "The Prophet lagged behind us in one of our travels. He caught up with us after we had delayed the afternoon prayer. We started to make ablution and were wiping over our feet, when the Prophet said, 'Woe to the heels, save them from the Hell-fire,' repeating it two or three times." (Related by al-Bukhari and Muslim.)

Needless to say, the preceding obligations are the ones that Allah has mentioned in *(al-Ma'idah:6)*.

Following the prescribed sequence. Allah mentioned the obligations in a specific order. He also differentiated the legs from the hands — though both of them have to be washed — from the head, which only needs to be wiped. The polytheists of Arabia would not differentiate items unless there was some benefit in doing so. The way Allah structured the ablution made it easier for them to comprehend it. *Al-Ma'idah*:6 explains what is obligatory and it falls under the generality of the Prophet's statement, "Begin with what Allah began with." The Prophet used to follow that sequence as one of ablution's principles. There is no such report that the Prophet, upon whom be peace, ever departed from that sequence. Ablution is part of worship, and in matters of worship there is no room for anything except doing what has been commanded.

THE SUNAN ACTS OF THE ABLUTION

This section deals with those acts connected with the ablution, but which are not obligatory, as the Prophet, upon whom be peace, did not rigorously stick to them or censure anyone for not doing them.[14] They are as follows:

Mentioning the name of Allah at the beginning. There are some weak *hadith* that mention this act, and all of the chains of these *hadith* point to the fact that there is some basis for this act. In any case, it is a good act in and of itself and, in general, it is part of the Islamic law.[15]

Dental Hygiene. This involves using a stick or similar object to clean one's teeth. The best type to use is that of the *arak* tree found in the Hejaz. Such a practice strengthens the gums, prevents tooth disease, helps digestion and facilitates the flow of urine. This *sunnah* is fulfilled by using any object which removes yellow stains on the teeth and cleans the mouth, such as a toothbrush, and so on. Abu Hurairah reported that the Prophet, upon whom be peace, said, "Were it not to be a hardship on my community, I would have ordered them to use a toothbrush for every ablution." (Related by Malik, ash-Shaf'i, al-Baihaqi and al-Hakim.) 'Aishah reported that the Prophet said, "The toothbrush purifies the mouth and is pleasing to the Lord." (Related by Ahmad, an-Nasa'i and at-Tirmidhi.)

Using a toothbrush is liked at any time, but there are five times in which it is especially liked: (1) ablution, (2) prayer, (3) reading the Qur'an, (4) rising from sleep, and (5) when the taste in one's mouth has changed. Fasting and non-fasting people may use it at the beginning, the end, or at any other time during the day. 'Amr ibn Rabi'ah said, "I have seen the Messenger of Allah, upon whom be peace, on countless occasions using a toothbrush while fasting." (Related by Ahmad, Abu Dawud and at-Tirmidhi.)

When one uses a toothbrush, it is *sunnah* to clean it afterwards. Said 'Aishah, "When the Prophet, upon whom be peace, used his

---

[14]This means that they are not obligatory, but their fulfillment is highly preferred and entails reward for the one who performs the act. - J.Z.

[15]Indeed, the different chains of the *hadith* strengthen each other to the extent that the *hadith* is no longer considered weak, but *hassan lighairibi*. The main *hadith* on this topic is, "There is no prayer for one who does not have ablution. And there is no ablution for one who does not mention Allah's name upon it." Since this *hadith* is *hassan*, some scholars augue that the pronouncement of the name of Allah at the beginning of the ablution is obligatory.

toothbrush, he would give it to me. I would wash it, use it, wash it again and give it back to him." (Related by Abu Dawud and al-Baihaqi.)

It is part of the *sunnah* that one who has no teeth may use his fingers to clean his mouth. Asked 'Aishah, "O Messenger of Allah, how should a toothless person cleanse his mouth?" "By putting his fingers into his mouth," he replied. (Related by at-Tabarani.)

Washing the hands three times at the beginning. This is based on the *hadith* of Aus ibn Aus al-Thaqafi who said, "I saw the Messenager of Allah make ablution, and he washed his hands three times." (Related by Ahmad and an-Nasa'i.) Abu Hurairah reported that the Prophet, upon whom be peace, said, "When one of you rises from his sleep, he should not put his hand into a pot until he has washed it three times, for he does not know where his hand was (while he slept)." (Related by "the group", al-Bukhari did not mention the number of times.)

Rinsing the mouth three times. Laqit ibn Sabrah reported that the Prophet said, "When one performs ablution, he should rinse his mouth." (Related by Abu Dawud and al-Baihaqi.)

Sniffing up and blowing out water three times. Abu Hurairah reported that the Prophet, upon whom be peace, said, "When one of you performs ablution, he should sniff water up his nostrils and then blow it out." (Related by al-Bukhari, Muslim and Abu Dawud.)

The *sunnah* is to put the water into the nostrils with the right hand and blow it out with the left. 'Ali once called for water for ablution, rinsed his mouth, sniffed up water into his nostrils and blew it out with his left hand. He did that three times and then said, "That is how the Prpohet, upon whom be peace, would purify himself." (Related by Ahmad and an-Nasa'i.)

This *sunnah* is fulfilled by putting water into the mouth and nostrils in any way. The practice of the Prophet was to do both acts at the same time. 'Abdullah ibn Zaid said, "The Prophet would rinse his mouth and nose with just one hand (at one time, together). He did that three times." In one narration it says, "He would rinse his mouth and nose with three scoops of water." (Related by al-Bukhari and Muslim.) It is also *sunnah* to be plentiful (with water) while performing this *sunnah*, except if one is fasting. Laqit asked the Prophet, "Inform me about your ablution." He replied, "Complete and perfect the ablution and (put water) between your fingers. Use lots of water while sniffing it up your nostrils, unless you are fasting." (Related by "the five." At-Tirmidhi said it is *sahih.*)

Running one's fingers through his beard. 'Aishah reported that the Messenger of Allah would run his fingers through his beard. (Related by Ibn Majah and at-Tirmidhi, who classified it as *sahih.*)

Anas said that when the Messenger of Allah performed ablution, he would take a handful of water and put it under his jaws and pass it through his beard. He said, "This is what my Lord, Allah, ordered me to do." (Related by Abu Dawud, al-Baihaqi and al-Hakim.)

Running water through one's fingers and toes. Ibn 'Abbas said that when the Messenger of Allah performed ablution, he would run his fingers through his fingers and toes. (Related by "the five," except Ahmad.) It is also related that it is preferable to remove jewelry, for example, rings, bracelets, and so on, while performing ablution. Even though these reports are not accepted as fully authentic, one must follow them, for they fall under the general category of completing and perfecting the ablution.

Repeating each washing three times. This is a *sunnah* that the Prophet, upon whom be peace, almost always followed. If he acted otherwise, it was just to show that the other acts are permissible. 'Amr ibn Shu'aib related on the authority of his father from his grandfather who said: "A bedouin came to the Messenger of Allah, upon whom be peace, and asked him about the ablution. He showed him how to wash each part three times and said, 'This is the ablution. Whoever does more than that has done wrong, transgressed and committed evil." (Related by Ahmad, an-Nasa'i and Ibn Majah.) 'Uthman also reported that the Messenger of Allah would repeat each washing three times. (Related by Ahmad, Muslim and at-Tirmidhi.) It is also proven that he performed each washing only once or twice. According to most of the reports, he wiped his head only once.

Beginning each action with the right side. Said 'Aishah, "The Messenger of Allah loved to begin with his right side while putting on his shoes, straightening his hair and cleaning (or purifying) himself." (Related by al-Bukhari and Musilm.) Abu Hurairah reported that the Prophet said, "When you clothe or wash yourself, begin with your right side." (Related by Ahmad, Abu Dawud, at-Tirmidhi, and an-Nasa'i.)

Rubbing the limbs with water. This means to rub the hands over the bodily parts with water. 'Abdullah ibn Zaid reported that the Messenger of Allah was brought a pot of water which he used to perform ablution, and then rubbed his arms. (Related by Ibn Khuzaimah.) He also related that the Messenger of Allah performed ablution, then rubbed his limbs. (Related by Abu Dawud at-Tayalisi, Ahmad, Ibn Hibban and Abu Ya'la.)

Close sequence. Each bodily part must be washed right after the other in the prescribed sequence (without separating the washing of the different parts of acts not related to the abution). This is the customary practice of the early and later generations of Muslims.

Wiping the ears. The *sunnah* is to wipe the interior of the ears with the index fingers and the exterior portions with the thumbs. The water used to wipe the head is also used for the ears, as the ears are part of the head. Al-Miqdam ibn Ma'd Yakrib reported that the Prophet, upon whom be peace, wiped his head and his ears, the interior and exterior, while making ablution. He also put his finger inside his ear. (Related by Abu Dawud and at-Tahawi.)

While describing the ablution of the Prophet, upon whom be peace, Ibn 'Umar said, "He wiped his head and ears with one wipe." (Related by Ahmad and Abu Dawud.) In one narration it states, "He wiped the inner portion of his ears with his index finger, and the outer portion with his thumb."

Elongating the streaks of light. This refers to washing the complete forehead, a practice which is more than what is obligatory in washing the face, and will increase the streak of light (on the Day of Judgement). It also refers to washing above the elbows and ankles. Abu Hurairah reported that the Messenger of Allah said, "My nation will come with bright streaks of light from the traces of ablution." Abu Hurairah then said, "If one can lengthen his streak of light, he should do so." (Related by Ahmad, al-Bukhari and Muslim.) Abu Zar'ah related that when Abu Hurairah made ablution, he washed his arms above his elbows and his feet up to his calves. He was asked, "Why do you do this?" He said, "This is the extent of the embellishment." (Related by Ahmad.) According to al-Bukhari and Muslim, its chain is *sahih*.

Economizing the use of water, even if one is in front of the sea. Anas said, "The Prophet, upon whom be peace, used to perform *ghusl* (the complete bathing) with a *sa'a* of water (1.616 cm^3) to 5 *madd* (each 4 *madd* equals one *sa'a*). He also used to make ablution with one *madd* (404 cm^{3}d) of water." (Related by al-Bukhari and Musim.) 'Ubaidullah ibn Abu Yazid narrated that a man asked Ibn 'Abbas, "How much water is sufficient for *ghusl*?" He answered, "One *madd*." "And how much is sufficient for *ghusl*?" He said, "One *sa'a*." The man said, "That is not sufficient for me." "Ibn 'Abbas said, "No? It was sufficient for one better than you, the Messenger of Allah, upon whom be peace." (Related by Ahmad, al-Bazaar and at-Tabarani in *al-Kabeer*. Its narrators are trustworthy.) 'Abdullah ibn 'Umar narrated that the Messenger of Allah passed by Sa'd while he was performing ablution and said, "What is this extravagance, Sa'd?" He said, "Is there extravagance in the use of water?" He said, "Yes, even if you are at a flowing river." (Related by Ahmad and Ibn Majah with a weak chain.)

Extravagance is to use water without any benefit, like washing the parts more than three times. Ibn Shu'aib's *hadith*, quoted earlier, illustrates the point in question. 'Abdullah ibn Mughaffal narrated that he heard the Prophet say, "There will be people from my nation who will transgress in making supplications and in purifying themselves." (Related by Ahmad, Abu Dawud and an-Nasa'i.)

Says al-Bukhari, "The scholars do not like one to use water beyond what the Prophet, upon whom be peace, used for ablution.

Supplication while performing ablution. There is nothing confirmed from the Prophet, upon whom be peace, regarding supplications during ablution save the *hadith* of Abu Musa al-Ash'ari who said, "I came to the Messenger of Allah with water. While he was performing ablution, I heard him supplicate, 'O Allah, forgive my sins. Make my residence spacious for me and bless me in my provisions.' I said, 'O Prophet of Allah, I heard you supplicating such and such.' He said, 'Did I leave anything out?'" (Related by an-Nasa'i and Ibn as-Sunni with a *sahih* chain.) An-Nawawi includes this event under the chapter, *What is to be said after one completes the ablution*, and Ibn as-Sunni has it under, *What is to be said when one is in the state of ablution*.

An-Nawawi holds that both meanings may be implied from the hadith.[16]

---

[16]There is no authentic *hadith* that states there is to be any supplications during the ablution. When Sabiq said that its chain is *sahih*, he was following what an-Nawawi stated in *Kitab al-Idhkar*. It is true that the narrators are trustworthy, but the chain

Supplication after ablution. 'Umar reported that the Prophet, upon whom be peace, said, "If one completes (and perfects) the ablution and then says, 'I testify that there is no god except Allah, the One Who has no partner, and that Muhammad is His slave and Messenger,'" the eight gates of paradise will be opened for him and he may enter any of them that he wishes." (Related by Muslim.)

Abu Sa'eed al-Khudri reported that the Prophet said, "Whoever makes ablution and says, 'Glory be to Thee, O Allah, and the praise be to Thee. I bear witness that there is no god except You. I beg Your forgiveness and I repent unto you,' will have it written for him, and placed on a tablet which will not be broken until the Day of Resurrection. This *hadith* is related by at-Tabarani in *al-Ausat*. Its narrators are of the *sahih*. An-Nasa'i has it with the wording, "It will be stamped with a seal, placed below the throne, and it will not be broken until the Day of Resurrection." The correct statement is that it is *mauqoof*.

As for the supplication, "Allah, cause me to be from among the repentant, and cause me to be from among the pure," it has been narrated by at-Tirmidhi who said, "Its chain is *mudhtarib* and there is nothing authentic concerning this (supplication)."

Praying two *rak'ah* after ablution. Abu Hurairah reported that the Messenger of Allah, upon whom be peace, said to Bilal, "O Bilal, tell me what good deed you have done in Islam that I hear the sound of your footsteps in Paradise?" Bilal said, "That after I purify myself during the day or night, I pray with that purification as much as Allah has destined for me." (Related by al-Bukhari and Muslim.) 'Uqbah ibn 'Aamr related that the Messenger of Allah, upon whom be peace, said, "If one performs and perfects his ablution and prays two *rak'ah* with his heart and face (completely on his prayer), Paradise becomes his." (Related by Muslim, Abu Dawud, Ibn Majah and Ibn Khuzaimah in his *Sahih*.) Khumran, the client of 'Uthman, added, "I saw 'Uthman call for water for ablution, pour it from the pot onto his right hand and wash it three times. He then put his right hand into the container, rinsed his mouth and nose and blew

---

is broken and, therefore, it is a weak *hadith*. This point was noted by Ibn Hajr in *Nata'ij al-Afkar* and supported by as-Suyuti in *Tuhfat al-Abrar bi Naqd al-Adhkar*. The fact that the Prophet made this supplication is true as mentioned in a *hassan hadith* recorded by at-Tirmidhi, but its relation to the ablution has not been confirmed. J.Z.

the water out. Then he washed his face three times, followed by his arms up to the elbows. Then he washed his feet three times and said 'I saw the Messenger of Allah, upon whom be peace, make ablution like this.' And then he would say, 'Whoever makes ablution like this and then prays two *rak'ah* without having any other concern on his mind, all his past sins will be forgiven." (Related by al-Bukhari, Muslim and others.)

Other practices (protecting the eyes and wrinkles, removing any rings, wiping the neck, and so on) have not been mentioned here as their narrations are still questionable. But, one may follow them as part of general cleanliness.

NULLIFICATION OF ABLUTION

It is not desirable that one who is making ablution should leave any of the *sunan* that have just been mentioned. The person would then lose the great reward of these (simple)acts. Anytime one abandons the *sunnah*, he has done a disliked deed.

The following acts render ablution null and void:

An excretion of the penis, vagina or anus. This would include urine, feces (Allah says, "...or one of you comes from relieving himself," thus proving that such an act obligates a new purification), and releasing gas from the anus. Abu Hurairah reported that the Messenger of Allah said, "Allah does not accept the prayer of a person who has released gas until he makes a new ablution. A person from Hadhramaut asked Abu Hurairah, "What does releasing gas mean?" He answered, "Wind with or without sound." (Related by al-Bukhari and Muslim.) He also narrated that the Prophet said, "If one of you finds a disturbance in his abdomen and is not certain if he has released any gas or not, he should not leave the mosque unless he hears its sound or smells its scent." (Related by Muslim.)

Hearing the escaping gas or smelling it is not a condition for nullifying ablution, but he stressed that one should be certain of the action. As for *al-Madhi* (prostatic fluid), the Prophet said, "Make ablution." Concerning sperm or *al-mani*, said Ibn 'Abbas "It requires *ghusl* and for *al-madhi* and *al-wadi*, wash your sex organs and make ablution." This was related by al-Baihaqi in his *Sunan*.

Deep sleep that makes a person completely unaware of his surroundings. If the person did not keep his bottocks firmly seated on the floor while sleeping, he must make a new ablution. Safwan ibn 'Asal said, "The Prophet, upon whom be peace, used to order us while we were travelling not to take our socks off unless we were in post-sex impurity (i.e. not for defecation, urination or sleep)." (Related by Ahmad, an-Nasa'i and at-Tirmidhi, who graded it *sahih*.) If one's buttocks has remained firmly on the floor during his sleep, no new ablution is necessary. This is implied by the *hadith* of Anas who said, "The companions of the Prophet were waiting for the delayed night prayer until their heads began nodding up and down (from drowsiness and sleep). They would then pray without performing ablution." (Related by ash-Shafi, Muslim, Abu Dawud and at-Tirmidhi.) The wording that at-Tirmidhi recorded from the chain of Shu'bah is, "I have seen the companions of the Prophet sleeping to the extent that one could hear some of them snoring. But, they would stand for prayer without a new ablution." Said Ibn al-Mubarak, "In our opinion, this happened when they were sitting."

Loss of consciousness. This nullifies the ablution regardless of whether it was owing to insanity, fainting, drunkenness, or some medicine. It also does not matter if one was unconscious for a short or long period of time, or if one was sitting, or fell to the earth, and so on. The aspect of unawareness here is greater than that of sleeping. The scholars are agreed on this point.

Touching the sexual organ without any "barrier" (clothes, and so on) between the hand and the organ. Busrah bint Safwan narrated that the Prophet, upon whom be peace, said, "Whoever touches his sexual organ cannot pray until he performs ablution." This *hadith* is related by "the five." At-Tirmidhi classified it as *sahih* and al-Bukhari called it the most authentic report on that topic. Malik, ash-Shafi, Ahmad and others also narrated it. Abu Dawud said, "I asked Ahmad, 'Is the *hadith* of Busrah authentic?' He said, 'Certainly it is authentic." In the narration of Ahmad and an-Nasa'i, Busrah heard the Prophet saying, "Ablution is to be made by the one who touches his sexual organ." This is general and encompasses touching one's own sexual organs or touching somebody else's. Abu Hurairah reported the Prophet as saying, "Whoever touches his sexual organ without any covering (between them) must perform ablution." (Related by Ahmad, Ibn Hibban and al-Hakim, who classified it as *sahih,* as did Ibn 'Abdul-Barr.)

Said Ibn as-Sakin, "That *hadith* is from the best of what has been related on this topic." Ash-Shafi related: "Any man who touches his penis must perform ablution.[17] Any women who touches her vagina must perform ablution." Commenting on its authenticity, Ibn al-Qayyim quotes al-Hazimi who says, "That chain is *sahih*." The Hanifiyyah are of the opinion, based on the following *hadith*, that touching the sexual organ does not nullify the ablution: "A man asked the Prophet if a man who touches his penis has to perform ablution. Said the Prophet, upon whom be peace, "No, it is just a part of you." (Related by "the five." Ibn Hibban classified it as *sahih*, and Ibn al-Madini said, "It is better than the *hadith of Busrah.*")[18]

ACTIONS THAT DO NOT NULLIFY THE ABLUTION

Touching a woman. 'Aishah related that the Messenger of Allah, upon whom be peace, kissed her while he was fasting and said, "Kissing does not nullify the ablution, nor does it break the fast." (Related by Ishaq ibn Rahawaih and al-Bazzar with a good chain.)

Evaluating its authenticity, 'Abdul-Haqq says, "I do not know of any defect in the *hadith* that could cause its rejection."

---

[17]Nowhere in the text does Sabiq make it clear that this is a statement of the Prophet. In fact, this is a *hadith* of the Prophet, upon whom be peace. Ad-Daraqutni also related it and it is *sahih*. - J.Z.

[18]This latter *hadith* was related by the companion Talq. On this topic as-San'ani wrote, "The *hadith* of Busrah is stronger. *Busrah's hadith* is supported by hadith related by twenty-seven companions that are recorded in the books of *hadith*... We interpret the *hadith* of (Talq) by saying that it was the original order that occurred early in the post-*hijrah* period before the Prophet had his mosque built. It is abrogated by the *hadith* of Busrah, as she entered Islam later. And a better argument than that of abrogation is that (Busrah's *hadith*) is stronger. Most scholars of *hadith* consider it authentic. It has more reports as supporting evidence for it: She related it in the home of the "emigrants" and "helpers" and none of them refuted her. And we know that some of them agreed with what she said. 'Urwah agreed with what she said, although before he objected to (that opinion). Ibn 'Umar used to relate it from her and he did not stop making ablution after touching his penis until he died. Says al-Baihaqi, "The following suffices to consider Busrah's *hadith* stronger than Talq's: The people of the Jahih did not relate from Talq. None of them argue by his narration. But all of them argue by the *hadith* of Busrah. Furthermore, the *hadith* of Talq has been narrated by Qais ibn Talq. Ash-Shaf'i said, "I asked the people about Qais ibn Talq, and I found no one knew him. How then can we accept his report?" Abu Hatim and Abu Zura said, "Qais ibn Talq is not a person who can be used as a proof." Cf., Muhammad as-San'ani, *Subul as-Salam*, volume 1, p. 149. Ash-Shaf'i, Abu Hatim, Abu Zura, ad-Daraqutni, al-Baihaqi and Ibn aj-Jauzi consider Talq's *hadith* as weak. Al-Hazimi, in *al-I'tibar*, is also of the opinion that Talq's *hadith* is abrogated.

'Aishah also said, "One night, I missed the Messenger of Allah in my bed, and so went to look for him. I put my hand on the bottom of his feet while he was praying and saying, 'O Allah, I seek refuge in Your pleasure from Your anger, in Your forgiveness from Your punishment, in You from You. I cannot praise you as You have praised Yourself" (related by Muslim and at-Tirmidhi, who classified it as *sahih.*), and she also reported, 'The Prophet kissed some of his wives and went to prayer, without performing ablution." (Related by Ahmad and "the four,"[19] and its narrators are trustworthy.) She also said, "I would sleep in front of the Prophet, upon whom be peace, with my feet in the direction of the *qiblah* (to him). When he made prostrations, he would touch me, and I would move my feet." In another narration it says, "When he wanted to prostrate, he would touch my legs."

Bleeding from an unusual place. This involves bleeding due to a wound, cupping or a nosebleed, and regardless of whether the amount of blood is small or large.

Said al-Hassan, "The Muslims still prayed even while wounded." (Related by al-Bukhari.) He also reported, "Ibn 'Umar squeezed a pimple until it bled, but he did not renew his ablution. Ibn Abi 'Uqiyy spat blood and continued his prayer. 'Umar ibn al-Khattab prayed while blood was flowing from him. 'Ibbad ibn Bishr was hit with an arrow while praying, but continued his prayers." (Related by Abu Dawud, Ibn Khuzaimah, and al-Bukhari in *mu'allaq* form.)

Vomit. Regardless of whether the amount of vomit was great or small, there is no sound *hadith* that it nullifies ablution.

Eating camel meat. That this does not nullify the ablution was the opinion of the four rightly guided caliphs, the companions and the following generation, although there is an authentic *hadith* that states one should make ablution after it.

Said Jabir ibn Sumrah, "A man asked the Prophet, 'Should we make ablution after eating mutton?' He said, 'If you wish, make ablution. If you do not, do not make ablution.' The man asked 'Should we make ablution after eating camel meat?' He said, 'Yes.'" Al-Barra' ibn 'Aazib related that someone asked the Prophet about praying in the dens of camels, and he said, "Do not pray therein, for they

---

[19]Meaning, an-Nasa'i, Abu Dawud, at-Tirmidhi and Ibn Majah. - J.Z.

are of the devils." He asked about the dens of sheep, and he said, "Pray therein, for they are blessings. (Related by Ahmad, Abu Dawud and Ibn Hibban.) Ibn Khuzaimah said, "I know of no dispute over the authenticity of this report." In summation, an-Nawawi can be quoted as saying, "This opinion has the strongest proof, although the majority of the scholars differ from it."

Of doubts whether or not one has released gas. This is the case where the person cannot quite recall if he is in a state of purity or not. Such a state of mind does not nullify ablution, regardless of whether the person is in prayer or not, until he is certain that he has nullified his ablution. 'Abbad ibn Tameem related that his uncle queried the Prophet about a person who feels something in his abdomen while praying. Said the Prophet, "He should not leave (the prayer) until he hears it or smells it." (Related by Muslim, Abu Dawud and at-Tirmidhi). It does not mean that its sound or bad smell nullifies ablution, but that the person must be certain about the fact that he has nullified his ablution. Says Ibn al-Mubarak, "If one is uncertain about his condition of purity, he does not need to perform a new ablution." If one is certain that he has nullified his ablution and doubts whether he has purified himself or not, he must perform a new ablution.

Laughing during prayer. This does not nullify ablution, for there are no confirmed reports that state such a thing.

Washing a dead person. This also does not require a new ablution, for the reports that say it nullifies ablution are weak.

ACTIONS THAT REQUIRE ABLUTION
AS A PREREQUISITE

Three actions require ablution in order for them to be accepted by Islamic law. These are:

Any type of ritual prayer. This involves only obligatory, voluntary, or funeral prayers, not the supplications *(du'a)*. This is based on Allah's statement, "O you who believe. When you get up to perform a prayer *(salah)* wash your face and your arms up to the elbows and wipe your head and feet to the ankles." Also, the Messenger of Allah, upon whom be peace, said, "Allah does not accept a prayer (that was performed while the person) was not in a state

of purity. Nor does he accept charity from misappropriated booty."
(Related by "the group," except for al-Bukhari.)

Circumambulating the Ka'bah. Ibn 'Abbas reported that the
Messenger of Allah said, "Circumambulation is a type of prayer, but
Allah has permitted speaking during it. Whoever speaks during it
should only speak good."

This *hadith* is related by at-Tirmidhi, ad-Daraqutni, al-Hakim,
Ibn as-Sakin and Ibn Khuzaimah, who classified it as *sahih*.

Touching a copy of the Qur'an. Abu Bakr ibn Muhammad
related from his father on the authority of his grandfather that the
Prophet, upon whom be peace, sent a letter to the people of Yemen
which stated, "No one is to touch the Qur'an except one who is
purified."

This *hadith* is related by an-Nasa'i, ad-Daraqutni, al-Baihaqi and
al-Athram. Of its chain, Ibn 'Abdul-Barr says, "It appears to be a
continuous transmission." 'Abdullah ibn 'Umar reported that the
Prophet, upon whom be peace, said, "No one is to touch the Qur'an
unless he has purified himself." (Al-Haithami mentioned it in
Majma' az-Zawaid and said its narrators are trustworthy.) Apparently, this *hadith* has a problem. The word "purify" must have one
particular meaning here. Therefore, to say that one who has a minor
defilement may not touch the Qur'an makes no sense. Concerning
Allah's statement, "...which none touches save the purified," *(al-
Waqi'ah: 79)*, apparently the pronoun refers to "the Book kept hidden" (from the preceding verse) and that is "the well-preserved
tablet" and the "purified" refers to the angels, which is similar to
the verses, "On honored scrolls, exalted, purified, (set down) by
scribes, noble and righteous" *('Abasah: 13-16)*. Ibn 'Abbas, ash-
Sha'bi, adh-Dhahak, Zaid ibn 'Ali, al-Mu'aiyad Billah, Dawud, Ibn
Hazm and Hammad ibn Abu Sulaiman are of the opinion that one
who has a minor defilement may touch the Qur'an. Most of the
scholars, however, agree that such people may recite the Qur'an
without touching it.

ACTIONS FOR WHICH A STATE OF
PURITY IS PREFERRED

It is preferred to have ablution for the following acts:

While mentioning the name of Allah. Al-Muhajir ibn Qunfudh
related that he greeted the Prophet, upon whom be peace, but that

the latter did not return his salutation until he had made ablution: "There is nothing that prevented me from responding to you except that I do no like to mention the name of Allah unless I am in a state of purity." Said Qatadah, "Because of this, al-Hassan hated to recite the Qur'an or mention Allah's name unless he had performed ablution. (Related by Amad, Abu Dawud, an-Nasa'i and Ibn Majah.) Raeported Abu Juhaim ibn al-Harith, "The Prophet, upon whom be peace, met a person at the well of Jaml, who greeted him, but he did not return his greeting until he had wiped his face and hands." (Related by Ahmad, al-Bukhari, Muslim, Abu Dawud and an-Nasa'i.) This action was one of preference, not of obligation. Mentioning the name of Allah is permissible for the one who is in a state of purity, one who has a minor impurity, a person in post-sex impurity, or one who is standing, sitting, and so on. Said 'Aishah, "The Messenger of Allah used to remember Allah at all times." (Related by "the five," except for an-Nasa'i.) Al-Bukhari recorded it in *mu'alliq* form.) Reported 'Ali, "The Messenger of Allah would come from relieving himself, recite to us and eat meat with us. Nothing would stop him from the Qur'an except post-sex impurity." (Related by "the five." At-Tirmidhi and Ibn as-Sakin categorized it as *sahih*.)

Going to sleep. Al-Barra' ibn 'Aazib reported that the Messenger of Allah, upon whom be peace, said, "When you go to your bed, perform ablution, lie on your right side and then say, 'O Allah, I submit my soul to You, and I turn my face to You. I entrust my affairs to You. I retreat unto You for protection with hope and fear in You. There is no resort and no savior but You. I affirm my faith in Your books which You revealed and in Your prophets you sent.' If you die during that night, you will be along the natural path. Make it your final statement (of the night). He reported that he repeated this supplication to the Prophet, upon whom be peace, and he said, "...and Your messengers." The Prophet interjected, "No,...'and the prophets You sent." (Related by Ahmad, al-Bukhari, and at-Tirmidhi.) This also applies to one who is in post-sex impurity . Ibn 'Umar asked the Prophet, "O Messenger of Allah, can one of us sleep while he is in post-sex impurity?" The Prophet answered, "Yes, if he makes ablution." Reported 'Aishah, "When the Prophet, upon whom be peace, wanted to sleep in a state of post-sex impurity, he would wash his private parts and perform ablution." (Related by "the group.")

To remove a sexual impurity. If a person in a state of post-sex impurity wants to eat, drink or have intercourse again, he should perform ablution.

Said 'Aishah, "When the Prophet, upon whom be peace, was in a state of impurity because of intercourse and wanted to eat or sleep, he would perform ablution." 'Ammar ibn Yasar reported that the Prophet permitted a person in post-sex impurity to eat, drink or sleep if he performed ablution first. (Related by Ahmad and at-Tirmidhi, who classified it as *sahih.*)

Abu Sa'eed reported that the Prophet, upon whom be peace, said, "If one has intercourse with his wife and wants to repeat the act, he should perform ablution." (Related by "the group," except for al-Bukhari. Ibn Khuzaimah, Ibn Hibban and al-Hakim recorded it with the addition, "It makes the return more vivacious.")

Before performing *ghusl.* It is preferred to perform ablution before *ghusl* regardless of whether that particular *ghusl* was an obligatory or a preferred act. Said 'Aishah, "When the Messenger of Allah, upon whom be peace, performed post-sex *ghusl*, he would begin by washing his hands and then pour water from his right hand to his left and wash his private parts. He would then perform ablution.." (Related by "the group.")

Before eating food touched by fire. Said Ibrahim ibn 'Abdullah ibn Qaridh, "I passed by Abu Hurairah while he was performing ablution and he said, 'Do you know why I am making ablution? It is because I ate some yoghurt dried over a fire, for I heard the Messenger of Allah say, 'Perform ablution before eating food touched by fire." (Related by Ahmad, Muslim and "the four.")

'Aishah related that the Prophet, upon whom be peace, said, "Perform ablution from whatever touches fire." (Related by Ahmad, Muslim, an-Nasa'i and Ibn Majah.) This order is one of preference as the following *hadith* makes clear: 'Amr ibn Umayyah adh-Dhamari said, "I saw the Messenger of Allah, upon whom be peace, cutting a piece of a sheep's shoulder and eating it. He was then called to prayer. He put the knife down, prayed, and did not perform another ablution." (Related by al-Bukhari and Muslim.)

Renewing the ablution for every prayer. Said Buraidah, "The Prophet, upon whom be peace, made ablution for every prayer. On the day of the conquest of Makkah, he made ablution, wiped over his socks and prayed a number of times with just one ablution. 'Umar said to him, 'O Messenger of Allah, you did something that you have not done (before).' He answered, 'I did it on purpose, 'Umar.'" (Related by Ahmad, Muslim and others.)

Said Anas ibn Malik, "The Prophet, upon whom be peace, used to make ablution for every prayer." He was asked, "And what did you people use to do?" Malik said, "We prayed the prayers with one ablution unless we nullified it." (Related by Ahmad and al-Bukhari.)

Abu Hurairah reported that the Prophet said, "Were it not to be a hardship on my people, I would order them to make ablution for every prayer." (Related by Ahmad with a *hassan* chain.)

Ibn 'Umar reported that the Prophet, upon whom be peace, said, "Whoever makes ablution while he is already in a state of purity will have ten good deeds written for him."[20] (Related by Abu Dawud, at-Tirmidhi, and Ibn Majah.)

NOTES OF IMPORTANCE

It is permissible to speak while performing ablution. There is nothing reported from the *sunnah* that prohibits it.

Making supplications while washing the extremities is based on false *hadith*. It is best for the person to use only the supplications mentioned under the *Sunnah Acts of Ablution*.

If the person who is making ablution has a doubt concerning how many times he has washed a particular part of the body, he should go by the number he is certain about.

If any barrier or substance with weight, such as wax, is found on the body, it would invalidate one's ablution unless it is removed and the ablution is performed again. Coloring, like henna, is permissible, as it does not affect the ablution's correctness.

People with unusual circumstances (i.e. women with "prolonged flows of blood"), people who cannot control their urine, people with flatulence, and so on, should perform one ablution for each prayer whether their problem exists all or part of the time. Their prayers will be acceptable even while their problems are occuring.

One may be assisted by others in performing ablution.

---

[20]This *hadith* is weak. This is the opinion of at-Tirmidhi, an-Nawawi, al-Bukhari, al-Baghawi, al-'Iraqi, Ibn Hajr, as-Suyuti, al-Munawi and al-Albani. Cf., al-Munawi, *Faidh al-Qadeer* (Dar al-Ma'rifah, Beirut, 1972), volume 6, pp. 109-110. - J.Z.

One may use a towel to dry himself during any time of the year.

WIPING OVER THE SOCKS

Proof of its legitimacy. Wiping over the socks is part of the *sunnah*. An-Nawawi states, "All those who qualify for *ijma'* (consensus) agree that it is allowed to wipe over the socks — during travelling or at home, if needed or not — even a woman who stays at home or a handicapped person who cannot walk can do so. The Shi'ah and Khawarij reject it, but their rejection is not valid. Says Ibn Hajr in *Fath al-Bari*, "All of the preservers (of *hadith*) are of the opinion that wiping over the socks has come through a continuous transmission. Some have collected all of its narrations (from among the companions), and its number exceeds eighty. This includes *hadith* from the ten pepole who were promised Paradise." The strongest *hadith* on this point has been related by Ahmad, al-Bukhari, Muslim, Abu Dawud and at-Tirmidhi on the authority of Hammam an-Nakha'i who said, "Jarir ibn 'Abdullah urinated, performed ablution and wiped over his socks." It was said to him, "You do that and you have urinated?" He said, "Yes, I saw the Messenger of Allah, upon whom be peace, urinate and then do likewise." Said Ibrahim, "They were amazed at that *hadith*, because Jarir had embraced Islam after *surah al-Ma'idah* was revealed (10 AH). One of its verses calls for washing one's feet. This *hadith* helps us understand the verse by confining it to one who is not wearing socks. This constitutes a particular case, and the person who wears socks can just wipe over them.

Wiping over slippers. It is allowed to wipe over slippers, as this has been related from many companions. Says Abu Dawud, "Wiping over sandals (has been done by) 'Ali ibn Abu Talib, Ibn Mas'ud, al-Barra' ibn 'Aazib, Anas ibn Malik, Abu Umamah, Sahl ibn Sa'd and 'Amr ibn Hareeth. It has also been related from 'Umar ibn al-Khattab and Ibn 'Abbas." 'Ammar, Bilal ibn 'Abdullah ibn Abu Aufi and Ibn 'Umar also have *hadith* on this subejct. In Ibn al-Qayyim's *Tahdhib as-Sunan*, he relates from Ibn al-Mundhir, "Ahmad made a statement about the permissibility of wiping over slippers because of his fairness and justice. Nevertheless, the basis of this permissibility is the practice of the companions and a manifest analogy. There is no real difference between socks and slippers. It is correct that they take the same ruling. Most scholars say that one can wipe over either one." Those who permit it include Sufyan al-Thauri, Ibn al-Mubarak, 'Ata, al-Hasan and Sa'eed ibn al-Musayyab. Commenting on this subject, Abu Yusuf and Muhammad said, "It is allowed to wipe over them if they are thick and completely hide what they cover."

Abu Hanifah did not approve of wiping over thick slippers, but he changed his mind three or seven days before his death. He wiped over his slippers during his illness and said to his visitors, "I did what I used to tell people not to do." Al-Mughirah ibn Shu'bah reported that the Messenger of Allah, upon whom be peace, made ablution and wiped over his socks and slippers. This is related by Ahmad, at-Tahawi, Ibn Majah and at-Tirmidhi, who called it *hassan sahih*. Abu Dawud graded it weak.[21]

As it is permissible to wipe over socks so is it permissible to wipe over any foot covering, which has been used to avoid the cold or protect the wound, and so on. Of its permissibility, Ibn Taimiyyah says, "It is all right to wipe over foot covering because it takes precedence over wiping socks or slippers, for usually a foot covering is used for some need and to protect the feet from some harm... If wiping over the socks and slippers is allowed, then wiping over any foot covering should come first. Whoever claims that there is a consensus on the inadmissibility of wiping over foot coverings does so with a lack of knowledge. Not to speak of a consensus, he cannot prove its forbiddance even from the works of ten famous scholars." He goes on to say, "Whoever ponders over the words of the Messenger of Allah, upon whom be peace, and gives analogy its proper place, will know that the license from him was spacious on this subject and in accord with the beauty of Islamic law and the monotheistic magnanimity with which the Prophet had been sent." Even if there are some holes or cuts in the socks, it is permissible to wipe over them, as long as the person has only such socks to wear. Says al-Thauri, "The slippers of the emigrants and helpers were not free of cuts or holes, like the slippers of the people (in general). If this were a matter of concern, it would have been mentioned and related by them."

Conditions for wiping over the socks. One must have put his socks (or whatever covering he is using) while in a state of purity.

Said al-Mughirah ibn Shu'bah, "I was with the Messenger of Allah, upon whom be peace, one night during an expedition. I poured water for him to make ablution. He washed his face and arms and wiped

---

[21]Al-Albani has discussed why Abu Dawud thought it was weak. Cf., Muhammad Nasiruddin al-Albani, *Irwa' al-Ghaleel* (Maktab al-Islami, Beirut, 1979), volume 1, p. 138. - J.Z.

his head. Then I went to remove his socks and he said, 'Leave them on, as I put them on while I was in a state of purity,' and he just wiped over them." (Related by Ahmad, al-Bukhari and Muslim).

Al-Humaidi related in his *Musnad* that al-Mughirah reported, "We said, 'O Messenger of Allah, may we wipe over our socks?' He said, 'Yes, if you put them on while you were in a state of purity." The stipulations by the jurists that the socks must completely cover the foot to the ankle, and that one must be able to walk (a distance) in them alone, has been shown by Ibn Taimiyyah in his *al-Fatawa* to be weak.

The place to be wiped. Islamic law prescribes that the top of the sock is to be wiped.

Said al-Mughirah, "I saw the Messenger of Allah, upon whom be peace, wipe over the top of his socks." (Related by Ahmad, Abu Dawud and at-Tirmidhi, who called it *hassan*.) 'Ali observed, "If the religion was based on opinion, the bottom of the sock would take preference in being wiped to the top of the sock." (Related by Abu Dawud and ad-Daraqutni with a *hassan* or *sahih* chain.) What is obligatory in the wiping is what is meant by the lexicographical meaning of the word "wipe." There are no specifications authentically mentioned with respect to the wiping.

The duration of the wiping. For the resident, this period is one day and night. For the traveller, it is three days and nights. Said Safwan ibn 'Assal, "We were ordered (by the Prophet) to wipe over the socks if we were in a state of purity when we put them on, for three days if we were travellers, and for one day and night if we were residents. We did not remove them unless we were in post-sex impurity." (Related by ash-Shaf'i, Ahmad, Ibn Khuzaimah, at-Tirmidhi, and an-Nasa'i, who graded it *sahih*.)

Shuraih ibn Hani said, "I asked 'Aishah about wiping over socks and she answered, 'For the traveller, three days and three nights; for the resident, one day and night." This *hadith* is related by Ahmad, Muslim, at-Tirmidhi, an-Nasa'i and Ibn Majah. Of its authenticity, al-Baihaqi says, "This is the most authentic report on this topic." Some say that the duration begins with the time of the wiping, while others say it begins from the time of nullifying the ablution after wearing the socks.

The description of the wiping. After the person completes his ablution and puts on his socks or slippers, it is proper for him to wipe over them later on when he wants to perform ablution. He is permitted to do that for one day and night if he is resident, and for three days and nights if he is a traveller. But if he is in post-sex impurity, he must remove his socks, in accordance with the preceding *hadith* of Safwan.

What invalidates the wiping. The following invalidates the wiping:

(i) The end of the permissible time period for wiping.
(ii) Post-sex impurity.
(iii) Removal of the socks. If (i) or (iii) occurs while the person was in a state of purity, he need only wash his feet.

THE COMPLETE ABLUTION
(AL-GHUSL)

Ghusl means to wash the entire body with water. Says Allah in the Qur'an, "If you are sexually impure, purify yourselves." And, "They question you concerning menstruation. Say: It is an illness, so let women alone at such times and do not have sex with them until they are cleansed" *(al-Baqarah: 222)*.

ACTIONS REQUIRING *GHUSL*

Such actions are five in number:

Discharge of *al-Mani* owing to stimulation while asleep or awake. The opinion of the jurists in general is that *ghusl* is a must should one have a discharge of *al-mani* (sperm) owing to stimulation while asleep or awake. Abu Sa'eed reported that he heard the Messenger of Allah, upon whom be peace, say, "Water (washing) is (needed) after (ejaculation of) sperm." (Related by Muslim.)

Umm Salamah reported that Umm Sulaim said, "O Messenger of Allah, Allah is not ashamed of the truth. Does a woman have to perform *ghusl* if she has a wet dream?" He said, "Yes, if she sees the liquid." (Related by al-Bukhari, Muslim and others.)

There are some other points of importance that need to be noted:

(i) If the sperm is discharged without any type of stimulation (owing to illness or extreme cold). In this case, *ghusl* is not obligatory. 'Ali reported that the Prophet, upon whom be peace, said to him, "If sperm is ejaculated, perform *ghusl*." (Related by Abu Dawud).

Said Mujahid, "We were in a meeting in the mosque with the companions of Ibn 'Abbas (Tawus, Sa'eed ibn Jubair and 'Ikrimah). When he stood to pray, a man came in and said, 'Is there one who can give a legal verdict?' We said, 'Ask your question.' He said, 'Whenever I urinate, a liquid always follows it.' We asked, 'Is it the type of liquid that gives birth to children?' He said, 'Yes.' We said, 'Then you have to perform *ghusl*.' The man went away. Ibn 'Abbas hurried to finish his prayer, after which he told 'Ikrimah to bring the man back. He turned to us and said, 'Is your verdict found in the Book of Allah?' We said, 'No.' He asked, 'Is it based on the sayings of the Prophet, upon whom be peace?' We said, 'No.' 'Then from what?' We said, 'From our opinion.' He said, 'That is why the Messenger of Allah said that one learned man is more difficult for Satan than a thousand worshippers.'[1] The man came and faced Ibn 'Abbas, who said to him, 'When that happens, is it owing to any stimulation?' He answered, 'No.' Ibn 'Abbas asked, 'Do you feel any numbness in your body?' He answered, 'No.' Said Ibn 'Abbas, 'That is from the cold. Ablution is sufficient.'"

(ii) If one has a wet dream but does not find any traces of ejaculation. There is no need for *ghusl* in this instance either. Ibn al-Mundhir said, "All of the knowledgeable people known to me agree on this point." The *hadith* of Umm Salamah mentioned earlier supports this proposition.

(iii) If one wakes from sleep and finds some moistness, but does not recall any wet dream, though he is sure it is sperm, what should he do? To be safe, he should perform *ghusl*. Said Mujahid and Qatadah, "There is no need for *ghusl* until he is sure that it is sperm, for his prior condition of purity is not ended by an uncertainty.

(iv) If a man squeezes his penis to prevent ejaculation. This also makes *ghusl* unnecessary. This is based on the *hadith* which states that *ghusl* is required if the sperm can be seen. But, if the person walks and cannot control his ejaculation, he must perform *ghusl*.

---

[1]This *hadith* (and therefore the story too) is not weak but fabricated.

(v) **Sperm on the clothes during prayer.** If a man does not know how the sperm got on his clothes, and he has already prayed, should he perform *ghusl* and repeat all of his prayers since the last time he slept? If he thinks that it happened before his most recent sleep, he should repeat all of his prayers since the supposed time of his ejaculation.

Touching the two circumcised parts. This refers to the penis and the vagina. If one's penis has entered his wife's vagina, *ghusl* is obligatory even if there was no ejaculation. Says Allah, "If you are sexually impure, purify yourselves." Commenting on the subject, ash-Shaf'i says, "In the Arabic language, sexual impurity refers to any type of sexual intercourse, regardless of whether sperm was ejaculated or not. If someone says, 'So and so is sexually impure due to so and so,' it refers to any type of sexual intercourse between them, even if there was no ejaculation. No one disagrees that the fornication which requires the prescribed punishment is sexual intercourse, even if there is no ejaculation."

Abu Hurairah reported that the Prophet, upon whom be peace, said, "When anyone sits between the four parts of her body and exerts himself (has intercourse), bathing becomes obligatory (for both)." (Related by Ahmad and Muslim.)

Sa'eed ibn al-Musayyab reported that Abu Musa al-Ash'ari said to 'Aishah, "I would like to ask you something, but I am embarrassed." She said, "Ask and don't be shy, for I am your mother." He asked about a man who had intercourse but did not ejaculate. She said, on the authority of the Prophet, "If the two circumcised parts encountered each other, *ghusl* is obligatory." This *hadith* is related by Ahmad and Malik with different wordings. There is no doubt that there must be insertion; if there is only touching, *ghusl* is not obligatory for either. All scholars agree on this point.

Women and their period. Concerning menstruation and childbirth bleeding, Allah says in the Qur'an, "Do not approach them until they become pure. When they are pure, go to them in the manner that Allah has prescribed for you." The Messenger of Allah, upon whom be peace, said to Fatimah bint Abu Habish, "Do not pray during your period. After it has ended, perform *ghusl* and pray." (Related by al-Bukhari and Muslim.)

Post-childbirth bleeding is treated in a similar manner, according to the consensus of the companions. If a woman gives birth and has no flow of blood afterwards, some scholars say that she must perform *ghusl*, while others say that it would not be necessary. There is no textual authority on this latter point.

Death. When a Muslim dies, it is obligatory to wash his or her body, according to the consensus of the Muslims. This will be discussed in more detail later on.

A non-Muslim upon embracing Islam. New converts to Islam must perform *ghusl*. Abu Hurairah reported that Thumamah al-Hanafi was captured. The Prophet, upon whom be peace, passed by him and said, "What do you have to say for yourself, O Thumamah?" He said, "If you kill me, you would be killing a relative. If you give me a bounty (set me free), I would be thankful. If you want wealth (as a ransom), we can give you what you wish." The companions of the Prophet preferred the ransom and said, "What would we get if we killed him?" One time when the Prophet passed by him, he finally embraced Islam. The Prophet, upon whom be peace, untied him and told him to go to the garden of Abu Talhah and perform *ghusl*. He performed *ghusl* and prayed two *rak'ah*. The Prophet said, "Indeed, your brother became a fine Muslim." This *hadith* is related by Ahmad. There is also a source for the story in reports by al-Bukhari and Muslim.

ACTS THAT ARE FORBIDDEN TO THE IMPURE

Such acts are the following:

Prayer.

Circumambulating the Ka'bah. The reasoning behind this can be found in *What actions require the ablution as a prerequisite.*

Touching or carrying the Qur'an. The companions were all agreed that it is forbidden to touch or carry the Qur'an while one is in a state of impurity. There are some jurists, such as Dawud ibn Hazm[2], who allow the physically unclean person, whether because of sex or menstruation, to touch or carry the Qur'an, and they see nothing wrong with this. He derives his support from a *hadith* in the two *Sahihs* in which it is stated that the Prophet sent a letter

---

[2]This is how it is stated in the text, but it is a misprint. It should be Dawud and Ibn Hazm. - J.Z.

to Heraclius saying, "In the name of Allah, the Compassionate, the Merciful...O people of the book, come to a statement that is common between us and you, that we should worship none but Allah, and that we shall ascribe no partner unto Him, and that none of us shall take others for lords besides Allah. If they turn away, then say 'Bear witness that we are they who have surrendered (unto Him)." *(al-'Imran: 64)*. Ibn Hazm concludes, "This is the letter the Messenger of Allah wrote, containing this verse, to the Christians, and of course they touched it." The majority of scholars answer him by stating that one is allowed to touch parts of the Qur'an that are used in letters, books, *tafsir*, and so on, as such things are not copies of the Qur'an, nor is it confirmed that such an action is forbidden.

Reciting the Qur'an. According to most scholars, one who is physically unclean (because of sex or menstruation) may not recite any portion of the Qur'an. This is based on a *hadith* from 'Ali, in which he stated that nothing kept the Messenger of Allah, upon whom be peace, from the Qur'an save being sexually impure. This is related by "the four." At-Tirmidhi graded it *sahih*. Says al-Hafez in *al-Fath*, "Some people declare some of its narrators weak. But, in fact, it is of the *hassan* class and it is satisfactory as a proof." He also related, "I saw the Messenger of Allah perform ablution and recite some of the Qur'an, after which he said, 'This is for the one who is not in post-sex impurity. If one is in post-sex impurity, he may not do so, not even one verse." Ahmad and Abu Ya'la related this *hadith* with that wording. With that wording, al-Haithami says, "Its narrators are trustworthy." Says ash-Shaukani, "If that (report) is authentic, that is proof enough that it is forbidden." The first *hadith* does not forbid it, for it just states that it was his practice not to recite the Qur'an while he was in post-sex impurity. Similar reports do not show that it is disliked. Therefore, how can it be used as a proof that it is forbidden?" Al-Bukhari, at-Tabarani, Dawud, and Ibn Hazm are of the opinion that it is permissible for one who is in post-sex impurity (or in menstruation) to recite the Qur'an. Says al-Bukhari, "Ibrahim said, 'There is no problem if a menstruating woman recites a verse.' Ibn 'Abbas did not see anything wrong with a sexually impure person reciting the Qur'an. The Prophet, upon whom be peace, used to mention Allah under all circumstances." In Ibn Hajr's notes to that work, he says, "There is no authentic *hadith* reported by the author (al-Bukhari) concerning the prohibition of reciting by one who is sexually impure or menstruating." The sum total of what has been related on this issue informs us on this point, though the interpretations differ.

Staying in the mosque. It is forbidden for one who is physically unclean (because of sex or menstruation) to stay in the mosque. 'Aishah said, "The Messenger of Allah, upon whom be peace, saw that his companions' houses were practically in the mosque. He said, 'Direct those houses away from the mosque.' He then entered the mosque, but the people did nothing, hoping that Allah would reveal to Muhammad that what they were doing was permissible. After he came out, he said , 'Direct those houses away from the mosque, for it is not permitted for a menstruating woman or sexually impure person to be in the mosque." (Related by Abu Dawud.)[3]

Umm Salamah related that the Prophet, upon whom be peace, came to the mosque's courtyard and said at the top of his voice, "The mosque is off limits to menstruating women and the sexually impure persons." (Related by Ibn Majah and at-Tabarani.) Such people can, however, pass through the mosque, for says Allah, "O you who believe, draw not near unto prayer when you are drunk until you know that which you utter, nor when you are impure save when journeying upon the road, until you have bathed" *(an-Nisa': 43).* Said Jubair, "One of us used to pass through the mosque though he was impure." (Related by Ibn Abu Shaibah and Sa'eed ibn Mansur in his *Sunan.*) Zaid ibn Aslam said, "The companions of the Messenger of Allah, upon whom be peace, used to walk through the mosques while they were sexually impure." (Related by Ibn al-Mundhir.) Yazib ibn Habib reported that the companions' doors opened up into the mosque, and that when they were sexually impure, they could find no water or any path to water save through the mosque. Then Allah revealed, "...nor when you are impure, save journeying upon the road..." (Related by at-Tabari.)

Commenting on the preceding reports, ash-Shaukani says,"The meaning is so clear that there is no room for doubt." Said 'Aishah, "The Prophet said to me, 'Hand me my cloth from the mosque.' I said, 'I am menstruating.' He said, 'Your menstruation is not in your hand." (Related by the group, except for al-Bukhari.) Said Maimunah, "The Messenger of Allah used to come to one of our rooms while we were menstruating and put his head on (his wife's) lap and recite the Qur'an. Then one of us would take his clothes and put them in the mosque while she was menstruating." (Related by Ahmad and an-Nasa'i. The report has supporting evidence.)

---

[3]This is a weak hadith. Cf., al-Albani's *Dha'eef Sunan Abu Dawud*, number 32. - J.Z.

ACTIONS FOR WHICH *GHUSL* IS PREFERRED

This category of actions involves a reward for performing *ghusl*, and no blame if he does not. Such actions are:

Before the Friday prayer. Muslims are encouraged to perform *ghusl* before they gather for the Friday prayer. In fact, Islamic law even goes to the extent of ordering one to perform *ghusl* at this time as part of the overall cleanliness and hygiene of the Muslim society. Abu Sa'eed reported that the Prophet said,"*Ghusl* on Friday is obligatory (*wajib*) on every adult, as is using a toothbrush and applying some perfume." (Related by al-Bukhari and Muslim.)

The meaning of "obligatory" here is that it is greatly recommended. This understanding of the Prophet's saying is derived from what al-Bukhari recorded about an incident from Ibn 'Umar about his father. One day, 'Umar ibn al-Khattab was standing and delivering the *khutbah* when 'Uthman, one of the people from among the emigrants and helpers, entered. 'Umar said to him, "What time is it now?" He said, "I was busy and could not return home. When I heard the call to prayer, I did not make more than the regular ablution." 'Umar said, "And the ablution only, when you know that the Messenger of Allah ordered us to perform *ghusl* ?" Commenting on the incident, says ash-Shaf'i, " 'Uthman did not leave the prayer to perform *ghusl*, nor did 'Umar order him to do so. This illustrates that the companions knew that this order was one of choice. It also shows that it is preferred."

Muslim recorded that Abu Hurairah reported the Prophet saying, "Whoever makes the ablution and perfects it and then goes to the Friday prayer and listens attentively, will have forgiveness during (the period)between the Friday and the next (Friday), and an additional three days." Says al-Qurtubi, "This *hadith* shows that *ghusl* is preferred. The mention of ablution, the reward and acceptability points to the fact that ablution alone is sufficient." Ibn Hajr states in *at-Talkhis*, "It is one of the strongest proofs that *ghusl* for the Friday prayer is not obligatory. The statement that it is preferred is built upon the fact that if one does not perform *ghusl*, it will not harm (his prayer). But, if others are harmed by his perspiration or bad smell from his clothes and body, *ghusl* becomes obligatory, and not performing it detracts from the rewards of *salah*. Some scholars say that the Friday *ghusl* is a duty even if its non-performance causes no harm (to others). Their basis for this opinion is the *hadith* related by Abu Hurairah in which the Prophet, upon whom be peace, said, "It is a duty upon every Muslim to perform *ghusl* once every seven days, by washing his head and body." Al-Bukhari and Muslim accept the *hadith* mentioned on the subject in their apparent meanings, and refute the ones contrary to the last *hadith* (of Abu Hurairah).

The time for the Friday *ghusl* is between dawn and the time of the Friday prayer. It is preferable to do it at the time of departure (to the mosque). If one loses his ablution after that, it is sufficient for him just to make a new ablution (he does not have to repeat the *ghusl*).

Says al-Athram, "I heard Ahmad being asked if a person performed *ghusl*, and then lost it, would the regular ablution be sufficient for him. He said, 'Yes, and I have not heard anything about that preferable to the *hadith* of Ibn 'Abzi," Ahmad is referring to the *hadith* related by Ibn 'Abzi Shaibah (with a *sahih* chain from 'Abdurahman ibn 'Abzi on the authority of his father, who was a companion.)He performed *ghusl* for the Friday prayer, and afterwards nullified his ablution. After that, he performed just the regular ablution, and did not repeat his *ghusl*. The time for the *ghusl* ends with the time of the prayer. If one performs *ghusl* after the prayer, it would not be the *ghusl* of the Friday prayer, and one who does so is not following the Prophet's order. Ibn 'Umar reported that the Prophet said, "Before you come to the Friday prayer, you should perform *ghusl*. (Related by "the group.") Muslim says, "When one of you wants to come to the Friday prayer, he should perform *ghusl*." Ibn 'Abdul-Barr related that there is a consensus on this point.

Performing *ghusl* for the 'Id prayers. Scholars also encourage Muslims to perform *ghusl* for the 'id prayers, even though there is no authentic *hadith* to support this opinion. It says in *al-Badr al-Muneer*, "The *hadith* concerning performing *ghusl* for the 'ids are weak. But there do exist good reports from the companions (on this point)."

***Ghusl* for washing a corpse.** According to many scholars, performing *ghusl* is also preferred for one who has washed a corpse. Abu Hurariah reported that the Prophet, upon whom be peace, said, "Whoever has washed a corpse must perform *ghusl*, and whoever carried him must perform ablution." (Related by Ahmad, Abu Dawud, at-Tirmidhi, an-Nasa'i, Ibn Majah and others.) However, there is some criticism of this *hadith*. 'Ali ibn al-Madani, Ahmad, Ibn al-Mundhir, ar-Rafi' and others say, "The *hadith* scholars did not classify anything on this topic as authentic." But Ibn Hajr quotes at-Tirmidhi and Ibn Hibban: "At-Tirmidhi called it *hassan* and Ibn Hibban called it *sahih*. And, due to its numerous chains, it is most likely *hassan*. An-Nawawi strongly refutes what at-Tirmidhi said." Says adh-Dhahabi, "The chains of this *hadith* are stronger than a number of chains of the *hadith* that the jurists argue by." The order in the *hadith* implies preference, based on what has been related by 'Umar, who said, "We used to wash the dead. Some of us would perform *ghusl* and some would not." (Related by al-Khateeb with a *sahih* chain.) When 'Asma bint Umaish washed the body of her deceased husband, Abu Bakr as-Siddiq, she asked if there were any among the emigrants present, and said, "This day is extremely cold and I am fasting. Do I have to make *ghusl*?" They said, "No." (Related by Malik.)

Making *Ghusl* for Hajj. According to the scholars, it is also preferable for one who is undertaking the pilgrimage or *'umrah* to perform *ghusl*. Zaid ibn Thabit related that he saw the Messenger of Allah, when he intended to perform the *hajj*, perform *ghusl*. (Related by ad-Daraqutni, al-Baihaqi and at-Tirmidhi, who called it *hassan*. As-Usaili regarded it as weak.)

Making *Ghusl* upon entering Makkah. It is preferable for whoever wants to enter Makkah to perform *ghusl*. It is reported that Ibn 'Umar, when going to Makkah, would spend the night in Tawa, and would enter Makkah during the day. He mentioned that the Prophet, upon whom be peace, also used to do this. (Related by al-Bukhari and Muslim.) Ibn al-Mundhir said, "All of the scholars say it is preferred to perform *ghusl* upon entering Makkah, but if one does not do so, there is no expiation for him to make. Most of them say that the regular ablution is sufficient.

Making *Ghusl* at Mount 'Arafah. Such an act is preferred while one stops there during the *hajj*. Malik ibn Nafa' reported that Ibn 'Umar used to do so before embarking upon the *hajj*, upon entering Makkah, and while stopping at 'Arafah.

THE PRINCIPLES OF *GHUSL*

There are only two things that the law requires:

The intention. This involves distinguishing the acts of worship from the customary acts. The intention is only in the heart, and should not be stated, as this would be tantamount to innovation.

Washing all bodily parts. This is based on the following: Says Allah, "If you are sexually impure, cleanse yourselves," that is, perform *ghusl,* and "They ask you concerning menstruation. Say: 'It is an illness, so leave women alone at such times and go not in unto them until they are cleansed," that is, until they perform *ghusl.* The proof that cleansing means *ghusl* is in the verse, "O you who believe, draw not unto the prayer when you are drunk until you know what you utter, nor when you are polluted, save when journeying upon the road, until you have bathed (*taghtasilu*)." This shows that *ghusl,* the washing of all bodily parts, is meant.

HOW *GHUSL* IS PERFORMED

According to the practice of the Prophet, upon whom be peace, the correct manner of performing *ghusl* is: (1) wash both hands three times, (2) wash the penis, (3) make a complete ablution (like the one made for prayer — the Prophet used to delay washing his feet until the end of his *ghusl* if he was using a tub, and so on), (4) rub water through one's hair three times, letting the water reach down to the roots of the hair, (5) pour water over the entire body, begining with the right side, then the left, washing under the armpits, inside the ears, inside the navel, inside the toes and whatever part of the body can be easily rubbed. This account is based on the following report from 'Aishah: "When the Prophet, upon whom be peace, took his bath after sexual intercourse, he would begin by washing his hands. Then he would pour water from his right hand to his left and wash his sexual organs, make the ablution for prayer, take some water and put his fingers to the roots of his hair to the extent that he sees that the skin is wet, then pour water over his head three times and then over the rest of his body." (Related by al-Bukhari and Muslim.) In one narration it states, "He used to rub his head with his hands until he was certain the water reached his skin, and then he poured water over it three times." It is also related that she said, "When the Prophet would perform *ghusl* after having had sexual intercourse, he would call for some water, which he would pour on his right hand to wash the right side of his head and then the left. He would then take water with both hands and pour it over his head." Said Maimunah, "I put water out for the Messenger of Allah to perform *ghusl.* He washed his hands two or three times, and then he poured water from his right hand to his left and washed his private parts, wiped his hands on the earth, rinsed his mouth and nose, washed his face and hands, washed his head three times, poured water over his body, and finally moved from his place and washed his feet. I brought him a towel, but he did not take it, for he shook the water off with his hands." (Related by "the group.")

Ghusl for Women

A woman performs *ghusl* just as a man does, except that if she has plaited hair she does not have to undo it, provided that the water can reach the roots of her hair. Umm Salamah said, "O Messenger of Allah, I am a woman who has closely plaited hair on my head. Do I have to undo them for *ghusl* after sexual intercourse?" He said, "No, it is enough for you to throw three handfuls of water on your head and then pour water over yourself. After doing this, you shall be cleansed." (Related by Ahmad, Muslim and at-Tirmidhi, who called it *hassan sahih*.) 'Ubaid ibn 'Umair reported that 'Aishah discovered that 'Abdullah ibn 'Amr was ordering the women to undo their plaits of hair (for *ghusl*). She observed, "It is amazing that Ibn 'Amr orders the woment to undo the plaits of hair for *ghusl*. Why doesn't he just order them to shave their heads? I and the Messenger of Allah used to bathe from one vessel, and all I did was pour three handfuls of water over my head." (Related by Ahmad and Muslim.)

It is preferrable for a woman performing *ghusl* to cleanse herself from menstruation or post-childbirth bleeding to take some cotton smeared with musk or perfume and wipe it over the traces of blood. This will remove the bad smell of the menstrual blood. 'Aishah reported, " 'Asma bint Yazid asked the Messenger of Allah about *ghusl* after menstruation has ended. He said, "She should use water mixed with the leaves of the lote-tree and cleanse herself. Then she should pour water over her head and rub it well till it reaches the roots of the hair, after which she should pour water over it. Afterwards, she should take a piece of cotton smeared with musk and cleanse herself with it." 'Asma asked, "How should she cleanse herself with it?" He said, "Praise be to Allah, she should cleanse herself with it." 'Aishah said in a subdued tone that she should apply it to the traces of blood. 'Asma then asked about bathing after sexual intercourse. He said, "She should take water and cleanse herself or complete the ablution, pour water on her head and rub it till it reaches the roots of her hair, and then she should pour water over herself." 'Aishah observed, "How good are the women of the 'helpers' that shyness does not keep them from learning their religion." (Related by "the group," except at-Tirmidhi.)

Questions Related to the *Ghusl*

It is sufficient to perform one *ghusl* for both menstruation and sexual impurity, or for the Friday prayer and the *'id* prayer, or for sexual impurity and the Friday prayer, if one has the intention for both of them. This is based on the Prophet's saying, "All acts are based on intentions."

If a person performed post-sex *ghusl* but did not make ablution, the *ghusl* will suffice. Said 'Aishah, "The Messenger of Allah did not perform ablution after *ghusl*." Ibn 'Umar said to a man who had told him that he performed ablution after *ghusl*, "You went too far." Says Abu Bakr ibn al-'Arabi, "There is no difference of opinion among the scholars that ablution falls under the category of *ghusl*. If the intention was to remove sexual impurity, it also includes the minor impurities, as what sexual impurity prevents is greater than what the minor impurities prevent. The smaller one falls under the greater one, and the intention for the greater one suffices."

It is acceptable for a person in post-sex uncleanliness or a menstruating woman to remove their hairs, cut their nails, go to the markets, and so on, without any dislike. 'Ata said that such people can get cupped, cut their nails and their hair, and that this is allowed even if he (or she) has not performed the regular ablution. (Related by al-Bukhari).

One may enter a public bathroom as long as he keeps his private parts from being seen, and he does not look at others' private parts. Says Ahmad, "If you know that everyone inside the bathroom is wearing a loincloth, you may enter. If not, then don't enter." The Prophet, upon whom be peace, said, "A man should not look at another man's private parts, and a woman should not look at another woman's private parts." There is no problem with mentioning Allah's name in the public baths, as mentioning the name of Allah under any circumstances is good, since there is no text prohibiting it. The Messenger of Allah used to remember Allah under all circumstances.

There is no problem in drying one's self with a towel or other cloth after performing ablution or *ghusl* during the summer or winter.

It is permissible for a man to use the water left over by a woman and vice-versa. This is derived from the fact that it is permissible for them to perform *ghusl* from the same container. Ibn 'Abbas narrated that some of the Prophet's wives were performing *ghusl* from a container. The Prophet came and performed his ablution or *ghusl* from it. They said to him, "We were sexually unclean." He said, "The water does not become impure." (Related by Ahmad, Abu Dawud, an-Nasa'i and at-Tirmidhi, who called it *hassan sahih*). 'Aishah used to wash with the Messenger of Allah from one container, and they would take turns taking water until he said, "Leave some for me, leave some for me."

It is not allowed to bathe in the nude in front of people. It is forbidden to uncover one's private parts. If you cover it with some clothes, it is permissible. The Messenger of Allah would cover Fatimah with a curtain when she performed *ghusl*. If one performs *ghusl* in the nude, far away from the people, it is not prohibited. The prophets Musa (Moses) and Ayyub (Job) did so, as al-Bukhari, Ahmad, and an-Nasa'i recorded.

DRY ABLUTION (AT-TAYAMMUM)

Definition. Literally *tayammum* means "aim, purpose." In Islamic law, it refers to "aiming for or seeking soil to wipe one's face and hands with the intention of preparing oneself to pray, and so on."

Proof of its legitimacy. This is proven by the Qur'an, *sunnah* and *ijma'* (consensus). The Qur'an says, "And if you are ill, or on a journey, or one of you comes from relieving himself, or you have touched women, and you do not find water, then go to high clean soil and rub your face and hands (therewith). Lo, Allah is Benign, Forgiving" *(an-Nisa': 43)*. From the *sunnah* we have the *hadith* related by Abu Umamah in which the Prophet, upon whom be peace, said, "All of the earth has been made for me and my nation a pure place of prayer. Whenever a person from my nation wants to pray, he has something with which to purify himself, that is, the earth." (Related by Ahmad.) Finally, there is a consensus that *tayammum* forms a legitimate part of the *shari'ah*, as it replaces ablution or *ghusl* under specific circumstances.

This form of ablution is viewed as a blessing from Allah to the Muslims. Jabir relates that the Prophet, upon whom be peace, said, "I have been given five things that were not given to anyone before me: I have been made victorious due to fear for a distance of one month's journey; the earth has been made a place of prayer for me — wherever and whoever of my nation wants to pray, he may pray; and the war booty has been made lawfal for me, and this was not lawful for anyone before me. I have been given permission to intercede. The prophets used to be raised for their own people only, but I have been raised for all of mankind." (Related by al-Bukhari and Muslim.)

The reason for its legitimacy. Said 'Aishah, "We went out with the Messenger of Allah on one of his journeys until we reached Baida'. At this place, one of my bracelets broke and fell somewhere. The Messenger of Allah and others began to look for it. There was no water at that place, nor did anyone have any water with him. The people went to Abu Bakr and said, "Do you see what your daughter has done?" Abu Bakr came to me, while the Prophet was sleeping on my thigh. He blamed me and said to me whatever Allah willed him to say. He also poked me in my side. I could not move, for the Prophet, upon whom be peace, was sleeping on my lap. He slept until the morning without any water available. Then, Allah revealed the verse of *tayammum*. As-Sayyid ibn Hudhain said, 'That was not the first blessing from the family of Abu Bakr.' The camel that I was on got up and we found the necklace underneath it." (Related by "the group," except for at-Tirmidhi.)

When it is permissible. *Tayammum* is, however, permissible only on specific occasions. These are:

(a) One cannot find water, or the amount one finds is insufficient for ablution. 'Imran bin Husain said, "We were with the Messenger of Allah during a journey. When he led the people in prayer, one man stayed apart. He asked him, "What prevented you from praying?" He said, 'I need a post-nocturnal bath and there is no water.' He said, 'Use the soil, for it is sufficient.'" (Related by al-Bukhari and Muslim.)

Abu Dharr related that the Prophet, upon whom be peace, said, "The soil is a purifier for a Muslim, even if he does not find water for twenty years." (Related by "the four." At-Tirmidhi grades it *hassan sahih*.) But before one makes *tayammum*, he must look for water from any posible source. If he is sure water is not to be found or it is too far away, he does not have to look for it.

(b) One is injured or ill. If one is in this condition, and believes water will worsen it (he does not have to be absolutely sure, but may base his opinion on past experience or what a knowledgeable person has told him), he may perform *tayammum*. Jabir said, "We were on a journey and one of us got injured. Later, he had a wet dream. He asked his companions, 'Can I perform *tayammum?*' They said, 'No, not if you have water.' He performed *ghusl* and died. When they came to the Messenger of Allah, they informed him of what had transpired. He said, 'They killed him, Allah will kill them. Do you not ask if you do not know? The rescue of the ignorant person is the question. He could have performed *tayammum* and dropped water on his wound or wrapped it with something and wipe over the wrapping, and wash the rest of his body." This is related by Abu Dawud, Ibn Majah, ad-Daraqutni and Ibn as-Sakin, who said it is *sahih*.

(c) **If the water is cold enough to physically harm the user.** This is only allowed on the condition that he can find no one to heat it, or is unable to use the public bathrooms. 'Amr ibn al-'Aas narrated that he was participating in an expedition. He had a wet dream during an extremely cold night, and was afraid that if he performed *ghusl* he would die. He prayed the morning prayer with his companions. He then went to the Messenger of Allah, upon whom be peace, to ask him about this. Muhammad said, "O 'Amr, did you pray with your companions while you needed a post-nocturnal bath?" 'Amr mentioned the verse, "Do not kill yourselves, Allah is merciful to you" to the Prophet. The Prophet just laughed and didn't say anything. (Related by Ahmad, Abu Dawud, al-Hakim, ad-Daraqutni, Ibn Hibban and al-Bukhari in *mu'allaq* form.) This example illustrated the Prophet's tacit approval.

(d) **When water is nearby, but one does not want to fetch it due to fear.** If one fears for his life, family, wealth, (for example, if an enemy is nearby — beast or human — or one is a prisoner, and so on), one may perform *tayammum*. This is also allowed if there is water but one lacks the proper means to get it, or if one fears some accusation against him if he gets it.

(e) **If one is saving his water for later use.** This could be for a hound, for dough, cooking or to remove an impurity that is not pardonable. Says Imam Ahmad, "Many of the companions performed *tayammum* to save their water for drinking." 'Ali said that a man who is travelling and becomes unclean because of sex or a wet dream can perform *tayammum* if he fears he will go thirsty: "He should perform *tayammum* and not *ghusl*." (Related by ad-Daraqutni.) Says Ibn Taimiyyah, "If a person needs to relieve himself but has only a small amount of water, it is best that he pray with *tayammum* and relieve himself, rather than keep his ablution and pray before relieving himself."

(f) One can get water, but fears that the prayer will be over by the time he gets it. He can perform *tayammum* and pray, and does not need to repeat his prayer (after he gets water).

(g) The soil used for *tayammum*. It must be pure soil: this can be sand, stone, gypsum, and so on. Says Allah, "Perform *tyammum* with pure soil," and all scholars of Arabic agree that "soil" is whatever covers the earth, dirt or otherwise.

How to perform *tayammum*. First, one must have the intention (see the section on ablution). Then, he mentions Allah's name, strikes the soil with his hands, wipes his face and his hands up to the wrist. Nothing is more authentic and clear than what 'Ammar related. He said, "We became sexually impure and had no water, so we rolled in the dirt and prayed. This was mentioned to the Prophet and he said, 'This would have been enough for you,' and he struck the earth with his hands, blew in them and then wiped his face and hands with them." (Related by al-Bukhari and Muslim). In another text he states, "It would have been enough for you to strike the ground with your hands, blow into them, then wipe your face and hands up to the elbows." (Related by ad-Daraqutni.)

This *hadith* shows that one strike of the earth is sufficient, and one only wipes the arms to the wrists. It is from the *sunnah* that one who· makes *tayammum* with dirt should blow into his hands first and not make his face dusty or dirty.

What *tayammum* makes permissible. After doing so, he is pure and may do any of the acts requiring prior purification, such as praying and touching the Qur'an. He does not have to perform it during the time of prayer, and he may pray as many prayers as he wishes (unless he nullifies it), exactly as he can after performing the regular ablution. Abu Dharr reported that the Prophet said, "The soil is a purifier for a Muslim, even if he does not find water for twenty years. Then if he touches water, that is, to make ablution, and so on, it would be good." This is related by Ahmad and at-Tirmidhi, who said it is *sahih*.

What nullifies *tayammum*. In addition to the presence of water, everything that nullifies the ablution nullifies *tayammum*.

If a person prays after performing *tayammum* and then finds water, he does not need to repeat his prayer even if there is time left to do so. Abu Sa'eed al-Khudri said, "Two men went out on a journey. The time of prayer came and, as they had no water, they performed *tayammum*. Then they found some water during the time of the same prayer. One of them repeated his prayer with ablution and the other did not. When they saw the Messenger of Allah, they asked him about the proper procedure in such a case. He said to the one who did not repeat his prayer, 'You have acted according to the *sunnah* and your prayer is sufficient for you.' He said to the other, 'You will get a double reward.'" (Related by Abu Dawud and an-Nasa'i.) If one comes across water before he prays or finishes his prayer with *tayammum*, his prayer becomes null and void, for he must make ablution with water. If a person is not clean because of sex or a wet dream, or a woman is menstruating, and they pray after performing *tayammum*, they need not repeat their prayer after finding water, but they must perform *ghusl* with water when they can. 'Umar said, "The Prophet led the people in prayer, and afterwards saw a man who had not prayed. He said, 'Why didn't you pray with us?' The man replied, 'I was sexually unclean and there was no water.' He told him, 'Use the soil, and it will be enough.' 'Imran then mentioned that they later found water. The Prophet, upon whom be peace, brought a bowl of water for the man and told him to perform *ghusl*. (Related by al-Bukhari.)

Wiping Over Casts, Wrappers and Similar Items.

It is allowable to wipe over any wrapper or diseased or injured bodily part. There are many *hadith* on this point, and although they are all weak, their many chains strengthen each other, making them valid to talk about. One *hadith*, that of Jabir (quoted earlier), relates a story about a man who was on a journey and suffered an injury. While he slept, he had a wet dream, after which he asked his companions if he could perform *tayammum*. They said he could not, so he made *ghusl* and died because of it. When that was mentioned to the Prophet, he said "They killed him, may Allah kill them. Do you not ask about what you do not know? ... It would have been enough for him to perform *tayammum* and drop a little water over his wound or else wipe it, then to wipe it and wash the rest of the body." This is related by Abu Dawud, Ibn Majah, ad-Daraqutni and Ibn as-Sakin, who classified it as *sahih*. Ibn 'Umar used to do this.

In fact, it is obligatory to wipe over such casts or wrappers in ablution or *ghusl* instead of washing the injured parts. This must be done even if he has to heat the water. But, if he believes that this would harm the diseased or injured part, or that his condition may worsen, or that his pain would increase, he may wipe the injured part with water. If he fears that this would also be harmful, he should wrap it and then gently wipe over it. It is not necessary for him to be in a state of purity while applying the cast or wrapper to be wiped. There is also no time limit for such wipings, for he can do so as long as his condition lasts. Removing the wrapper or cast nullifies the wiping, as does the final cure.

The Prayer of One Who Has no Means of Purifying Himself

Whoever cannot get water or soil may pray in whatever state he is in, and he will not have to repeat his prayer later. This is based on what Muslim related from 'Aishah. She had borrowed some jewelry from 'Asma and it broke (and fell). The Messenger of Allah, upon whom be peace, sent some people to search for it. The prayer time came and they had to pray without ablution. When they came to the Prophet, they complained to him and the verses of *tayammum* were revealed. Usaid ibn Hudhair said, "May Allah give you good recompense. Allah never reveals an order with respect to you except that He removes by it some hardship and gives the Muslims some benefit." The companions prayed while in a state of impurity, but the Prophet did not admonish them nor did he order them to repeat their prayers. Says an-Nawawi, "That is the strongest statement of proof (on this question)."

MENSTRUATION (HAIDH)

In Arabic, the word for menstruation (*haidh*) literally means "running." Here it refers to the discharge of blood during a woman's state of health, not from giving birth or breaking the hymen.

Most scholars say that its time begins at the age of nine. If blood is seen before that age, it is not menstrual blood, but is considered to be putrid blood. As there is no evidence about when a woman stops menstruating, if an elderly lady finds blood flowing it is considered menstrual blood.

For the blood to be so considered, it must be one of the following colors:

(a) Dark. Once, when Fatimah bint Abu Habash had a prolonged flow of blood, the Prophet told her, "If it is the blood of menstruation, it will be dark and recognizable. If it is that, then leave the prayer. If it is other than that, then make ablution and pray, for it is only due to a vein." This is related by Abu Dawud, an-Nasa'i, Ibn Hibban and ad-Daraqutni, who said all of its narrators are trustworthy. Al-Hakim also related it, and said that it meets Muslim's standards.

(b) Red. It is the original color of blood.

(c) Yellow. It is a liquid, like pus.

(d) A muddy color. It is an intermediate color between black and white, like dirt.

Malik and Muhammad al-Hassan (and al-Bukhari in *mu'allaq* form) recorded that women would send 'Aishah small boxes with yellow-stained cotton, and she would tell them, "Do not be in haste until you see the pure white cotton." If the discharge is yellow or muddy during the days of menstruation, it is to be considered as part of the menses. During other days, it is not regarded as such. Umm 'Atiyyah said, "After we were pure, we did not consider the yellow or muddy discharge to be anything." This is related by Abu Dawud and al-Bukhari, but without the words "...after we were pure..."

There is no stated minimum or maximum length of time for the menses, and all statements dealing with this topic have no sound backing. If a woman has a customary length of time for her menses, she should according to it. Umm Salamah asked the Prophet about a woman with a prolonged flow of blood. He said, "She should look for the number of days and nights that she usually has her menses and the time of the month during which it occurs. Then she should leave the prayer (during those days, and then afterwards) perform *ghusl*, tie something around her vagina and pray." (Related by "the five," except for at-Tirmidhi.) If she has no customary period to go by, then she can try to distinguish between the different types of blood. This practice is based on the previously quoted *hadith* of Fatimah bint Abu Hubaish, which states that menstrual blood is distinguishable and well-known to women.

All scholars agree that there is no minmum or maximum time limit between two menstrual periods. Some say that the latter period is fifteen days, while others say it is three days.

POST-CHILDBIRTH BLEEDING

Such bleeding occurs after the birth of a child, regardless if the child survived the birth or not. This type of bleeding has no minimum duration, for it could stop right after the birth, or there could even be no blood. Therefore, her confinement would end and she would be obliged to fast, pray, and so on. The maximum duration is forty days. Said Umm Salamah, "During the lifetime of the Prophet, the post-childbirth woman would be in confinement for forty days." (Related by "the five," except for an-Nasa'i.)

After recording the *hadith*, at-Tirmidhi states, "The knowledge-able companions, the following generation and those that came later agree that a woman experiencing post-childbirth bleeding had to stop praying for forty days unless her blood stopped. If her bleeding stops before that time, she is to make *ghusl* and start praying. If she sees blood after forty days, most scholars say that she is not to stop praying."

Forbidden Acts for Women Experiencing Menstruation and Post-Childbirth Bleeding

All acts forbidden for a person who has not yet cleansed himself from sex or a wet dream are prohibited to women in these two conditions, as these are considered major impurities. But, there are also two further prohibitions:

(i) **They cannot fast.** If women fast, their fasting will be considered null and void. If they fast during the month of Ramadan, they will still have to make those days of fasting up later on. Mu'adhah said, "I asked 'Aishah, 'Why must we make up the fasts missed due to our menstruation, and not the prayers?' She said, 'That was what the Messenger of Allah told us to do. We were ordered to make up the fasts, and we were ordered not to make up the prayers." (Related by "the group.")

(ii) **She can not engage in sexual intercourse.** Said Anas, "When a Jewish woman was menstruating, her husband would not eat or sleep with her. The companions asked the Prophet, upon whom be peace, about that, and Allah revealed: "They question you concerning menstruation. Say: 'It is an illness, so let women alone at such times and go not in unto them until they are cleaned. And when they have purified themselves, then go in unto them as Allah has enjoined upon you. Truly, Allah loves those who turn unto Him and loves those who have a care for cleanliness" *(al-Baqarah: 222)*. The Messenger of Allah also said, "Do everything except intercourse." (Related by "the group," except for al-Bukhari.)

In his comments on the subject, an-Nawawi states, "If a Muslim believes it is permissible to have intercourse with his menstruating wife, he becomes an unbelieving apostate. If he does it, not thinking that it is permissible, but out of forgetfulness or not knowing that it is forbidden or not knowing that his wife was menstruating, then there is no sin or expiation upon him. If he does it on purpose, knowing that it is forbidden, he has committed a grave sin and must repent. There are two opinions on this: the more correct one is that there is to be expiation." He further says, "All scholars say that one may touch anything above the navel or below the knees. Most scholars say that it is permissible to touch what is between the navel and the knees, but not the vagina or anus." An-Nawawi concludes that it is permitted but hated, as that is the strongest position from the evidence. This evidence is based upon the practice of the Prophet's wives: when he wished to be with them during their period, they would put something over their vagina. (Related by Abu Dawud.) Al-Hafez observes, "Its chain is strong." Masruq ibn al-Ajda' asked 'Aishah, "What is off limits to me sexually during my wife's menstruation?" She said, "Nothing, except the vagina." (Related by al-Bukhari in his *Tarikh*.)

Women with Prolonged Flows of Blood

Islam defines such an occurrence as the flowing of blood outside of the regular time. This usually happens in three specific cases. In the first case, the woman knows that her flow of menstrual blood is lasting longer than usual. In such a case, she will act according to her customary period, and the remainder will be considered days of prolonged blood flows. This is based on the *hadith* of Umm Salamah, in which she asked the Messenger of Allah, upon whom be peace, about this condition. He said, "She should wait for the days and nights of her normal period and figure them out of the month, and she should leave the prayer during those days. (Afterwards) she should perform *ghusl*, tighten something around her vagina and then pray." (Related by Malik, ash-Shafi and "the five," except for at-Tirmidhi.)

Evaluating the report, an-Nawawi says, "Its chain meets the conditions (of al-Bukhari and Muslim)." Al-Khattabi holds, "That regulation is for the woman who is experiencing prolonged blood flows. If the blood is flowing, the Prophet ordered her to leave the prayer during her regular period, and to perform *ghusl* after her customary time has passed. Then, she becomes just like any other purified person."

In the second case, a woman does not know her period well enough to determine if she is experiencing menstrual bleeding or a prolonged flow of blood. In that case, her menstruation is considered to be six or seven days, which is the most common among women.

Said Jamnah bint Jahsh, "I had a very strong prolonged flow of blood. I went to the Prophet to ask him about it. When I asked him if I had to stop praying and fasting, he said 'Tie around a cloth, and it will stop.' I said, 'It is greater than that.' He said, 'Curb it.' I said, 'It flows greatly.' He then said, 'You may do one of two things: either one will suffice. Which one you are able to do you know best. This is a strike from Satan.[4] Be on your period for six or seven days, which Allah knows, and then perform *ghusl* until you see that you are clean. Pray for fourteen nights or thirteen nights and days and fast, and that will be sufficient for you. Do that every month as the other women become pure and menstruate. If you can, you may delay the noon prayer and hasten the afternoon prayer. Perform *ghusl* and pray the noon and afternoon prayers together. Then delay the sunset and hasten the night prayers and pray them together. Perform *ghusl* for the morning prayer and pray it. This is how you may pray and fast if you have the ability to do so..." And he said, "That is the more loved way to me."

As to the authenticity of the *hadith*, it is related by Ahmad, Abu Dawud and at-Tirmidhi, who grades it as *hassan sahih*. He says, "I asked al-Bukhari about it, and he called it *hassan*." Ahmad ibn Hanbal says it is *hassan sahih*.[5]

Al-Khattabi observes, in a note to this *hadith*, that this is for the woman who is a "beginner" and does not know her regular days of menstruation. The Prophet told her to act according to the customary situation of women, and to consider herself as having her period only once a month, like most women. His statement, 'As women menstruate and as they become pure' points to this fact. This is by analogy to the affairs of women with respect to each other in menstruation, pregnancy, maturity and other affairs of theirs."

In the third case, a woman has a regular period, but she is able to distinguish the blood. She should, therefore, behave according to the type of blood she sees. Fatimah bint Abu Hubaish had a prolonged flow of blood, and the Prophet told her, "If it is menstrual blood, it is dark and recognizable. If you have that, abstain from the prayer. If it is other than that, make ablution and pray, for it is a vein."

Women who fall into any of these categories must abide by the following regulations:

Ghusl. She does not have to perform *ghusl* for every prayer, except for the one time when her period or blood flow has ended.

---

[4]Because it makes the woman doubt whether she should be praying or not, and so on. - J.Z.

[5]This is probably a mistake. I've never heard of Ahmad ever using the term *hassan sahih*. - J.Z.

She must make ablution for every prayer. Said the Prophet, "Make ablution for every prayer." According to Malik, this is only preferred and not obligatory (unless she nullifies her ablution, of course).

Keeping the blood in check. She is to wash her vagina before she makes ablution, and she should wear something which soaks up the blood. It is preferred for her to do what she can to keep the blood in check.

Ablution. She should not make ablution before the prayer's time begins.

Sex. She may have intercourse with her husband even while the blood is flowing, according to most scholars, because there is no evidence to the contrary. Said Ibn 'Abbas, "If she can pray, her husband can have intercourse with her." Al-Bukhari says that if she is pure enough for prayer, she certainly must be pure enough for intercourse. Abu Dawud and al-Baihaqi related that 'Akramah bint Hamnah had a prolonged flow of blood and that her husband had intercourse with her. An-Nawawi holds its chain to be *hassan*.

What she can do. She is to be considered a pure person, and she may pray, fast, remain in the mosque, recite the Qur'an, touch a copy of the Qur'an, and so on.

PRAYER (SALAH)

The prayer is a type of worship consisting of specific statements and actions. It is begun by pronouncing the greatness of Allah, and is concluded with salutations of peace. As prayer is the essence of Islam, we will discuss it here in detail.

To state it simply, prayer must exist, for without it Islam can not stand. The Prophet, upon whom be peace, said, "The head of the matter is Islam, its pillar is the prayer, and the top of its hump is *jihad* in the way of Allah." It was the first act of worship that was made obligatory by Allah. Its obligation was revealed directly to the Prophet, during his ascension to heaven. Said Anas, "The prayers were made obligatory on the Prophet, upon whom be peace, the night of his ascension to heaven. At first, they were fifty in number, but were reduced several times until they were five. Then it was proclaimed, 'O Muhammad, the order is not changed. These five are (equivalent) to the fifty."

As to the authenticity of the report, it is related by Ahmad, an-Nasa'i and at-Tirmidhi, who said it is *sahih*.

Salah is the first act that the person will be held accountable for. 'Abdullah ibn Qart related that the Messenger of Allah, upon whom be peace, said "The first act that the slave will be accountable for on the Day of Judgement will be prayer. If it is good, then the rest of his acts will be good. And if it is evil, then the rest of his acts will be evil." (Related by at-Tabarani.) It is the last thing that the

Prophet, upon whom be peace, recommended to his nation before he died, saying, "Prayer, prayer and what your right hand possesses." It will be the last thing taken away from the religion. When it perishes, Islam will perish. The Messenger of Allah, upon whom be peace, said, "If Islam were stripped away, piece by piece, people would hold tight to the next one. The first thing taken would be ruling and governance, and the last thing would be prayer." (Related by Ibn Hibban from the *hadith* of Abu Umamah.) In many verses of the Qur'an, Allah follows up prayer with the remembrance of Allah. "Lo! Worship preserves (one) from lewdness and iniquity, but verily, remembrance of Allah is more important." *(al-'Ankabut: 45);* "He is successful who grows and remembers the name of his Lord, so pray *(al-A'la: 14-15);* "So serve Me and establish worship for My remembrance" *(Taha: 14).* Sometimes He mentions prayer along with *zakah:* "Establish prayer and pay *zakah" (al-Baqarah: 110).* And at times, with patience: "Seek help in patience and prayer" *(al-Baqarah: 45),* and with *hajj:* "So pray unto your Lord and sacrifice" *(al-Kauthar: 2);* "Say: Lo! my worship and my sacrifice and my living and my dying are for Allah, Lord of the Worlds. He has no partner. This am I commanded, and I am the first of those who surrender (unto Him)" *(al-An'am: 162-163).* At other times, Allah begins the acts of piety with prayers and ends with them, as in the verses about the *ma'arij* (ascension to heaven): "Successful indeed are the believers who are humble in their prayers," and the verses, "And who pay heed to their prayers. These are the heirs who will inherit Paradise. There will they abide" *(al-Mu'minun: 1-2, 9-11).*

The importance of *salah* is so great that one is ordered to observe it while travelling or not, while one is safe or in fear: "Be guardians of your prayers, and of the mid-most prayer, and stand up with devotion to Allah. And if you go in fear, then (pray) standing or on horseback. When you are safe, remember Allah, as He has taught you that which (heretofore) you knew not" *(al-Baqarah: 238-239).* Allah explains how to pray during fear, safety or wartime: "And when you are among them and arrange their prayers for them, let only a party of them stand with you (to worship) and let them take their arms. Then, when they have performed their prostrations, let them fall to the rear and let another party come to pray with you, and let them take their precautions and arms. They who disbelieve long for you to neglect your arms and your baggage, that they may attack. It is no sin for you to lay aside your arms, if rain impedes you or if you are sick. But take your precautions. Lo! Allah prepares for the disbelievers shameful punishment. When you have performed your prayer, remember Allah, standing, sitting and reclining. And when you are in safety, observe your prayer properly. Prayer at fixed hours has been enjoined on the believers" *(an-Nisa': 102-103).*

Allah also strongly warns those who tamper with their prayers or are heedless. Says Allah in the Qur'an, "Now there has succeeded them a later generation who have ruined their prayers and have followed lusts. But they will meet deception" *(Maryam: 59);* "Ah, woe unto worshippers who are heedless of their prayers" *(al-Ma'un: 4-5).*

Prayer is one of the most important acts in Islam, and thus it requires a special guidance. Ibrahim asked his Lord to give him descendants who abided by their prayers: "My Lord! Cause me and (some) of my offspring to remain constant in prayer. And O our Lord! Accept my supplication" *(Ibrahim: 40).*

One Who Ignores His Prayers

Not praying and denying its obligation is seen as disbelief and places the person outside the religion of Islam. All scholars agree on this piont. They base their opinion on several *hadith,* some of which are:

Jabir reports that the Prophet, upon whom be peace, said, "Between a person and disbelief is discarding prayer." (Related by Ahmad, Muslim, Abu Dawud, at-Tirmidhi and Ibn Majah.)

Buraidah reported that the Prophet, upon whom be peace, said, "The pact between us and them is prayer. Whoever abandons it is a disbeliever." (Related by Ahmad, Abu Dawud, at-Tirmidhi, an-Nasa'i and Ibn Majah.)

'Abdullah ibn 'Amr ibn al-'Aas reported that the Prophet, upon whom be peace, one day mentioned the prayer and said, "Whoever guards and observes his prayer, they will be a light and a proof and a savior for him on the Day of Resurrection. Whoever does not guard and obvserve them, they will not be a light or a proof or a savior for him. On the Day of Resurrection, he will be with Qarun, Fir'aun, Haman and Ubayy ibn Khalf." (Related by Ahmad, at-Tabarani and Ibn Hibban. Its chain is excellent.)

That one who does not pray will be with the leaders of the unbelievers in the Hereafter makes it evident that such a person is an unbeliever. Says Ibn al-Qayyim, "The one who does not pray may be preoccupied with his wealth, kingdom, position or business. If one is kept away from his prayers by his wealth, he will be with

Qarun. One whose kingdom keeps him away from the prayers will be with Haman, and one whose business keeps him away from the prayers will be with Ubayy ibn Khalf."

Says 'Abdullah ibn Shaqiq al-'Aqeely, "The companions of Muhammad, peace be upon him, did not consider the abandonment of any act, with the exception of prayer, as being disbelief." (Related by at-Tirmidhi and al-Hakim, who said it met al-Bukahri's and Muslim's conditions.)

Says Muhammad ibn Nasr al-Mirwazi, "I heard Ishaq say, 'It is authentic (that) the Prophet (said or ruled): One who does not pray is an unbeliever." It is from the Prophet himself that one who intentionally does not pray until the time for the prayer is over is an unbeliever."

Says Ibn Hazm, "It has come from 'Umar, 'Abdurahman ibn 'Auf, Mu'adh ibn Jabal, Abu Hurairah and other companions that anyone who skips one obligatory prayer until its time has finished becomes an apostate. We find no difference of opinion among them on this point." This was mentioned by al-Mundhiri in *at-Targheeb wa at-Tarheeb*. Then he comments, "A group of companions and those who came after them believed that an intentional decision to skip one prayer until its time is completely finished makes one an unbeliever. The people of this opinion incude 'Umar ibn al-Khattab, 'Abdullah ibn Mas'ud, 'Abdullah ibn 'Abbas, Mu'adh ibn Jabal, Jabir ibn 'Abdullah and Abu ad-Darda'. Among the non-companions who shared this view were Ibn Hanbal, Ishaq ibn Rahwaih, 'Abdullah ibn al-Mubarak, an-Nakha'i, al-Hakim ibn 'Utaibah, Abu Ayyub as-Sakhtiyani, Abu Dawud at-Tayalisi, Abu Bakr ibn Abu Shaibah, Zuhair ibn Harb, and others.

Some *hadith* make it clear that such a person should be killed. For example:

Ibn 'Abbas reported that the Prophet, upon whom be peace, said, "The ties of Islam and the principles of the religion are three, and whoever leaves one of them becomes an unbeliever, and his blood becomes lawful: testifying that there is no god except Allah, the obligatory prayers, and the fast of Ramadan." (Related by Abu Ya'la with a *hassan* chain.[6]) Another narration states, "If anyone leaves one of them, by Allah he becomes an unbeliever and no voluntary deeds or recompense will be accepted from him, and his blood and

---

[6]This *hadith* is weak. Its problem lies both in its chain and in its text. Cf., al-Albani, *Silsilat al-Ahadith adh-Dha'eefah*, number 94. In *Kitab al-Khaba'ir*, adh-Dhahabi mentions it as a statement of Ibn 'Abbas, which is probably more sound. - J.Z.

wealth become lawful." This is a clear indication that such a person is to be killed.

Ibn 'Umar related that the Messenger of Allah, upon whom be peace, said, "I have been ordered to kill the people until they testify that there is no god except Allah, and that Muhammad is the Messenger of Allah, and they establish prayer and pay the *zakah*. If they do that, their blood and wealth are protected from me save by the rights of Islam. Their reckoning will be with Allah." (Related by al-Bukhari and Muslim.)

Umm Salamah related that the Prophet, upon whom be peace, said, "There will be rulers over you who will do good and evil things. Whoever hates these (latter) acts will be innocent of them. Whoever denies them will be safe, but (not) one who accepts and follows them." They asked, "Should we kill them?" He said, "Not if they pray." (Related by Muslim.) Therefore, he made it unlawful to kill even an unjust ruler who observes his prayers.

Abu Sa'eed reported that 'Ali, while he was in Yemen, sent the Prophet some gold, which he then divided among four people. A man said, "O Messenger of Allah, beware of Allah." The Prophet said, "Woe to you. Of all the people of the earth, am I not the most dutiful in being aware of Allah?" Khalid ibn al-Walid said, "O Messenger of Allah, shall I kill him?" He said, "Perhaps he is one of those who pray." Khalid said, "How many people say with their tongues what is not in their hearts?" The Prophet said, "I have not been ordered to look into the hearts of people, nor to rip open their bellies." (Abridged from al-Bukhari and Muslim.) In this *hadith* also, prayer is given as the reason for not killing a person. It is understood, therefore, that not praying would have resulted in the person's killing.

Even though the preceding *hadith* clearly rule that one who discards *salah* becomes an unbeliever and should be killed, many early and later scholars (excluding Abu Hanifah, Malik and ash-Shaf'i) believe that such people become evildoers who must repent. If such a person does not repent, he is to be killed, that being the prescribed punishment, according to Malik, ash-Shaf'i and others. Abu Hanifah maintains that such a person is not to be killed, but must be given a minor punishment and confined until he prays. They say the *hadith* that calls such people unbelievers refer to those who deny the prayers, and so on. They say that any other interpretation is contradicted by other texts. For example, Allah says, "Lo! Allah does not pardon one who gives Him partners. He pardons all save whom He wills" *(an-Nisa': 116)*. There is also a *hadith* related by Abu

Hurairah and recorded by Ahmad and Muslim in which the Prophet, upon whom be peace, said, "Every prophet has a special supplication that is answered. Every prophet hastened to make his supplication, but I concealed mine and will use it for my nation on the Day of Resurrection. It will be granted — Allah willing — to whoever dies without associating any partners with Allah." Al-Bukhari also recorded that Abu Hurairah reported that the Prophet, upon whom be peace, said, "The person who will be the happiest due to my intercession is the one who says, 'There is no god but Allah' sincerely from his heart."

Says ash-Shaukani, "The truth of the matter is that he becomes an unbeliever who is to be killed for his unbelief. The *hadith* authenticates that Islamic law calls one who does not pray an unbeliever. It has also put the performance as the barrier between a believer and an unbeliever. Abandoning prayer means he may be called an unbeliever. We need not concern ourselves with arguments presented by those of the opposing opinion. We can say to them: It is not impossible that some types of unbelievers may obtain forgiveness or may have a right to intercession, such as the unbelief of those who pray to (our) *qiblah*. Nevertheless, the fact remains that they commit some sins which the Islamic law views as unbelief. To turn to the other narrow interpretations is just redundant."

Who Must Pray

Prayer is obligatory upon every sane, adult Muslim. 'Aishah related that the Messenger of Allah, upon whom be peace, said, "The pen is raised for three (meaning: there is no obligation upon three): one who is sleeping until he wakens, the child until he becomes an adult, and one who is insane until he becomes sane."

As to the authenticity of this report, it is recorded by Ahmad, Abu Dawud, at-Tirmidhi, an-Nasa'i, Ibn Majah, and al-Hakim, who grades it *sahih* according to the criterion of al-Bukhari and Muslim. At-Tirmidhi classifies it as *hassan*.

Although it is not obligatory for a child to pray, it is a must that his guardian order him to do so when he is seven, and he should beat him if he does not pray after he reaches the age of ten. A minor should practice praying until he reaches puberty. 'Amr ibn Shu'aib related from his father on the authority of his grandfather that the Prophet, peace be upon him, said, "Order your children to pray when they reach the age of seven. Beat them (if they don't pray) when they reach the age of ten. And have them sleep separately."

The *hadith* is related by Ahmad, Abu Dawud, and al-Hakim. The latter grades it *sahih* according to Muslim's criteria.

The Number of Obligatory Prayers

The number of prayers prescribed by Allah is five. Ibn Mahyraiz narrated that al-Makhdaji, from the tribe of Kananah, heard Abu Muhammad — a man in ash-Shams — saying, "The *witr* prayer is obligatory."[7] He said he went to 'Ubadah ibn as-Samit and informed him of this. 'Ubadah corrected him, saying, "Abu Muhammad is mistaken.[8] I heard the Messenger of Allah, upon whom be peace, say 'Allah has laid five prayers upon His slaves. Whoever fulfills them and does not miss any of them will have a pact with Allah that He will let him enter Paradise. Whoever does not come with them will have no pact with Allah. If He wishes, He may punish him, and if He wishes, He may forgive him." (Related by Ahmad, Abu Dawud, an-Nasa'i and Ibn Majah.) In one version it states, "Or one who comes with a deficiency in them or who degrades their duties." Talhah ibn 'Ubaidullah narrated that a bedouin with un- kempt hair came to the Messenger of Allah, upon whom be peace, and said, "O Messenger of Allah, inform me of what Allah has made obligatory on me as regards praying." He said, "Five prayers, unless you do others voluntarily." He asked the Prophet to inform him about fasting, and he said, "The fast of Ramadan, unless you do others voluntarily." Then he asked him about charity...and the Messenger of Allah informed him of the Islamic legislations. The bedouin then said, "By the One who has honored you, I shall not voluntarily add anything to it, nor shall I be deficient in what Allah has ordered me to do." The Messenger of Allah, upon whom be peace,

---

[7]The text says *witr* is one (*wahid*) instead of obligatory (*wajib*). *Obviously, this is just a typographical error. - J.Z.*

[8]The companions often used the word *kadhb* in the sense of "mistaken." This is a very important distinction and many Arabic writers have failed to make this distinc- tion. A famous case which concerns the use of this expression is that of 'Ikrimah, the client of Ibn 'Abbas. See Ibn Hajr's discussion in *Hadyu as-Sari* (Maktabah as- Salifiyyah, Kuwait), p. 425. And see the mistake made by Muhammad Haras in his footnotes to al-Mundhiri's *at-Targheeb wa at-Tarheeb* (Maktabah al-Jamhuriyyah al-Arabiyyah, no date), volume 1, p. 615. In this particular case the man referred to as Abu Muhammad was Mas'ud ibn Zaid who was a companion of the Prophet, and no companion has been accused of lying. Therefore, "lie" here definitely means "mistaken." Cf., Ibn al-Athir, *an-Nihayah fi Ghareeb al-Hadith (al-Maktabah al-Is- lamiyyah, no city or date), volume 4, p. 159. - J.Z.*

then said, "He will enter Paradise if he is truthful (to what he said)." (Related by al-Bukhari and Muslim.)

The Times of the Prayers

Each prayer has its own particular time at which it must be performed. Says Allah, "Prayer at fixed hours has been enjoined upon the believers" *(an-Nisa': 103)*.

The Qur'an itself points to these different times. Allah says, "Pray at the two ends of the day and in some watches of the night. Lo! Good deeds annul evil deeds. This is a reminder for the mindful" *(Hud: 114)*. Surah *al-Isra' states, "Establish prayer at the setting of the sun until the dark of the night, and (the recital) of the Qur'an at dawn. Lo! The recital of the Qur'an at dawn is ever witnessed"* *(al-Isra': 78)*, and "Celebrate the praises of your Lord before the rising of the sun and before its setting. Glorify Him some hours of the night and at the two ends of the day, that you may find acceptance" *(Taha: 130)*. This verse specifically refers to the dawn prayer and the afternoon prayer, as it is recorded in the two *Sahihs*. Jarir ibn 'Abdullah al-Bajali reported, We were sitting with the Messenger of Allah and we looked at the moon on a clear night. The Prophet said, 'You will see your Lord as you see this moon, and you will not be harmed by seeing Him. So, if you can, do not let yourselves be overpowered in the case of prayer before the rising of the sun and its setting,' and he recited the above verse."

Those are the times of the prayers that the Qur'an mentions. From the *sunnah*, we have the following:

'Abdullah ibn 'Amr reported that the Messenger of Allah, upon whom be peace, said, "The time of the noon prayer is when the sun passes the meridian and a man's shadow is the same length as his height. It lasts until the time of the afternoon prayer. The time of the afternoon prayer is until the yellowing of the sun (during its setting). The time of the evening prayer is as long as twilight. The time of the night prayer is to the middle of a night of medium duration. And the time of the morning prayer is from the appearance of the dawn until the time of sunrise. When the sun rises, abstain from praying, as it rises between the horns of Satan." (Related by Muslim.)

Jarir ibn 'Abdullah narrated that the angel Gabriel came to the Messenger of Allah and said to him, "Stand and pray," and they prayed the noon prayer when the sun had passed its meridian. He then came to him for the afternoon prayer and said, "Stand and pray," and they prayed the afternoon prayer while the length of a shadow of something was similar to the length of the object. Then he came at sunset and said, "Stand and pray," and they prayed the sunset prayer when the sun had just disappeared. Then he came at night and said, "Stand and pray," and they prayed the night prayer when the twilight had disappeared. He came again when dawn broke (and they prayed the morning prayer). Then Gabriel came on the next day at noon and said (to the Messenger of Allah), "Stand and pray," and they prayed the noon prayer when the length of the shadow of something was close to the length of the object. Then he came for the afternoon prayer and said, "Stand and pray," and they prayed when the shadow of something was twice as long as the length of the object. Then he came at the same time (as the previous day) for the sunset prayer, without any change. Then he came for the night prayer after half of the night had passed ("or," he said, "one-third of the night"). Then he came when the sky was very yellow and said, "Stand and pray," and they prayed the morning prayer. Then Gabriel said, "Between these times are the times for the prayers."

As to the authenticity of the report, it is recorded by Ahmad, an-Nasa'i and at-Tirmidhi. Al-Bukhari observes, "It is the most authentic report concerning the prayer times."

The Time for the Noon Prayer (*Dhuhr*)

The previous two *hadith* make it clear that the noon prayer begins when the sun passes its meridian and it continues until an object's shadow is approximately the same length as the object itself. If it is extremely hot, it is preferred to delay the noon prayer until it is cooler. This is done in order to retain the humility and awe of the prayer. If this is not the case, it should be prayed early in its time. This opinion is based on the following *hadith*: Reported Anas, "If it was extremely cold, the Prophet, upon whom be peace, would pray early. If it was extremely hot, he would wait for it to cool down." (Related by al-Bukhari.) Abu Dharr relates, "We were with the Prophet, upon whom be peace, on a journey. When the caller to prayer wanted to give the *adhan*, the Prophet said 'Let it cool down.' This happened two or three times, until we saw the shadows of the hills. Then the Prophet said, 'The extreme heat is from the fragrance of Hell. If the heat becomes extreme, delay the prayer until it becomes cool." (Related by al-Bukhari and Muslim.)

However, this delay does have a limit. According to Ibn Hajr's *Fath al-Bari*, "The scholars differ over how long one may wait to let the temperature cool. Some say, 'Until the shadow of an object becomes an arm's length,' or 'Until the shadow becomes one-fourth of one's height.' Others say one-third or one-half, and so on. Its ruling is according to its basic principle, and it changes with different circumstances, provided that the prayer is not delayed until the end of its time."

The Time for the Afternoon Prayer ('*Asr*)

This prayer begins in the afternoon when the shadow of an object is of the same length as the object itself, and continues until the sun sets. Abu Hurairah reported that the Prophet, upon whom be peace, said, "Whoever catches one *rak'ah* of the afternoon prayer before the sun sets and then prays the remainder of the prayer after the sun has set has not missed the afternoon prayer."

The best and most preferred time to pray the afternoon prayer ends when the sun becomes yellowish on the horizon. This is implied by the preceding *hadith* of Jabir and 'Abdullah ibn 'Umar. To delay the prayer until the sun becomes yellowish, although it is permissiable, is greatly disliked, unless there is some need to do so. Anas reported that he heard the Prophet, upon whom be peace, say, "The following is the prayer of the hypocrite: he waits until the sun is between the horns of Satan, then he gets up and prays four quick *rak'ah*, and he does not remember Allah therein save a little bit." (Related by "the group," except for al-Bukhari and Ibn Majah.)

Says an-Nawawi in his commentary on *Sahih Muslim*, "Our companions ((the Shaf'iyyah) hold that the afternoon prayer time can be divided into five categories: the most virtuous time, the preferred time, the allowable time in which there is no disliked aspect, the allowable time that contains some aspect of dislike, and the time that is due to some excuse or necessity. The most virtuous time is at the beginning of the permissible time. The preferred time is until the shadow of an object is twice the length of the object itself. The permissible time without any aspect of dislike is from the time the sun becomes yellowish. The permissible time with some aspect of dislike is from the time the sun becomes yellowish until the setting of the sun. The time of excuse or necessity begins, in fact, at the time of the noon prayer for one who is to combine the noon and afternoon prayers, due to travelling or rain. If the afternoon prayer is made during any of those times, it has been fulfilled properly. If all of those times pass and the sun has set, then one must make up the prayer."

On a cloudy day, it should be prayed earlier in its time. Buraidah al-Aslami reported, "We were with the Messenger of Allah, upon whom be peace, during a battle and he said, "Hasten in praying on a cloudy day, for one who misses the afternoon prayer has destroyed all of his works." (Related by Ahmad and Ibn Majah.)[9]

Of the subjecat, Ibn al-Qayyim says, "Leaving the prayer is of two types: leaving it completely and never praying it (which destroys all of one's deeds), and leaving it during a particular day, which destroys all of the deeds of that day."

The Afternoon Prayer is the "Mid-most" Prayer

Says Allah in the Qur'an, "Observe and guard the prayers and the mid-most prayer, and stand with total submission to Allah. Authentic *hadith* have made it clear that the afternoon prayers is the "mid-most" prayer.

'Ali reported that the Prophet, upon whom be peace, said on the day of al-Ahzab (the battle of the clans), "May Allah fill their graves and houses with fire, as they kept us preoccupied from the "mid-most" prayer until the sun had set." (Related by al-Bukhari and Muslim. Muslim, Abu Dawud and Ahmad have "the afternoon prayer" inserted after "the mid-most" prayer.")

Explaining the context of this *hadith* , Ibn Mas'ud said, "The idol-worshippers kept the Prophet from the afternoon prayer until the sun had become reddish and yellowish. The Messenger of Allah said, "They kept us preoccupied from the "mid-most" prayer, the afternoon prayer — may Allah fill their bellies and graves with fire.'" (Related by Ahmad, Muslim, and Ibn Majah.)

The Time for the Sunset Prayer (*Maghrib*)

The time for the sunset prayer begins with the disappearance of the sun and lasts until the red twilight ends. 'Abdullah ibn 'Amr reported that the Prophet, upon whom be peace, said, "The time for the sunset prayer is when the sun has disappeared and the twilight has not gone." (Related by Muslim.) Abu Musa related that a man

---

[9]The first part of this *hadith* is weak. The second part has also been mentioned in other authentic *hadith*. See al-Albani, *Irwa' al-Ghaleel, number 255.*

asked the Prophet about the prayer times, and he mentioned the *hadith* which states that he ordered the sunset prayer when the sun had set and, on the next day, he prayed it when the red twilight was ending and he said, "The time (for the sunset prayer) is between these two times."

An-Nawawi says in his commentary on *Sahih Muslim,* "It is the opinion of the research scholars of our companions (the Shafiyyah) that ... it is allowed to delay it as long as it is twilight. It is allowed to begin the prayer at any time during that period. There is no sin in delaying it from its earliest time."[10] Concerning the earlier quoted *hadith* in which Gabriel led the prayers and prayed the sunset prayer at the same time on both days, it only shows that it is greatly preferred to perform the sunset prayer as early as possible. This point is made clear by some other *hadith*:

As-Sa'ib ibn Yazid related that the Messenger of Allah, upon whom be peace, said, "My nation will always be along the natural path as long as they pray the sunset prayer before the stars appear." (Related by Ahmad and at-Tabarani).

In Ahmad's *Musnad* it is related from Abu Ayyub al-Ansari that the Prophet said, "Pray the sunset prayer when the fasting person breaks his fast and when the stars are about to appear."

In *Sahih Muslim* it is related from Rafa' ibn Khadeej that "We prayed the sunset prayer with the Messenger of Allah, and one of us would leave (afterwards) and would still be able to see where he shot his arrow, (because there was still so much light left in the sky)."

In *Sahih Muslim* it is recorded from Salamah ibn al-Aku' that the Messenger of Allah, upon whom be peace, would pray the sunset prayer when the sun had set and disappeared (behind the horizon).

The Time of the Night Prayer ('Isha)

This prayer begins when the red twilight disappears and continues up to half of the night. Reported 'Aishah, "They used to pray the night prayer between the disappearance of the twilight and the final third of the night's beginning." (Related by al-Bukhari.) Abu

---

[10]The fact that this statement is made by people of the Shafi school of thought has some importance, because Imam ash-Shafi, while he was in Baghdad and during his early period in Egypt, was of the opinion that the only time allotted for the sunset prayer is the time it takes to make ablution and to pray the obligatory and *sunnah* prayers immediately after the sun had set. Later, in Egypt, he had changed his mind on this question.

Hurairah reported that the Messenger of Allah, upon whom be peace, said, "If it were not to be a hardship upon my nation, I would order them to delay the night prayer until a third or a half of the night had passed." (Related by Ahmad, Ibn Majah and at-Tirmidhi, who said it is *sahih*.) Reported Abu Sa'eed, "Once, we waited for the Messenger of Allah to lead the night prayer until half the night had passed, at which time he came and prayed with us. He said, 'Stay in your places of sitting while the people have gone to their places of lying down (for sleep), for you are in prayer as long as you are waiting for the prayer. If it were not for the weakness of the weak, the illness of the ill and the need of those who have needs, I would have delayed the time of this prayer to a half of the night."

As to the authenticity of this report, it is recorded by Ahmad, Abu Dawud, Ibn Majah, an-Nasa'i and Ibn Khuzaimah. Its chain is *sahih*). The *hadith* describes the best time to pray. As for the allowable time and the time due to need, it lasts until dawn. Abu Qatadah reported that the Messenger of Allah, upon whom be peace, said, "There is no negligence in sleeping, but the negligence lies in not praying a prayer until the time of the next prayer has come." (Related by Muslim.) This *hadith* shows that the time of every prayer continues until the beginning of the time for the next prayer, except for the morning prayer, as all scholars agree that its time lasts only until sunrise.

Delay is Preferred

It is most virtuous to delay the night prayer until the end of the preferred time for it, which is half the night. Reported 'Aishah, "One night the Prophet, upon whom be peace, prayed the night prayer after most of the night had gone and most of the people in the mosque had fallen aleep. Then he came out, prayed, and said, "This would be the proper time if it were not a hardship on my nation."' (Related by Muslim and an-Nasa'i.) The Prophet, upon whom be peace, did not do this on a regular basis, as he heard that it would be a hardship on his nation. He would take into consideration the situation of those in the mosque. Sometimes he would hasten in performing the prayer and at other times he would delay it. Said Jabir, "The Messenger of Allah would pray the noon prayer during the hottest time of noon, the afternoon prayer when the sun was clear, the sunset prayer when the sun had gone down, and the night prayer he would sometimes delay and sometimes hasten if he found people gathered (in the mosque). If he noticed that they were lingering, he would delay

it. He would pray the morning prayer while it was still dark."
(Related by al-Bukhari and Muslim.)

Sleeping Before the Night Prayer Is Forbidden

One should not sleep before the night prayer, nor have discussions after it. Abu Barza al-Aslami related that the Prophet, upon whom be peace, loved to delay the night prayer (which was called darkness, *al-'atmah*) and he hated sleeping before it and talking or discussions after it." (Related by "the group.") In another saying by Ibn Mas'ud, it is reported, "The Messenger of Allah ordered us not to talk after the night prayer." (Related by Ibn Majah.)

The reasons behind this are: sleep may make a person miss the night prayer in its best time, or it may cause him to miss the congregational prayer, and talking and socializing afterwards would cause one to misappropriate a time from which he could greatly benefit. If one wants to sleep and has someone to wake him up, or he is discussing a beneficial matter, then it is not disliked. Said Ibn 'Umar, "The Prophet would discuss with Abu Bakr some of the affairs of the Muslims during the night, and I was with him." (Related by Ahmad and at-Tirmidhi, who said it is *hassan*.) Reported Ibn 'Abbas, "I slept in the home of Maimunah one night when the Prophet, upon whom be peace, was there. I watched to see how the Prophet prayed during the night. He talked with his wife for a while and then slept." (Related by Muslim.)

The Time of the Morning Prayer *(Fajr)*

The time of the morning prayer begins with the true dawn and lasts until sunrise. It is preferred to pray it early in its permissible time. Abu Mas'ud al-Ansari reported that the Messenger of Allah prayed the morning prayer in the darkness (of the dawn). Another time, he prayed it when the dawn was shining (or glowing). Then after that, he always prayed in the darkness (of the dawn) until he died." (Related by Abu Dawud and al-Baihaqi. Its chain is *sahih*.) Said 'Aishah, "Believing women would pray the morning prayer with the Prophet, upon whom be peace, being enveloped in their clothing. They would return to their homes after the prayer and no one could recognize them due to the darkness (of the dawn)." (Related by "the group.")

Rafa' ibn Khadeej related a *hadith* in which the Prophet, upon whom be peace, said, "Make the morning prayer at daybreak, as your reward will be greater." In another version it states, "Make the morning prayer at the shining (time of the dawn), as your reward will be greater." (Related by "the five." At-Tirmidhi and Ibn Hibban grade it as *sahih*.) It refers to the time that one finishes the prayer, not the time when one begins it. That is, one should make the recital long so that one is in prayer until the dawn becomes "shiny." This is what the Prophet, upon whom be peace, used to do, for he would recite between 60 and 100 verses. It also means to make sure that the dawn has come.

Performing One *Rak'ah* During the Time of Prayer

Whoever catches a *rak'ah* of prayer before its time has expired has caught the entire prayer in its time. Abu Hurairah reported that the Prophet, upon whom be peace, said, "Whoever catches one *rak'ah* of the prayer has caught the prayer." (Related by "the group.") This refers to any of the prayers. Al-Bukhari has recorded, "Whoever of you catches one prostration of the afternoon prayer before the sun has set should complete his prayer. If one of you catches one prostration of the morning prayer before the sun has risen, he should complete his prayer." Here the meaning of prostration is *rak'ah*. The clear meaning of the *hadith* is that one who catches one *rak'ah* of the morning or afternoon prayer should complete the prayer even if the sun is setting or rising, also those are times in which it is not liked to pray. If one *rak'ah* is performed, then the prayer is to be completed and the obligation of prayer will have been fulfilled, although it is not allowed to intentionally delay those prayers until such times.

Sleeping Through or Forgetting the Prayer

Whoever sleeps through or has forgotten to pray a certain prayer should pray it when he wakes up or remembers the prayer. Abu Qatadah related that sleeping through the prayer time was mentioned to the Prophet, upon whom be peace, and he said, "There is no negligence in sleep, but negligence occurs while one is awake. If one of you forgets a prayer or sleeps through its time, then he should pray it when he remembers it."

As to the authenticity of the report, it is recorded by an-Nasa'i and at-Tirmidhi, who said it is *sahih*.

Anas related that the Prophet, upon whom be peace, said, "Whoever forgets a prayer should pray it when he remembers it, and there is no expiation for it save that." (Related by al-Bukhari and Muslim.) Reported 'Imran ibn Husain, "We went with the Messenger of Allah during the night. When the last portion of the night came, we became tired and fell asleep. We did not wake until we felt the heat of the sun. Some of us tried hurriedly to purify ourselves. The Prophet ordered us to be calm. Then we rode on until the sun had risen and we made ablution. He ordered Bilal to make the call to prayer, and then prayed two *rak'ah* before the (obligatory) morning prayer. Then we stood and prayed. We said, 'O Messenger of Allah, should we not repeat it tomorrow in its proper time?' He said, 'Would your Lord the Most High forbid you from interest and accept it from you?'" (Related by Ahmed and others.)

The Times in Which the Prayers are Prohibited

It is forbidden to pray after the morning prayer until the sunrise and from the sunrise until the sun has completely risen to the length of a spear above the horizon, and when the sun is at its meridian until it moves sightly to the west, and after the afternoon prayer until the sun sets. Abu Sa'eed reported that the Prophet, upon whom be peace, said, "There is no prayer after the morning prayer until the sun rises." (Related by al-Bukhari and Muslim.) 'Amr ibn 'Abbas related that he said, "O Prophet of Allah, inform me about the prayers." He said, "Pray the morning prayer and then abstain from prayer until sunrise and the sun has completely risen, for it rises between the horns of Satan. That is when the unbelievers prostrate to it. Then pray, as your prayer will be witnessed and attended to until the shadow of a spear becomes less than its length. At that time stop praying, for at that time the hell-fire is fed with fuel. When the shade comes, you may pray, for your prayer will be witnessed and attended (to by angels) until you pray the afternoon prayer. Then abstain from praying until the sun sets, for its sets between the horns of Satan, and that is when the unbelievers make prostrations to it." (Related by Ahmad and Muslim.)

Said 'Uqbah ibn 'Amr, "There are three times during which the Prophet prohibited us from praying or burying our deceased: sunrise until the sun has risen (some distance), when the sun is at its meridian, and when the sun is setting until it has completely set." (Related by "the group," except for al-Bukhari.)

The Opinions of the Jurists Concerning Prayer
After the Morning and Night Prayers

Most scholars agree that one can make up missed prayers after the morning or afternoon prayers. This is based on the Prophet's words, "If someone forgets the prayer, he should pray it when he remembers it." (Related by al-Bukhari and Muslim.)

Concerning voluntary prayers, the following companions disliked such prayers during those times: 'Ali, Ibn Mas'ud, Abu Hurairah and Ibn 'Umar. 'Umar used to beat those who offered two *rak'ah* after the afternoon prayers (in the presence of other companions), and was not rebuked. Khalid ibn al-Waleed also used to do this. Those *tabi'een* who disliked such prayers were al-Hassan and Sa'eed ibn al-Musayyab. Abu Hanifah and Malik also hated such prayers. Ash-Sahf'i reasoned that prayers at such times are allowable if the person has a reason for that prayer (the prayer of salutation to the mosque, or the prayers after one performs the ablution, and so on). He uses as a proof the fact that the Prophet, upon whom be peace, prayed the two noon *sunnah rak'ah* after the afternoon prayers. The Hanbaliyyah say that it is forbidden to pray during such times even if one has a reason to do so, except in the case of the two *rak'ah* for the circumambulation of the Ka'bah. This is based on the *hadith* from Jabir ibn Mut'am that the Prophet said, "O tribe of 'Abd Manat, do not prevent anyone from circumambulating this house (the Ka'bah) or from praying therein at any time they wish."

As to the authenticity of thie report, it is related by Abu Dawud, an-Nasa'i, at-Tirmidhi and Ibn Majah. At-Tirmidhi and Ibn Khuzaimah called it *sahih*.

About Praying at Sunrise, Sunset and While the Sun is at its Meridian

The Hanifiyyah are of the opinion that prayer during such times is not valid, regardless of whether the prayer was obligatory or voluntary, or if one was making up a prayer or fulfilling a require-ment. But, they make an exception for the afternoon prayer of that particular day and the funeral prayer (if the funeral is at any of these times, the funeral prayer is still to be made). They also permit the prostration in response to Qur'anic recitation if the respective verses were recited at such times. Abu Yusuf also makes an exception for voluntary prayers on Friday while the sun is at its meridian. The Shaf'iyyah say that voluntary prayers which are not offered for a particular reason are disliked at such times. Obligatory prayers, voluntary prayers because of some occasion, voluntary prayers on Friday when the sun is at its meridian and the prayer of the cir-cumambulation of the Ka'bah are all permissible at such times without any disliked aspects. The Malikiyyah say that voluntary prayers during sunrise and sunset are forbidden, even if there is some occasion for them. The same applies to a prayer that was vowed, prostration owing to Qur'anic recitation, and the funeral prayer (unless they fear some decay or alteration in the deceased). But they always allow prayer, voluntary or obligatory, at the time when the sun is at its meridian. Al-Baji wrote in his commentary to *al-Muwatta*, "In *al-Mubsut* it is related from Ibn Wahb that Malik was asked about praying at mid-day and he said, 'I found the people praying at mid-day of Friday. Some *hadith* do not consider it desirable (to pray at such times), but I do not stop the people from praying. I do not like to pray at that time because it is not desirable to do so." The Hanbaliyyah say that no voluntary prayers should be made during such times, regardless of whether or not there is a reason for such prayers, and regardless of whether it is Friday or not, save for the prayer of salutations to the mosque on Friday (they allow this without any disike for it while the sun is at its meridian or while the *imam* is making his address). They also say that the funeral prayer is forbidden at that time, unless there is a fear of alteration or decay in the corpse. They allow the making up of missed prayers, the vowed prayers and the prayer of the circumabulation of the Ka'bah (even if it is voluntary) at any of these three times.

Voluntary Prayer at Dawn Before the Morning Prayer

Yasar, the client of Ibn 'Umar, said, "Ibn 'Umar saw me while I was praying after the dawn had begun, and he said, 'The Messenger of Allah came to us while we were praying at this time and he said, 'Let your witness reach those who are absent that there is no prayer after (the beginning of) the dawn except two *rak'ah*."

As to its place in the corpus of *hadith*, it is recorded by Ahmad and Abu Dawud. Although the *hadith* is weak, its numerous chains strengthen each other.

We can conclude from this that it is disiked to make voluntary prayers beyond the two *sunnah rak'ah* after the dawn has begun. This was stated by ash-Shaukani. Al-Hassan, ash-Shaf'i, and Ibn Hazm say voluntary prayers are permissible at that time without any aspect of dislike. Malik openly allowed prayers during that time for those who missed the voluntary prayers during the night due to some excuse. It is mentioned that it reached him that 'Abdullah ibn 'Abbas, al-Qasim ibn Muhammad, and 'Abdullah ibn 'Aamar ibn Rabi'ah would pray the *witr* prayer after the dawn had begun. Said 'Abdullah ibn Mas'ud, "It does not bother me if they make the *iqamah* (the second call) to prayer while I am praying *witr*." Yahya ibn

Sa'eed reported, " 'Ibadah ibn as-Samit was the *imam* for the people. One day he went to the morning prayer and the caller to prayer made the *iqamah* for the prayer. 'Ibadah kept quiet until he prayed the *witr* prayer and then he led them in the morning prayer." Sa'eed ibn Jubair reported that Ibn 'Abbas slept (one night), woke up and told his servant, "Look to see what the people are doing." (By that time he had lost his eyesight). The servant returned and told him that they were dispersing from the morning prayer. Ibn 'Abbas then stood, prayed *witr* and prayed the morning prayer.

Voluntary Prayers while the *Iqamah* Is Being Made

If the prayer has already started, it is disliked to preoccupy one's self with voluntary prayers. Abu Hurairah reported that the Prophet, upon whom be peace, said, "If the prayer is beginning, there is no prayer save the obligatory one." In another narration it states, "Save for the one for which *iqamah* has been made." (Related by Ahmad, Muslim, Abu Dawud, at-Tirmidhi, an-Nasa'i and Ibn Majah.) Reported 'Abdullah ibn Sarjis, "A man entered the mosque while the Prophet was leading the morning prayer. The man prayed two *rak'ah* at the side of the mosque and then entered (the congregation) behind the Messenger of Allah. When the Prophet had finished the prayer he said, 'O so and so, which of the two prayers do you count — the one you prayed by yourself or the one you prayed with us?" (Related by Muslim, Abu Dawud and an-Nasa'i.) The Messenger objected to this act, but he did not order him to repeat his prayer. This shows that such a prayer is valid but disliked. Reported Ibn 'Abbas, "I was praying while the caller to prayer was making the *iqamah*. The Messenger of Allah pulled me and said, 'Do you pray four *rak'ah* for the morning (obligatory) prayer?" The *hadith* is related by al-Baihaqi, at-Tabarani, Abu Dawud, at-Tayalisi and al-Hakim, who said it is *sahih* according to the criterion of al-Bukhari and Muslim. Abu Musa al-Ash'ari related that the Prophet saw a man praying two *rak'ah* of the morning prayer while the caller to prayer was making the (second) call. The Prophet touched his elbow and said, "Shouldn't this be before that?" (Related by at-Tabarani. Al-'Iraqi says it is good.)

THE CALL TO PRAYER (ADHAN)

The *adhan* is a call to inform others in specific words that the time for a prayer has begun. It is a call to the congregation, and is an expression of the Islamic practices. It is obligatory or highly preferred. Al-Qurtubi and others have said that the *adhan*, although it has very few words, covers all essentials of the faith. It begins by proclaiming the greatness of Allah, pointing to His existence and perfection. It mentions His oneness and the denial of polytheism, and it confers the messengership of Muhammad, upon whom be peace. It calls to specific acts of obedience after testifying to Muhammad's messengership, and it calls to a prosperity which is everlasting, pointing to the return to Allah. Then, in a manner of emphasis, it repeats some of what was already mentioned.

Its Virtues and Excellence.

Many *hadith* describe the virtues of the *adhan* and the one who calls it. Such *hadith* include the following:

Abu Hurairah reported that the Prophet said, "If the people knew what was in the *adhan* and the first row (of the prayer in virtue), and that they could not get it save by drawing lots, they would draw lots. If they knew the reward for praying the noon prayer early in its time, they would race to it. And if they knew the reward for the night and the morning prayers in congregation, they would come to them even if they had to crawl." (Related by al-Bukhari and others.)

Mu'awiyyah reported that the Prophet, upon whom be peace, said, "The callers to prayer will have the longest necks of all people on the Day of Resurrection." (Related by Ahmad, Muslim, and Ibn Majah.)

Al-Barra' ibn 'Aazib reported that the Prophet, upon whom be peace, said, "Allah and His angels pray upon those in the first rows. And the caller to prayer is forgiven, for as far as his voice reaches and whoever hears him will confirm what he says. He will get a reward similar to those who pray with him." This *hadith* is related by Ahmad and an-Nasa'i. Al-Mundhiri says its chain is good.

Abu ad-Darda' reported that he heard the Prophet, upon whom be peace, say, "If three people do not make the *adhan* and establish the prayer among themselves, Satan gains mastery over them." (Related by Ahmad.)

Abu Hurairah reported that the Prophet, upon whom be peace, said, "The *imam* is a guarantor, and the caller to prayer is one who is given the trust. O Allah, guide the *imam* and forgive the caller to prayer."

'Uqbah ibn 'Aamar said he heard the Prophet, upon whom be peace, say, "Your Lord, the Exalted, is amazed (and pleased) by one who is watching sheep in his pasture, then goes to the mountain to make the call to prayer and pray. Allah, the Exalted, says, 'Look at my slave there who makes the call to prayer and establishes the prayer out of fear of Me. I have forgiven my slave and have allowed him to enter Paradise.'" (Related by Ahmad, Abu Dawud and an-Nasa'i.)

The Event Behind Its Legislation

The *adhan* was made part of the *shari'ah* during the first year after the migration to Madinah. The *hadith* clarify what led up to its institution.

Nafa' related that Ibn 'Umar said, "The Muslims would gather and calculate the time of prayer, and no one would call them. They spoke about that one day. Some said, 'We should have a bell like the Christians.' Others said, 'We should have a horn like the Jews.' Suggested 'Umar, 'Why don't we have one person call the others to prayer?' The Messenger of Allah said, 'Stand, Bilal, and make the call to prayer.'" (Related by Ahmad and al-Bukhari.)

Reported 'Abdullah ibn (Zaid ibn) 'Abd Rabbih, "When the Prophet was to order the use of a bell to call the people to prayer, he disliked it because it resembled the Christian practice. While I was sleeping, a man came to me carraying a bell. I said to him, 'O slave of Allah, will you sell me that bell?' Said he, 'What would you do with it?' I replied, 'I would call the people to prayer with it.' Said he, 'Shall I not guide you to something better than that?' I said, 'Certainly.' Said he, 'You should say, *Allahu akbar, Allahu akbar, Allahu akbar, Allahu akbar. Ashhadu alla ilaha illal-lah, ashhadu alla ilaha illal-lah, Ashhadu anna Muhammad ar-Rasool-lal-lah, ashhadu anna Muhammadar-Rasool-lal-lah. Hayya 'alas-salah, hayyah 'alas-salah. Hayya 'alal-falah, hayya 'alal-falah. Allahu akbar, Allahu akbar. La ilaha illal-lah.'* Then he went a short distance away and said, 'When you stand for the prayer, say, *'Allahu akbar, Allahu akbar. Ashhadu alla ilaha illal-lah, Ashhadu anna Muhammad ar-Rasool-lal-lah Hayya 'alas-salah, hayya 'alal-falah. Qad qaamatis-salah, qad qaamatis-salah. Allahu akbar, Allahu akbar. La ilaha illal-lah.'* When the morning came, I went to the Messenger of Allah to tell him what I had seen. He said, 'Your dream is true, Allah willing. Go to Bilal, tell him what you have seen, and tell him to make the call to prayer, for he has the best voice among you.' I went to Bilal and told him what to do, and he made the call to prayer. 'Umar was in his house when he heard it. He came out with his cloak, saying 'By the One who has raised you with the truth, I saw similar to what he saw.' The Prophet, upon whom be peace, said, 'To Allah is the praise." The *hadith* is related by Ahmad, Abu Dawud, Ibn Majah, Ibn Khuzaimah and at-Tirmidhi, who called it *hassan sahih*.

How It Is Made

There are three ways to make the *adhan*:

a) Make four *takbir* at the beginning and say the rest of the phrases twice, without any repetition, except for the last statement of *la illaha illa-lah*. So, the *adhan* would be made up of fifteen phrases, as in the preceding *hadith* of 'Abdullah.

b) Make four *takbir* and then repeat *ashhadu an la ilaha illal-lah, twice, and ashhadu anna Muhammad ar-Rasool-lal-lah* twice, in a low voice, then repeat them again in a louder voice. Abu Mahdhura reported that the Prophet, upon whom be peace, taught him an *adhan* consisting of nineteen phrases. This *hadith* is related by "the five." At-Tirmidhi called it *hassan sahih*.

c) Make two *takbir* and repeat the "statements of witness," making the number of phrases seventeen. Muslim records that Abu Mah-dhurah related that the Prophet, upon whom be peace, taught him the following *adhan: Allahu akbar, Allahu akbar. Ashhadu alla ilaha illal-lah, ashhadu alla ilaha illal-lah. Ashhadu anna Muham-mad ar-Rasool-lal-lah, ashhadu anna Muhammad ar-Rasool-lal-lah.* Then repeat *ashhadu alla ilaha illal-lah* (twice), *ashhadu anna Muhammad ar-Rasool-lal-lah* (twice), *hayya 'alas-salah* (twice), *hayya 'alal-falah* (twice). *Allahu akbar, Allahu akbar. La ilaha illal-lah."*

At-Tathweeb: (Saying "Prayer is better than sleep" in the Morning *Adhan*).

It is part of the *shari'ah* that the caller to prayer say, *"as-salaatu khairun min an-naum* (prayer is better than sleep) in the morning *adhan.* Abu Mahdhurah asked the Prophet, upon whom be peace, to teach him the *adhan,* and he told him, "If it is the morning *adhan,* say, *as-salaatu khairun min an-naum, as-salaatu khariun min an-naum. Allahu akbar, Allahu akbar. La illaha illal-lah."* (Related by Ahmad and Abu Dawud.) It is to be said only in the morning *adhan.*

Iqamah

There are three ways to perform the *iqamah*:

1) Saying the first *takbir* four times and everything else twice, with the exception of the last statement of *la ilaha illal-lah.* Abu Mahdhura said that the Prophet, upon whom be peace, taught him the *iqamah* consisting of seventeen phrases: *Allahu akbar* (4 times), *ashhadu alla ilaha illal-lah* (twice), *ashhadu anna Muhammad ar-Rasool-lal-lah* (twice), *hayya 'alas-salah* (twice), *hayya 'alal-falah* (twice), *qad qaamatis-salah* (twice), *Allahu akbar, Allahu akbar. La ilaha illal-lah.* This is related by "the five." At-Tirmidhi grades it *sahih.*

2) To say the beginning and ending *takbir,* and the phrase *qad qaamatus-salah* twice. Everything else is to be said once, making eleven phrases. This is based on the preceding *hadith* of 'Abdullah ibn Zaid: "When you stand for the prayer, say *"Allahu akbar, Allahu akbar. Ashhadu alla illaha illal-lah, ashhadu anna Muhammad ar-Rasool Allah. Hayya 'alas-salah, hayya 'alal-falah. Qad qaamatis-salah, qad qaamatis-salah. Allahu akbar, Allahu akbar. La illaha*

illal-lah.

3) The same as in the preceding, but *Qad qaamatus-salah* is said only once, making a total of ten phrases. Imam Malik chose this way, because he found the people of Madinah performing it thus. But says Ibn al-Qayyim, "It is not proven that the Messenger of Allah ever said '*Qad qaamatus-salah*' only once." Ibn 'Abdul-Barr is of the view, "In every case, it is said twice."

What Is Said During the *Adhan*

It is preferred that whoever is listening to the *adhan* repeat it with the caller, except for the two *hayya 'alas-salah, hayya 'alal-falah* phrases, after which he should say *La haula wa la quwatah illa billah* (there is no power or might save Allah).

Says an-Nawawi, "Our companions hold that it is preferable for the listener to repeat after the caller (to prayer), except when he comes to the two preceding phrases, for this shows that he approves of what the caller is saying. Those two statements are calls to the prayer, and it is only proper for the caller to prayer to say them. It is preferable for the listener to say something, such as *La haula wa la quwatah illa billah*. It is confirmed in the two *Sahihs* from Abu Musa al-Ash'ari that the Prophet, upon whom be peace, said, '*La haula wa la quwatah illa billah* is a treasure from the treasures of Paradise.' Our companions say that to repeat the call to prayer is preferred for everyone who hears the call, whether clean or unclean, in a state of post-sexual uncleanliness or menstruating, and so on, as it is a remembrance and all of those people who can should make it. Those who can not do so are the ones who are praying, who are relieving themselves, or are having sexual intercourse. If one is reciting the Qur'an, or making remembrance of Allah (*dhikr*) or studying and so on, he should stop what he is doing and repeat after the caller to prayer. He may then return to what he was doing, if he wishes, or he can pray a voluntary or obligatory prayer." Says ash-Shaf'i, "One should not repeat after the call to prayer, but when he finishes he should repeat what he has said." In *al-Mughni*, it says, "If one enters the mosque and hears the *adhan*, it is best that he wait until the caller finishes it before he begins to repeat it. This way he will catch both good deeds. If he does not repeat after the call but starts praying, there is no problem. This is what Ahmad says on the subject."

The Muslim should pray for the Prophet, peace be upon him, after the call is over in any of the manners that have been related, and ask Allah to give him the place of *wasilah*.[1] 'Abdullah ibn 'Amr related that the Messenger of Allah, upon whom be peace, said, "If you hear the call to prayer, repeat after it. Then supplicate for me, for whoever makes one supplication for me, Allah makes ten for him. Then ask Allah to grant me the place of *wasilah*. It is a place in Paradise reserved for a slave from among the slaves of Allah. I hope to be him, and whoever asks Allah to grant me the place of *wasilah*, my intercession becomes permissible for him." (Related by Muslim.) Jabir reported that the Prophet said, "Whoever says (after) hearing the call to prayer, 'O Allah, Lord of this complete call and of the estabished prayers, grant Muhammad the place of *wasilah*, the most virtuous place and raise him to a praiseworthy position that you have promised him,' will have my intercession made permissible for him on the Day of Judgement. (Related by al-Bukhari.)

The Supplication After the *Adhan*

After the *adhan*, one should make individual supplications, as that is the time when they will most likely be accepted. Anas reported that the Prophet, upon whom be peace, said, "A supplication made between the *adhan* and the *iqamah* is not rejected."

As to the authenticity of this report, it is related by Abu Dawud, an-Nasa'i, and at-Tirmidhi, who called it *hassan sahih*, and added "They asked, 'What should we say, O Messenger of Allah?' He responded, 'Ask Allah for forgiveness and well-being in this world and the Hereafter." 'Abdullah ibn 'Amr related that a man said, "O Messenger of Allah, the callers to prayer get more virtues than us." He said, "Say what they say and when they finish, ask and it shall be given." (Related by Abu Dawud with a *sahih* chain.)

On the same subject, reported Umm Salamah, "The Prophet, upon whom be peace, taught me to say (after)the sunset call to prayer, 'O Allah, this is the beginning of Your night and the end of Your day. I have supplicated to You, so forgive me."

During the *Iqamah*

It is preferred that one who hears the *iqamah* repeat the words, except when *Qad qaamatus-salah* is said, he should say, "Allah

---

[1]This is a special place of intercession on the Day of Judgment.

establishes it and makes it everlasting." Some of the companions reported that when Bilal said this phrase, the Prophet would say "Allah establishes it and makes it everlasting."

Conditions To Be Met By The Caller to Prayer

It is preferred that he meet the following conditions:

1) It is a must that he make the *adhan* for Allah's sake and not for wages. 'Uthman ibn Abu al-'Aas asked the Messenger of Allah, upon whom be peace, to appoint him as the *imam* of his people. He replied, "You are their *imam*. Be careful about the weak amongst them, and appoint a caller to prayer who does not accept wages for his *adhan*.

This *hadith* is related by Abu Dawud, an-Nasa'i, Ibn Majah and at-Tirmidhi, with a slightly different wording, who called it *hasan*. He also said that the scholars agree with this, and that they hate to see the caller receive wages for the *adhan*.

2) He should be clean from major or minor impurities. Al-Muhajir ibn Qanfadh reported that the Prophet, upon whom be peace, said to him, "Nothing prevented me from returning (your salutations) except that I dislike to mention the name of Allah when I am not clean. This report has come from Ahmad, Abu Dawud, an-Nasa'i, Ibn Majah and Ibn Khuzaimah. The latter grades it *sahih*.

According to the Shaf'iyyah, making the call while one is not in a state of cleanliness is permissible although disliked. According to Ahmad, the Hanafiyyah and others, it is permissible and is not disliked.

3) He should be standing and facing the *qiblah* (the direction of the Ka'bah). Said Ibn al-Mundhir, "There is agreement that it is *sunnah* for the caller to be standing, for then he can be heard far away. It is also *sunnah* that he face the *qiblah* while making the *adhan*. If he turns away from the *qiblah*, his *adhan* will be sound, but the act will be disliked.

4) He should turn with his head, neck and chest to the right upon saying *"Hayya 'alas-salah"* and to the left upon saying *Hayya 'alal-falah."* Says an-Nawawi, "It is the most authentic form."

Reported Abu Juhaifah, "Bilal made the *adhan*, and I saw the movement of his mouth from this side to that side upon saying *"Hayya 'alas-salah"* and *"Hayya 'alal-falah."* (Related by Ahmad, al-Bukhari and Muslim.)

According to al-Baihaqi, this turning is not documented through sound chains. In *al-Mughni*, it states from Ahmad that the caller should not turn to the left or to the right unless he is at the top of a minaret, so that the people on both sides can hear him.

5) He should insert his index fingers into his ears. Talking of his practice, Bilal said, "I put my index fingers into my ears and made the *adhan*. (Related by Abu Dawud and Ibn Hibban.)

Says at-Tirmidhi, "The scholars prefer the callers to put their index fingers into their ears while making the *adhan*."

6) He should raise his voice for the call, even if he is alone in the desert. 'Abdullah ibn 'Abdurahman related from his father that Abu Sa'eed al-Khudri said to him, "I see that you love the sheep and the desert. If you are with your sheep or in the desert, then raise your voice while making the call to prayer, for any jinn, human or thing within hearing distance of your voice will be a witness for you on the Day of Resurrection...I heard the Messenger of Allah say that." (Related by Ahmad, al-Bukhari, an-Nasa'i and Ibn Majah.)

7) He should pause between each phrase during the *adhan* and be quick in making the *iqamah*. Many narrations have reported that this act is preferred.

8) He should not speak during the *iqamah*. Some scholars dislike that he should even speak during the *adhan*, although al-Hasan, 'Ata and Qatadah permit it. Says Abu Dawud, "I asked Ahmad, 'May a man speak during his *adhan*?' He said, 'Yes.' 'May he speak during the *iqamah*?' He said, 'No,' and that is because it is preferred that he make it quickly."

The *Adhan* Before and at the Beginning of the Prayer Time

The *adhan* is to be made exactly at the beginning of the prayer time, except for the morning prayer, when it may be said before dawn (provided that the people are able to distinguish between the early *adhan* and that of the proper time). 'Abdullah ibn 'Umar related that the Prophet, upon whom be peace, said, "Bilal makes the *adhan* during the night, so eat and drink until you hear the *adhan* of Ibn Umm Maktum." (Related by al-Bukhari and Muslim.) The wisdom behind allowing the morning *adhan* a little earlier is made clear in a *hadith* recorded by Ahmad and others from Ibn

Mas'ud: "None of you should let Bilal's *adhan* prevent you from the pre-dawn meal, as he is making the *adhan* for those who are praying to stop and for those who are sleeping to get up." But Bilal made his *adhan* in exactly the same way as the regular *adhan*. At-Tahawi and an-Nasa'i relate that the time difference between Bilal's *adhan* and that of Ibn Umm Maktum was the time it took for one to come down from the *minaret* and for the others to get up to it.

Enough time should be left between the *adhan* and *iqamah* for people to prepare themselves for prayer and get to the mosque. The *hadith* that state the time difference are weak. Al-Bukhari has a section entitled *How Much Time Is There Between the Adhan and Iqamah?*, but no specific length of time has been confirmed therein. Ibn Batal said, "There is no time limit set, except that of the time beginning and the people gathering for the prayer." Jabir ibn Sumra said, "The callers to prayer of the Prophet would make the *adhan* and then leave some time, making the *iqamah* only when they saw the Prophet, upon whom be peace, coming (to the place of prayer). (Related by Ahmad, Muslim, Abu Dawud, and at-Tirmidhi.)

Whoever Makes the *Adhan* May Make the *Iqamah*

This is so because the caller to prayer takes precedence in making the *iqamah*. Says Ash-Shaf'i, "If a man made the *adhan*, he should follow it up with the *iqamah*." Of this, at-Tirmidhi says, "Most of the scholars agree with this opinion."

When One Should Stand for the Prayer

Malik states in *al-Muwatta*, "I have not heard anything concerning the specific time to stand for prayer. I have seen some peope lagging and others being quick." Ibn al-Mundhir recorded that Anas would stand when *Qad qaamtus-salah* was said.

Leaving the Mosque After the *Adhan* (and Before the Prayer)

It is not allowed to leave the call unanswered or to leave the mosque after it has been made, unless there is some excuse or one has the intention to return for the prayer. Abu Hurairah related that the Prophet, upon whom be peace, told them, "If one of you is in the mosque and the call is made, he should not leave the mosque until he prays." (Related by Ahmad with a *sahih* chain.) It is also related that Abu Hurairah said about a man who left the mosque after the call had been made, "That man has disobeyed Abu al-Qasim (the Prophet, upon whom be peace)." This is related by Muslim and others. Mu'adh at-Jahni related that the Prophet said, "It is the utmost apathy and sign of disbelief and hypocrisy that one who hears the call of Allah to salvation does not respond."[2] (Related by Ahmad and at-Tabarani.)

Commenting upon this, at-Tirmidhi says, "It has been related from more than one of the companions that one who hears the call and does not respond will have no prayer. Some said that this is the maximum imposition, which shows that there is no excuse for one who does not attend the congregational prayer without a valid reason."

The *Adhan* and *Iqamah* for Those
Who Missed the Proper Time of Prayer

One who sleeps through the time of a prayer or who forgets a prayer may make *adhan* and *iqamah* when he desires to pray. In a story recorded by Abu Dawud, when the Prophet, upon whom be peace, and his companions slept through the time of the morning prayer, he ordered Bilal to make the *adhan* and *iqamah* for the prayer. If one has missed many prayers, it is preferred to make one *adhan* at the beginning followed by an *iqamah* for each prayer. Says al-'Athram, "I heard Abu 'Abdullah (Ahmad) being asked what a man who had missed a prayer should do about the *adhan*. He mentioned the *hadith* of Hushaim from Abu az-Zubair...that the idol-worshippers kept the Prophet busy during four of his prayers during the Battle of the Clans. When part of the night had passed, he ordered Bilal to make the *adhan* and the *iqamah* and they prayed the afternoon, sunset, and night prayers in succession, each time followed by the *iqamah*.[3]

The Adhan and *Iqamah* for Women

Said Ibn 'Umar, "There is no *adhan* or *iqamah* for women." (Related by al-Baihaqi with a *sahih* chain.) This was the opinion of Anas, al-Hassan, Ibn Sireen, an-Nakha'i, al-Thauri, Malik, Abu Thaur

---

[2]This *hadith* is weak. See *Faidh al-Qadeer* by al-Munawi, number 3620.

[3]The chain of this *hadith* has Abu az-Zubair in it who committed *tadlis* and this *hadith* is from him in *mu'an'an* form; therefore, the chain is weak although it might have supporting evidence elsewhere. - J.Z.

and the people of "juristic reasoning." Ash-Shaf'i, Ishaq and Ahmad said if they make the *iqamah* and *adhan*, there is no problem. It is related from 'Aishah that she would make the *adhan* and *iqamah* and lead the women in prayer, standing in the middle of the row. (Related by al-Baihaqi.)

Entering the Mosque After the Prayer Is Finished

The author of *al-Mughni* states, "If one enters the mosque after the prayer is finished, he may make the *adhan* and *iqamah*. Ahmad's practice, based on what al-'Athram and Sa'eed ibn Mansur recorded from Anas,[4] was to ask a person to make the *adhan* and *iqamah*, after which he would pray with (some people) in congregation. If a person wishes, he may pray without making the *adhan* and *iqamah*. Says 'Urwa, "If you reach a mosque wherein the people have already prayed, you may base your prayer on their *adhan* and *iqamah*, as theirs are sufficient for those who come after them." This was the opinion of al-Hassan, ash-Sha'bi and an-Nakha'i. Al-Hassan, however, said, "I prefer that he makes the *iqamah*. If he makes the *adhan*, he should do so in a low voice and not aloud, for some people may consider it out of place."

The Time Between the *Iqamah* and the Prayer

It is permitted to talk between the *iqamah* and the prayer. One need not repeat the *iqamah*, even if the interval is long. Reported Anas ibn Malik, "The *iqamah* was made while the Messenger of Allah was talking to a man in the corner of the mosque. He did not come to the prayer until the people had fallen asleep." (Related by al-Bukhari.) One time, the Messenger of Allah, upon whom be peace, remembered that he was in post-sex impurity after the *iqamah* had been made, so he went to make *ghusl* and came back to lead the prayer without (a new) *iqamah*.

The *Iqamah* of One Who Is Not the Designated Caller

If someone other than the appointed caller wants to make the *adhan*, he must obtain the latter's permission. If the appointed or regular caller is late and they fear that they will miss the time of

---

[4]Al-Bukhari also recorded it in *mu'allaq* form.

the *adhan*, another person may make the call.

Extraneous Additions

The *adhan* is a form of worship. Muslims are not allowed to add or subtract anything from it. There is an authetic *hadith* which states, "Whoever introduces something to this affair of ours will have it rejected." We will discuss some of these acts here:

The caller saying, "I bear witness that our leader (Muhammad)is the Messenger of Allah." Ibn Hajr is of the opinion that the word 'leader' may not be added, although it is permissible on other occasions.

Shaikh Isma'il al-'Ajluni records in *Kashf al-Khafa'*, "Wiping the eyes with the index fingers and then kissing them after hearing the caller say 'I bear withess that Muhammad is the messenger of Allah,' and with the listener saying, 'I bear witness that Muhammad is His slave and messenger. I am pleased with Allah as Lord, with Islam as religion, and with Muhammad as the Prophet," is based on ad-Dailami's report from Abu Bakr that when he heard the caller say, "I bear witness that Muhammad is the Messenger of Allah," he would say the same, kiss the inside of his index fingers and wipe his eyes. The Prophet then said, "Whoever does what my friend (Abu Bakr) did, then my intercession will be permissible for him." In *al-Maqasid* it says, "This is not true. And what Abu Bakr ar-Raddad al-Yamani al-Mutasawaf recorded in *Mujibat ar-Rahmah wa Aza'im al-Maghfirah* is not true. Its chain is of unknown narrators and, moreover, the chain is broken." There is another report of equally dubious import from al-Khidr[5] and mentioned in the preceding book: "Whoever says, upon hearing the caller say, 'I bear witness that Muhammad is the Messenger of Allah,' 'Welcome O my love and the coolness of my eyes, Muhammad ibn 'Abdullah, upon whom be peace,' and then kisses his index fingers and wipes his eye with them, he well never go blind; nor will he never be afflicted with an eye infection.'" None of these practices can be attributed to the Prophet or his companions.[6]

---

[5]The companion of Moses. - J.Z.

[6]This shows the difference between al-'Ajluni and as-Sakhawi (the author of *al-Maqasid al-Hassanah*). Although this *hadith* is clearly a fabrication, al-'Ajluni simply

To "sing" the *adhan* or to state it in improper Arabic by adding a letter or lengthening the sound of a vowel, and so on, is disliked. If it changes or obscures the meaning of what is said, it becomes forbidden.

Reported Yahya al-Baka', "I saw Ibn 'Umar say to a man, 'I am mad at you for the sake of Allah.' Then he said to his companions, 'He sings in making his *adhan*, and he takes wages for it.'"

Making *dhikr*, supplications, and practices of a similar nature before the morning *adhan* are innovations to the *sunnah*. In *al-Iqna* and its commentary, a book of Hanbali *fiqh*, it is stated, "What some callers do before the morning *adhan* (i.e. *dhikr*, chanting, loud supplications and so on) are not part of the *sunnah*. No scholar has said that it is preferred to do such acts. In fact, they are hateful innovations introduced after the time of the Prophet and his companions. No one is to order such acts, and no one is to blame one who avoids such acts. If one has left money for such acts, it is not permissible to use it for those acts, as they contradict the *sunnah*. In *Talbis Iblis* by Ibn al-Jauzi, it states, "I have seen people staying up a part of the night on the minaret admonishing the people, making *dhikr* and reciting the Qur'an in a loud voice. They keep people from sleeping and disturb those who are making late-night prayers. These are rejected and evil actions." Ibn Hajr says in *Fath al-Bari*, "What is done in the way of *dhikr* before the morning *adhan*, the Friday prayers and the prayers for the Prophet is derived neither from the *adhan* nor from the Islamic law.

To say aloud "Peace and blessings upon the Messenger" after the *adhan*. This is a hated innovation. Ibn Hajr says[7] in *al-Fatawa al-Kubra*, "Our shaikhs and others have given a legal verdict about the prayers and salutations for the Prophet after the *adhan* and how the callers to prayer do it. Their verdict is that (the prayers for the Prophet) has its root in the *sunnah*, but the manner in which they perform it is an innovation." Muhammad 'Abduh was asked about

---

mentions that it was reported by ad-Dailami from Abu Bakr. He was just recording information without making any evaluation of the report. As-Sakhawi, on the other hand, was a *mujtahid* who was able to clearly state the status of the *hadith*, although he did not always do so in *al-Maqasid*.

[7]This is Ibn Hajr al-Haithami, the jurist and scholar of *hadith*, and it is not Ibn Hajr al-Asalani, the scholar of *hadith* and jursit, who wrote *Fath al-Bari*.

saying the prayers and salutation for the Prophet subsequent to the *adhan* and he said, "The *adhan*, as mentioned in *al-Khaniyyah*, is only for the prescribed prayers. It consists of fifteen phrases, the last being *La ilaha illal-lah*. Whatever is mentioned before or after it is an innovation. It has been introduced for rhythm, and nothing else. There is hardly a scholar who has allowed it, nor does it make any sense to say that it is a good innovation, for every innovation in matters of worship is evil. Whoever claims that it is not for melody is lying."

PREREQUISITES OF THE PRAYER (SALAH)

A person must fulfill several requirements for his prayer to be acceptable. These are:

Knowledge that the time for prayer has begun. If one is certain or fairly certain that the time has begun, he may pray. How he reached his decision is not important.

Purity From Major and Minor Impurities. Says Allah in the Qur'an, "O you who believe, when you rise for the prayer, wash your faces, your hands up to the elbows, and lightly rub your hands and (wash) your feet up to the ankles. If you are unclean, purify yourselves." Ibn 'Umar reported that the Prophet said, "Allah does not accept any prayer that was not performed while in a state of purity, nor does he accept charity from what has been stolen from booty." (Related by "the group.")

Purity of the Body, Clothes and Place. Such objects should be clean of physical impurities as much as possible. If one can not remove them, he may pray with the impurities present and does not have to repeat the prayer later. Concerning bodily purity, Anas related that the Prophet upon whom be peace, said, "Stay clean of urine, as the majority of punishment in the grave is due to it." This is related by ad-Daraqutni, who said it is *hassan*.

Reported 'Ali, I used to have a great deal of prostatic fluid flowing, so I asked a man to ask the Prophet about it (as I was shy to ask him, due to my relationship with him through his daughter). He asked him and the Prophet, upon whom be peace, said, "Make ablution and wash your penis." (Related by al-Bukhari and others.)

'Aishah also related that the Messenger of Allah said to women with a prolonged flow of blood, "Wash the blood from yourself and pray."

Concerning purity of clothing, we have the following: Says Allah, "And purify your raiment" *(al-Muddathir: 4).* Jabir ibn Sumrah reported that he heard a man ask the Prophet, "May I pray in the same clothes that I had on during intercourse with my wife?" He said, "Yes, but if you see some stains on it, you must wash it." This *hadith* is related by Ahmad and Ibn Majah. Its narrators are trustworthy. Reported Mu'awiyyah, "I asked Umm Habibah, 'Did the Prophet pray in the same clothes that he wore when he had intercourse?' She said, 'Yes, if there were no stains on it.'"(Related by Ahmad, Abu Dawud, an-Nasa'i and Ibn Majah.) Abu Sa'eed reported that the Prophet removed his shoes and the people behind him did likewise. When he finished the prayer, he asked, "Why did you remove your shoes?" They said, "We saw you remove yours." He said, "Gabriel came to me and informed me that there was some filth on them. Therefore, when one of you comes to the mosque, he should turn his shoes over and examine them. If one finds any dirt on them, he should rub them against the ground and pray with them on." Th *hadith* is related by Ahmad, Abu Dawud, al-Hakim, Ibn Hibban and Ibn Khuzaimah. The latter grades it as *sahih.*

This *hadith* shows that if one enters the mosque (with his shoes on) and is unaware of some impurity or has forgotten it, and he suddenly remembers it during the prayer, he must try to remove it and proceed with the prayer. He does not have to repeat it later on.

Concerning the purity of the place where one is praying, Abu Hurairah said, "A bedouin stood and urinated in the mosque. The people got up to grab him. The Prophet said, 'Leave him and pour a container full of water over his urine. You have been raised to be easy on the people, not to be hard on them." (Related by "the group," except for Muslim.)

Commenting on this subject, ash-Shaukani says, "If what has been produced of proof is firmly established, then one would know that it is obligatory to have one's clothes free of impurities. Whoever prays and has impurities on his clothing has left one of the obligations of the prayer. But his prayer would not be voided." In *ar-Raudhat an-Nabiyyah* it states, "The majority of scholars are of the opinion that it is obligatory to purify three things: the body, the clothes, and the place of prayer. Some are of the opinion that this is a condition for the soundness of the prayer, and others say that it is just a *sunnah*. The truth of the matter is that it is obligatory. Whoever intentionally prays with impurities on his clothing has left one of the obligations (of the prayer), but the prayer is still valid."

Covering the *'Aurah.* Says Allah in the Qur'an, "O Children of Adam, take your adornment (by wearing proper clothing) for every mosque" (*al-A'raf: 31*). The meaning of "adornment" here is the covering of the *'aurah*. The meaning of "mosque" is "prayer." Therefore, it means "Cover your *'aurah* for every prayer." Salamah ibn al-Aku' said to the Prophet, "O Messenger of Allah, may I pray in a long shirt?" He said, "Yes, but button it, even with just a thorn." (Related by al-Bukhari in his *Tareekh*.)[8]

A man must cover the front and back of his pubic region. There is disagreement about the navel, thighs and knees. The reports seem to contradict each other. The following *hadith* are used to prove that such parts are not part of the man's *'aurah*:

Says 'Aishah, "The Prophet was sitting with his thigh exposed when Abu Bakr asked, and received, permission to enter. The same thing happened with 'Umar. However, when 'Uthman sought permission to enter, the Prophet covered himself with his clothes. When they left, I said, 'O Messenger of Allah, you permitted Abu Bakr and 'Umar to enter while your thigh was exposed. When 'Uthman asked permission to enter, you covered yourself with your clothes.' He said, 'O 'Aishah, should I not be shy of a man who, by Allah, even the angels are shy of?" (Related by Ahmad and al-Bukhari in *mu'allaq* form.)

Says Anas, "During the battle of Khaibar, the Prophet's gown was withdrawn from his thigh until I could see its whiteness." (Related by Ahmad and al-Bukhari.)

Says Ibn Hazm, "It is correct to say that the thigh is not part of

---

[8]Al-Bukhari, of course, had many more works than just the *Sahih*. The *Tareekh* is his collection of narrators, weak or trustworthy. Therefore, just because this *hadith* was not mentioned by al-Bukhari in one of his works does not necessarily mean that it is not *sahih*.

the *'aurah*. If it were so, why would Allah allow His Prophet, who is protected (from sin), to uncover his so that Anas and others could see it? Allah would have kept him from doing this. According to Jabir as recorded in the two *Sahihs*, when the Prophet was young (before his prophethood), he was one time carrying the stones of the *Ka'bah*, wearing only a loincloth. His uncle al-'Abbas said to him, 'O nephew, why don't you untie your waistcloth and put it on your shoulder for padding?' The Prophet did so and fell unconscious. He was never seen naked again after that.'"

Muslim records from Abu al-'Aliya that 'Abdullah ibn as-Samit struck his thigh and said, "I asked Abu Dharr, and he struck my thigh as I struck yours, and he said, 'I asked the Messenger of Allah, upon whom be peace, and he struck my thigh as I have struck yours and said, 'Perform the prayer in its time...'" Ibn Hazm said, "If the thigh was *'aurah*, why would the Messenger of Allah touch it?" If the thigh was *'aurah* according to Abu Dharr, why would he have struck it with his hand? The same can be asked for 'Abdullah ibn as-Samit and Abu al-'Aliya. It is not allowed for a Muslim to strike with his hand another man's pubic area, or the clothes over the pubic area. Nor can a man touch the clothing over a woman's *'aurah*.

Ibn Hazm mentions that Hubair ibn al-Huwairith looked at Abu Bakr's thigh when it was uncovered, and that Anas ibn Malik came to Qas ibn Shamas when his thigh was uncovered.

However, the following *hadith* are used to show that the thighs and so on are part of the *'aurah*:

Reported Muhammad Jahsh, "The Messenger of Allah, upon whom be peace, passed by Ma'mar while his thighs were uncovered. He said, to him, 'O Ma'mar, cover your thighs, for they are (part of the) *'aurah.*" This is related by Ahmad, al-Hakim and al-Bukhari in *Tareekh* and in *mu'allaq* form in his *Sahih*.

Reported Jurhad, "The Messenger of Allah passed by me when the cloak I was wearing did not cover my thigh. He said, 'Cover your thigh, for it (is part of the) *'aurah.*" This is related by Ahmad, Abu Dawud and at-Tirmidhi, who called it *hassan*, and by al-Bukhari in *mu'allaq* form in the *Sahih*.

These are the two sides of the issue.[9] Which one is the best is a

---

[9] It should be noted that the author has not completely covered the stance of the two sides. For example, he could have added the *hadith* in which the Prophet told 'Ali

matter of opinion. However, it is safer for the person who wants to pray to cover what is between the navel and the knees. Says al-Bukhari, "Anas's *hadith* is stronger, but Jurhad's is safer."

There is no such dispute over what constitutes a woman's *'aurah*. It is stated that her entire body is *'aurah* and must be covered, except her hands and face. Says Allah in the Qur'an, "And to display of their adornment only that which is apparent (do not expose any adornment or beauty save the hands and face)." It has been authentically related from Ibn 'Abbas, Ibn 'Umar and 'Aishah that the Prophet said, "Allah does not accept the prayer of an adult woman unless she is wearing a headcovering (*khimar, hijab*)." This is related by "the five," except for an-Nasa'i, and by Ibn Khuzaimah and al-Hakim. At-Tirmidhi grades it as *hassan*.

It is related from Umm Salamah that she asked the Prophet, "Can a woman pray in a long shirt (like a night shirt) and headcovering without a loincloth?" He said, "If the shirt is long and flowing and covers the top of her feet." This is related by Abu Dawud. The scholars say it is *sahih* in *mauqoof* form (as a statement of Umm Salamah and not that of the Prophet.)

It is also related that 'Aishah was asked, "In how many garments is a woman to pray?" She answered, "Ask 'Ali ibn Abu Talib and then return to me and tell me what he said." 'Ali's answer was, "In a headcover and a long flowing shirt." This was told to 'Aishah and she said, "He has told the truth."

The clothes worn must cover the *'aurah*, even if they are tight enough to highlight those features. If the clothes are so thin that one's skin color can be seen, they are not suitable for prayer.

It is preferred for a person to wear at leat two garments, but he can wear just one if that is all he has. Ibn 'Umar reported that the Prophet, upon whom be peace, said, "If one of you is going to pray, he should wear two garments, for Allah has the most right that you should look good for Him. If one does not have two garments, he shoud cover himself with a cloak when he prays, but not like the Jews do." (Related by at-Tabarani and al-Baihaqi.)

'Abdurazaq related that Ubayy ibn Ka'b and 'Abdullah ibn Mas'ud had an argument. Ubayy thought it was permissible to pray in one garment, while Ibn Mas'ud said that that was allowed only if one had no other clothes. 'Umar mounted the pulpit and said, "The

---

'Ali not to look at the thigh of any person, dead or alive, and so on. (Related by Muslim.) - J.Z.

correct position is: If Allah gives you more provisions, you should wear more clothes. A man can gather his clothes about him, or pray in a waist cloth and a cloak, or in a waist cloth and a shirt, or in a waist cloth and a caftan, or in trousers and a cloak, or in trousers and a shirt, or in trousers and a caftan, or in leather trousers and a caftan, or in leather trousers and a shirt.' And I (a narrator) think he said, 'Leather trousers and a cloak."

Buraida reported that the Prophet forbade one to pray using an improperly-affixed sheet to cover his *'aurah*, and to pray in trousers while not wearing a cloak. (Related by Abu Dawud and al-Baihaqi.) It is related that when al-Hassan ibn 'Ali prayed, he would wear his best clothes. He was asked about that and he said, "Verily, Allah is beautiful and He loves beauty, so I beautify myself for my Lord." Such a view is in accord with Allah's words, "And wear your adornment for every prayer."

Uncovering the Head During the Prayer. Ibn 'Asakir related that the Prophet would sometimes remove his cap and place it in front of him as a *sutrah*. According to the Hanifiyyah, one can pray with his head uncovered. In fact, they prefer this if it is done out of a sense of humility and awe.[10] There is no evidence whatsoever that it is preferred to cover one's head while praying.

Facing the *Qiblah*. All scholars agree that one must face the *Masjid al-Haram* (in Makkah) during every prayer. Says Allah in the Qur'an, "Direct your face to the *Masjid al-Haram*. Wherever you may be, turn your faces to it" (*al-Baqarah: 144*).

Reported al-Barra', "We prayed with the Messenger of Allah, upon whom be peace, for about sixteen or seventeen months towards Jerusalem, after which time he turned towards the *Ka'bah*." (Related by Muslim.)

If one can see the *Ka'bah*, he must face that particular direction.

---

[10]May Allah reward Sabiq for explicitly mentioning the position of the Hanafiyyah on this question. I have met many misinformed Muslims who insist on covering their heads in prayer because (they claim) they are following the Hanafi school of thought. - J.Z.

If he can not see it, he must turn in its direction, as this is all that
he is able to do. Abu Hurairah reported that the Prophet said, "The
qiblah is between the East and the West." This is related by Ibn
Majah and at-Tirmidhi. The latter considers it *hassan sahih*. This
hadith refers to the people of Madinah and whoever has a position
similar to them (i.e., the people of Syria, the Arabian Peninsula and
Iraq. For the people of Egypt, the *qiblah* is between the East and
the South.)[11]

If one can not determine the direction of the *qiblah*, he should ask
one who knows. If he finds no one to ask, he should try his best to
determine it. In such a case, his prayer will be valid, and he need
not repeat it even though he discovers later on that he had faced in
the wrong direction. If it is made clear to him while he is praying
that he is facing the wrong direction, he need only turn in the proper
direction without stopping his prayer. This is based on the following
incident: Ibn 'Umar reported that the people were praying the morning prayer in the Quba' mosque when a person came to them and
said, "Allah has revealed some of the Qur'an to the Prophet in which
we have been ordered to face the *Ka'bah*, so face it." They immediately
turned their faces from Syria to the *Ka'bah*." (Related by al-Bukhari
and Muslim.)

If one prays according to what he determined and then wants to
make another prayer, he should again try to determine the *qiblah's*
direction. If it turns out to be different from what he had determined
earlier, he should pray in the new direction without repeating his
earlier prayer.

There are only two cases in which one doesn't have to face the
Ka'bah. The first one is performing voluntary prayers while riding
(an animal, car and so on). The rider may bend his head slightly for
the bowings and prostrations of the prayer, but he should bend a
little bit lower for the prostrations. He may face in whatever direction
his ride is going.

Reported 'Amr ibn Rabi'ah, "I saw the Messenger of Allah, upon
whom be peace, pray while riding, and he faced the direction in
which he was going." This *hadith* is related by Muslim, at-Tirmidhi
and al-Bukhari. The latter added that "he bent his head slighty."

He did not, however, do this for the obligatory prayers. Ahmad,

---

[11]The current reasoning in the United States is that the direction of the *qiblah* is
approximately North by Northeast since that is the direction of the shortest route
between the US and Makkah. Some still pray or allow the prayer to be made in the
Southeast direction. Allah knows best. - J.Z.

Muslim and at-Tirmidhi recorded that he would pray on his mount while travelling from Makkah to Madinah, facing away from Makkah. Upon this, Allah revealed, "Wherever you turn, you will find Allah's face." Says Ibrahim an-Nakha'i, "They would pray on their mounts and animals in the direction in which they were facing." Ibn Hazm comments, "This has been related from the companions and those of the following generation, during travel and residence."

The second case is praying while having to deal with forced conditions, illness and fear. Under such circumstances, it is allowed to pray without facing the *qiblah*. The Prophet, upon whom be peace, said, "If I order you to do something, do what you are capable of doing." Says Allah, "If you go in fear, then (pray) standing or on your mounts..." *(al-Baqarah: 239)*. Ibn 'Umar added, "Facing the *qiblah* or not facing it." (Related by al-Bukhari.)

THE STATE OF PRAYER (*SALAH*)

There are many prophetic *hadith* on this topic.[12] Here, we will mention just two of them, one describing his actions and other quoting his statements.

'Abdullah ibn Ghanam related that Abu Musa al-Ash'ari gathered together his people saying, " O Tribe of Ash'ari, gather together, and gather your women and children to teach them how the Messenger of Allah, upon whom be peace, prayed with us in Madinah." They all gathered to watch him perform ablution. After it, he waited until the sun had just passed the meridian and there was some shade, and then he made the *adhan*. He put the men in the row closest to him, the children in a row behind the men, and the women in a row behind the children. After the *iqamah*, he raised his hands and made the *takbir*, silently recited *Surah al-Fatihah* and another *surah*, repeated the *takbir* and bowed while saying, "Glory be to Allah and Praise be to Him" three times, after which he said, "Allah hears him who praises Him" and stood straight. He then made the *takbir* and prostrated, made another *takbir*, raised his head (and sat), repeated the *takbir* and prostrated again, after which he said the final *takbir* and stood up. In the first *rak'ah* he made six *takbir*, and he made another one when he stood for the second *rak'ah*. When he finished the prayer, he turned to his people and said, "Guard the

---

[12]The most important of this is his statement, "Pray as you have seen me pray." (Related by al-Bukhari.) - J.Z.

number of my *takbir* and learn my bowings and prostrations, for this is how the Prophet prayed with us during this part of the day." (Then he said) when the Prophet, upon whom be peace, finished the prayer, he turned toward the people and said, "O people, listen and understand. Allah has slaves who are neither prophets nor martyrs, but both the prophets and martyrs envy them for their closeness to Allah." A bedouin stepped forward, pointed to the Messenger of Allah and said, "O Messenger of Allah, tell us about these people." The Prophet was pleased with the bedouin's request and said, "They are from various peoples and tribes who have no ties of relationship between them. They love each other purely for the sake of Allah. On the Day of Resurrection, Allah will present them pulpits of light for them to sit on. Their faces will be light and their clothes will be light. The people will be scared on the Day of Resurrection, but they will not be scared. They are the friends of Allah who will not have any fear upon them nor will they grieve.

As to the authenticity of this report, it is related by Ahmad and Abu Ya'la with a *hassan* chain. Al-Hakim says its chain is *sahih*.

Reported Abu Hurairah, "A man entered the mosque and, after praying, went to the Prophet, upon whom be peace. The Prophet, upon whom be peace, responded to his salutations and said, 'Return and pray, for you have not prayed.' This happened three times, and the man finally said, 'By the One who sent you with the Truth, I do not know any better than that, so teach me.' He said, 'When you stand for the prayer, make the *takbir* and then recite what you can from the Qur'an. Then bow until you attain calmness and then come up again until you are standing straight. Then prostrate until you attain calmness in your sitting, and prostate until you attain calmness in your prostration. Do that during all of your prayer." (Related by Ahmad, Muslim and al-Bukhari.)

These are general *hadith* that describe how the Prophet, upon whom be peace, prayed or what he said about its performance. Now we shall discuss those acts of the prayer which are obligatory and those which are *sunnah*.

OBLIGATORY ACTS
OF THE PRAYER (SALAH)

For it to be acceptable, the method of prayer must conform to the norms spelled out in the Islamic law. These are:

Intention. Says Allah, "And We did not command them save to worship Allah, making the religion sincerely for Him" *(al-Bayinah: 5)*. The Prophet, upon whom be peace, said, "Every action is based upon intention. For everyone is what he intended. Whoever made the migration to Allah and His Prophet, then his migration is to Allah and His Prophet. Whoever's migration was for something of this world or for the purpose of marriage, then his migration was to what he migrated to." (Related by al-Bukhari.)[13]

In *Ighatha al-Lufan*, Ibn al-Qayyim states, "The intention is the aim and purpose of something. It is a condition of the heart, and it does not come from the tongue. For that reason, the Prophet and his companions never spoke their intentions. What has been introduced into this matter during the actions of purity and the prayer comes from Satan and is a trap for those who are unsure about how to make it. You will find them repeating it over and over, but that is not part of the prayer at all."

---

[13]With this wording, the *hadith* was related by Muslim and others and not al-Bukhari.
-J.Z.

Saying the Opening *Takbir* and Beginning the Prayer. 'Ali reported that the Prophet, upon whom be peace, said, "The key to prayer is purity. What puts one into its inviolable state is the *takbir*, and the *tasleem*[14] releases one from it."

As to the authenticity of the report, it is related by ash-Shaf'i, Ahmad, Abu Dawud, Ibn Majah and at-Tirmidhi, who called it the most authentic report on this topic. Al-Hakim and Ibn as-Sakin consider it as *sahih.* The *takbir* consists of saying *Allahu akbar.*[15] Abu Hameed reported that when the Prophet stood for prayer, he would stand straight, raise his hands and say, "*Allahu akbar.*"

This is related by Ibn Majah, and in the *Sahihs* of Ibn Khuzaimah and Ibn Hibban. Al-Bazzar related something similar to it, but with a chain that is *sahih* according to Muslim's criterion. 'Ali and others also reported this.

Standing During the Obligatory Prayers. One must stand during the prayer, if at all possible. Says Allah, "Guard and preserve the prayers and the mid-most prayer, and stand for Allah with devotion." Reported 'Umar ibn Hussain, "I had some physical problem, so I asked the Prophet, upon whom be peace, about the prayer, and he said, 'Pray standing; if you are not able to; pray sitting, if you are not able to; pray (while lying) on your side." (Related by al-Bukhari.) Most scholars say that one should not put his feet together while standing in prayer.

For voluntary prayers, one can pray sitting even if he can stand, but one who stands receives a larger reward than one who sits. 'Abdullah ibn 'Umar related that the Prophet, upon whom be peace, said, "The prayer of one who sits is half of the prayer." (Related by al-Bukhari and Muslim.)

If one can not stand, he may pray according to what he is capable of doing, as Allah does not burden a soul beyond its ability. He will get a complete reward for the prayer. Abu Musa reported that the Prophet said, "If a slave (of Allah) is sick or travels, he will get a reward for those acts similar to what he would get if he was healthy and at home."

Reciting *al-Fatihah* in Every *Rak'ah* of the Prayer. There are

---

[14]Saying *as-Salamu 'alaikum wa rahmatullah* at the end of the prayer. - J.Z.

[15]Some Hanafiyyah allow other statements such as *Allahu 'Adheem*, but their opinion on this point seems to be incorrect. - J.Z.

many authentic *hadith* which state that it is obligatory to recite *al-Fatihah* in every *rak'ah*. Thus, there is no difference of opinion on this point. Some of these *hadith* are:

'Ibadah ibn as-Samit related that the Prophet said, "There is no prayer for one who does not recite the opening of the Book *(al-Fatihah)*." *This is related by "the group."*

Abu Hurairah reported that the Prophet said, "Whoever prays a prayer and does not recite the opening chapter of the Qur'an has not prayed correctly." (Related by Ahmad, al-Bukhari and Muslim.) Ad-Daraqutni also recorded a *hadith* with a *sahih* chain with almost exactly the same wording.

Said Abu Sa'eed, "We were ordered to recite the opening chapter of the Qur'an and what (else) was easy (for us)." This is related by Abu Dawud. Al-Hafez and Ibn Sayyid an-Nass consider its chain as *sahih*.

In some of the narrations dealing with the prayer's incompleteness, it states, "And then recite the 'Mother of the Book' *(al-Fatihah)*," and he said, "And do that in every *rak'ah*."

It is confirmed that the Prophet, upon whom be peace, recited *al-Fatihah* in every *rak'ah* of every prayer, obligatory or superogatory. Since this is an act of worship, we can only follow what he did. And the Prophet said, "Pray as you have seen me pray." (Related by al-Bukhari.)

The scholars are agreed that the *bismillah* (the words "In the name of Allah, the Compassionate, the Merciful) is a verse in *Surah al-Naml*, but they differ over whether or not it constitutes a verse of every *surah*. There are three opinions on this point:

a) It is a verse of *al-Fatihah* and of every *surah* of the Qur'an. Therefore, it is to be recited with al-Fatihah during those prayers that are said aloud or quietly. The strongest support of this opinion comes from the *hadith* of Na'em al-Mujammir who said, "I prayed behind Abu Hurairah and he recited, 'In the name of Allah...' and then he recited *al-Fatihah*." At the end of the *hadith*, he is quoted as saying, "By the One in whose Hand is my soul, I have done what resembles how we prayed with the Messenger of Allah."

As to the authenticity of the report, it is related by an-Nasa'i, Ibn Khuzaimah and Ibn Hibban. In *Fath al-Bari*, Ibn Hajr said, "That is the most authentic *hadith* concerning the verbal recitation of the *bismillah.*"[16]

b) It is a verse by itself and was revealed to demarcate different *surahs*. It is allowed to recite it with *al-Fatihah* (in fact it is preferred), but it is not *sunnah* to recite it aloud. Anas said, "I prayed behind the Messenger of Allah, Abu Bakr, 'Umar and 'Uthman, and they did not recite it aloud."

This *hadith* is related by an-Nasa'i, Ibn Hibban and at-Tahawi with a *sahih* chain according to the criterion of the two *Sahihs*.

c) It is not a verse of *al-Fatihah* or of any other *surah*. It is disliked to recite it aloud or quietly during the obligatory prayers, but not for the superogatory prayers. This opinion, however, is not strong.

Ibn al-Qayyim has reconciled the first and second opinions by saying, "Sometimes the Prophet would recite it aloud, but most of the time he would say it quietly and not aloud."

One Who Cannot Recite Properly. Says al-Khattabi, "Basically, one's prayer does not suffice if he does not recite *al-Fatihah*. If one can recite neither *al-Fatihah* nor other portions of the Qur'an, he should recite at least seven verses of a similar meaning from the Qur'an. If he can not learn any part of the Qur'an (due to some innate inability, poor memory, or because it's a foreign language), he should say the *tasbeeh* (*Subhaan Allah* - Glory be to Allah), the *tamheed* (*al-Hamdu lillah* - All praise is due to Allah), and *tahleel* (*La ilaha illal-lah* - There is no God except Allah). It is related that he said, "The best remembrancce after the speech of Allah is *Subhaan Allah, al-Hamdu lillah, La ilaha illal-lah* and *Allahu akbar*." This is supported by Rafa'ah ibn Rafa', who narrated that the Prophet said, "If you have something from the Qur'an, recite it. If not, then say the *tamheed, takbir* and the *tahleel* and then bow."

This *hadith* is related by Abu Dawud, at-Tirmidhi, an-Nasa'i and al-Baihaqi. The former considers it as *hassan*.

Ar-Ruku' (Bowing Down). There is a consensus on the obligatory nature of the *ruku'*. Says Allah, "O you who believe, bow down and

---

[16]Statements of this nature do not mean that the *hadith* referred to is necessarily *sahih*. It could be the case that all of the *hadith* related on a certain topic are weak, though one of them may be the strongest and as such will be called, "The most authentic *hadith* on this topic," and so on. - J.Z.

prostrate yourselves..." The position of *ruku'* is established by bending over, putting one's hands on one's knees, and remaining in that position until he attains "calmness." In another *hadith* the Prophet said, "Then bow until you attain calmness while your are bowing." Abu Qatadah related that the Prophet, upon whom be peace, said, "The worst pepole are the thieves who steal part of the prayer." He was asked how this was done, and he replied, "He does not complete his bowings and prostrations," or he said, "He does not straighten his back during his bowings and prostrations."

As to its authenticity, the report is related by Ahmad, at-Tabarani, Ibn Khuzaimah and al-Hakim, who consider its chain as *sahih*.

Abu Mas'ud al-Badri reported that the Prophet, upon whom be peace, said, "The prayer of one who does not straighten his back in his bendings and prostrations is not accomplished." This *hadith* is related by "the five," and Ibn Khuzaimah, Ibn Hibban, at-Tabarani and al-Baihaqi, who consider its chain as *sahih*, while at-Tirmidhi grades it as *hassan sahih*.

Knowledgeable companions act according to the principle that a person is to make his back straight during his bowings and prostrations. Hudhaifah saw someone who did not straighten his back during his bowings and prostrations, and told him, "You have not prayed. And if you were to die, you would not die in the way of Allah and His Messenger." (Related by al-Bukhari.)

Standing Erect After the Bowing. This is based on Abu Humaid's description of the Prophet's prayer: "He would raise his head from his bowing, then stand straight until all of his backbones returned to their places." (Related by al-Bukhari and Muslim.)

'Aishah related that when the Prophet raised his head from bowing, he would not prostrate until his back was straight. (Related by al-Bukhari and Muslim.)

Abu Hurairah reported that the Prophet said, "Allah does not look at the prayer of a person who does not straighten his back between his bowings and his prostrations." (Related by Ahmad. al-Mundhiri considers its chain as good.)

Prostration. We have already stated the Qur'anic verse dealing with this obligatory act. The Prophet explained it in a *hadith* by saying, "Then prostrate until you attain calmness in your prostration, then rise (and sit) until you attain calmness in your sitting, and then prostrate until you gain calmness in your prostration. The first prostration, sitting afterwards, the second prostration and calmness during all of these acts are obligatory in every *rak'ah* of every obligatory or superogatory prayer.

How to Attain Calmness. The "calmness" comes from sitting in the position until the bones are set and still. Some scholars say that, at a minimum, this would take as long as it takes to say one *Subhaan Allah*.

Bodily Parts That Touch the Ground During Prostration. These parts are: the face, hands, knees and feet. Al-'Abbas ibn 'Abdul-Mutallib reported that he heard the Prophet say, "When a slave (of Allah) prostrates, seven bodily parts prostrate with him: his face, his hands, his knees and his feet." (Related by "the group," except for al-Bukhari.) Said Ibn 'Abbas, "The Prophet ordered us to prostrate on seven bodily parts and not to fold back the hair or clothing: the forehead, the hands, the knees and the feet." In another wording, the Prophet said, "I have been ordered to prostrate on seven bodily parts: the forehead, and he pointed to his nose, the hands, the knees and the ends of the feet." (Related by al-Bukhari and Muslim.) In another narration, he said, "I have been ordered to prostrate on seven bodily parts and not to fold back the hair or clothing: the forehead, the nose, the hands, the knees and the feet." (Related by Muslim and an-Nasa'i.)

Abu Humaid reported that when the Prophet, upon whom be peace, prostrated, he placed his nose and forehead on the ground. This *hadith* is related by Abu Dawud and at-Tirmidhi who said, "The scholars act according to this: a person prostrates on his nose and forehead." According to some scholars, if one prostrates on just the forehead without the nose touching the ground, it will still be sufficient. Others say that it would not be sufficient until his nose touches the ground.

The Final Sitting and Recital of the *Tashahud*. The Prophet's practice illustrates that when the final sitting of the prayer has been made, one must recite the *tashahud* at that time. In one *hadith*, he said, "When you raise your head from the last prostration and sit for the *tashahud*, you have completed your prayer."

Says Ibn Qudamah, "It has been related that Ibn 'Abbas said, 'We used to say, before the *tashahud* was made obligatory upon us, 'Peace be upon Allah before His slaves, peace be upon Gabriel, peace be upon Mikhail.' The Prophet, upon whom be peace, said, 'Do not say, 'Peace be upon Allah,' but say, 'Salutations to Allah.' This proves that the *tashahud* was made obligatory, although before it was not."

The most authentic report concerning the *tashahud* is Ibn Mas'ud's, who said, "When we would sit with the Prophet in the prayer, we would say, 'Peace be upon Allah before His slaves, peace be upon so and so.' The Prophet said, 'Do not say peace be upon Allah, for Allah is peace. When one of you sits, he should say salutations be to Allah, and the prayers, and the good deeds, peace be upon us and upon Allah's sincere slaves (if you say that, it applies to all of Allah's sincere slaves in the heavens and the earth). I bear witness that there is no god except Allah. I bear witness that Muhammad is His slave and Messenger.' Then you may choose whatever supplication you desire." (Related by "the group.")

Says Muslim, "The people are in agreement over the *tashahud* of Ibn Mas'ud, and the companions do not differ over it." At-Tirmidhi, al-Khattabi, Ibn 'Abdul-Barr and Ibn al-Mundhir all agree that Ibn Mas'ud's *hadith* is the most authentic one on this topic.

Said Ibn 'Abbas, "The Messenger of Allah used to teach us the *tashahud* like he taught us the Qur'an. He would say, 'Salutations, blessings, prayers and good deeds for Allah. Peace be upon you, O Prophet, and the mercy of Allah and His blessings. Peace be upon us and the sincere slaves of Allah. I bear witness that there is no god except Allah. I bear witness that Muhammad is His slave and messenger." (Related by ash-Shaf'i, Muslim, Abu Dawud and an-Nasa'i.)

Says ash-Shaf'i, "Different *hadith* have been related about the *tashahud*, but that one is the best in my opinion, for it is the most complete. Al-Hafez states, "Ash-Shaf'i was asked about this choice and the *tashahud* of Ibn 'Abbas, and he replied, 'I have found it to be the most encompassing. I have heard it from Ibn 'Abbas (through) authentic (chains). To me, it is more complete...'"

There is another form of the *tashahud* that Malik chose. In *al-Muwatta*, it is stated that 'Abdurahman ibn 'Abdul-Qari heard 'Umar ibn al-Khattab teaching the people, from the pulpit, this *tashahud*: "Salutations to Allah, purifications to Allah, the good deeds and prayers be to Allah. Peace be upon you, O Prophet, and the mercy of Allah and His blessings. Peace be upon us and Allah's sincere slaves. I testify that there is no god but Allah, and I testify that Muhammad is His slave and messenger."

Commenting on the stature of such *hadith*, an-Nawawi says, "Those *hadith* concerning the *tashahud* are all *sahih*. *Hadith* scholars are agreed that the strongest of them is the *hadith* of Ibn Mas'ud, and then the *hadith* of Ibn 'Abbas." Ash-Shaf'i said that any *tashahud* one uses will suffice, for the scholars agree that every one of them is permissible."

The *Salaam* (Peace Be Upon You and the Mercy of Allah) at the Prayer's End. Saying the *salaam* at the end of the prayer is obligatory. 'Ali related that the Prophet said, "The key to prayer is purity. One enters into its inviolable state by the *takbir* and leaves it by the *salaam*."

As to its authenticity, the report is related by Ahmad, ash-Shaf'i, Abu Dawud, Ibn Majah and at-Tirmidhi who said, "That is the most authentic report on this topic and the best."

'Amr ibn Sa'd related that his father said, "I saw the Prophet making the *salaam* on his right side and on his left side until I could see the whiteness of his cheeks." (Related by Ahmad, Muslim, an-Nasa'i and Ibn Majah.)

Reported Wa'il ibn Hajr, "I prayed with the Messenger of Allah. He would make the *salaam* on his right side by saying, 'Peace be upon you and the mercy of Allah." In *Bulugh al-Maram*, Ibn Hajr says that Abu Dawud related it with a *sahih* chain.

It is obligatory to say one *salaam*, and it is preferred to say two. Ibn al-Mundhir comments that all scholars agree that making only one *salaam* is permissible. Ibn Qudamah writes in *al-Mughni*, "There is no clear text from Ahmad that states that two *salaams* are obligatory. He only said, 'Two *salaams* are the most authentic act from the Messenger of Allah.' It is permissible to say that this is the regualtion, although it is not obligatory, and others have the same opinion. This is also pointed out in another of his statements where he said, 'Two *salaams* are more loved by me. But 'Aishah, Salamah ibn al-Aku' and Sahl ibn Sa'd narrated that the Prophet, upon whom be peace, made only one *salaam*." We can reconciliate these differences by stating that it is *sunnah* to say two *salaams*, but it is obligatory to say one. This is the consensus that Ibn al-Mundhir mentioned, and we have no option to reject that. Says an-Nawawi, "It is the opinion of ash-Shaf'i and most of the early and later scholars that it is *sunnah* to say two *salaams*." Malik and a group of scholars say that only one *salaam* is *sunnah*. They adduce this from a weak *hadith* that can not be used as a proof. If something of this nature had been confirmed from the Prophet, the act was probably done just to show that it is permissible to say only one *salaam*. Scholars are agreed that only one *salaam* is obligatory. If one makes only one *salaam*, he should turn to his right for the first one and to the left for the second one. He should turn until his cheeks can be seen from behind. That is the most authentic form and it is said, "If one says the two *salaams* to the right or to the left while facing forward, or the first one on the left and the second one on the right, then his prayer would still be valid and he would have fulfilled the act of the two *salaams*. But, he would have lost the virtue of how they are to be performed."

THE SUNNAH ACTS
OF THE PRAYER

The prayer also has certain acts which are *sunnah*. It is preferred that the person performs them to get their reward. These are:

Raising the Hands. This must be done at the beginning of each prayer's *takbir*. Says Ibn al-Mundhir, "All scholars agree that the Prophet raised his hands at the beginning of his prayer."

Commenting upon this report, Ibn Hajr says, "The Prophet's raising his hands at the beginning of his prayer has been narrated by fifty companions, inluding the ten who were given the tidings of Paradise. " Al-Baihaqi related that al-Hakim said, "I do not know of any *sunnah* other than this one which is accepted by the four rightly-guided *khalifahs*, the ten companions who were given the tidings of Paradise, and other companions scattered across many lands." Summing up his evaluation of the report, al-Baihaqi says, "And it is as our teacher Abu 'Abdullah has said."[17]

How to Raise the Hands. Many narrations have been recorded concerning this subject. Many scholars have chosen the following

---

[17]"Abu 'Abdullah" is usually used for Ahmad ibn Hanbal. In this case, it is a reference to al-Baihaqi's teacher, Abu 'Abdullah al-Hakim an-Naishapoori, the scholar of *hadith*. - J.Z.

forms: the hands are raised to the shoulders with the fingertips parallel to the button of the ears. Says an-Nawawi, "This is how ash-Shaf'i combined the *hadith* (on this question), and the people found it to be good." It is preferred that one extends the fingers while raising the hands. Abu Hurairah said, "When the Prophet, upon whom be peace, stood for prayer, he would raise his hands (with them being) open." (Related by "the five," except for Ibn Majah.)

When to Raise the Hands. One must raise the hands at about the same time he makes the *takbir.* Nafa' related that when Ibn 'Umar would begin his prayer he would say the *takbir* and raise his hands. The Prophet also did this. (Related by al-Bukhari, an-Nasa'i and Abu Dawud.) He also reported that the Prophet, upon whom be peace, would raise his hands upon making the *takbir* until they were parallel to his shoulders or close to that. (Related by Ahmad and others.)

As for raising the hands just before the *takbir*, Ibn 'Umar reported, "When the Prophet, upon whom be peace, stood for prayer, he would raise his hands until they were parallel to his shoulders and would make the *takbir.* (Related by al-Bukhari and Muslim.) A *hadith* from Malik ibn al-Huwairith has the wording, "Make the *takbir* and then raise your hands." (Related by Muslim.) This implies that the *takbir* comes before the raising of the hands, but Ibn Hajr says, "I have not met anyone who holds that the *takbir* comes before the raising of the hands."

It is preferred to raise one's hands while going to bow and upon coming up from the bow. Twenty-two companions narrated that the Prophet, upon whom be peace, did so. Reported Ibn 'Umar, "When the Prophet, upon whom be peace, stood to pray, he would raise his hands until they were the same height as his shoulders and then he would make the *takbir.* When he wanted to bow, he would again raise his hands in a similar fashion. When he raised his head from the bowing, he did the same and said, 'Allah hears him who praises Him.' (Related by al-Bukhari, Muslim and al-Baihaqi.) Says al-Bukhari, "He would not do that when he was going to prostrate nor when he came up from his prostration." Al-Bukhari also says, "He would not raise his hands between the two prostrations." Al-Baihaqi has the addition, "He did not stop doing that until he met Allah." Ibn al-Madini said, "In my opinion, that *hadith* is a proof for the whole creation. Whoever hears it must act by it. There is nothing wrong with its chain." Al-Bukhari wrote a pamphlet on this topic, and related from al-Hassan and Humaid ibn Hilal that the companions used to (perform their prayers)in this manner.

On the contrary, the Hanafiyyah say that one should only raise his hands at the beginning. This is based on the *hadith* of Ibn Mas'ud, who reported, "I prayed with the Prophet, upon whom be peace, and he raised his hands only once." This is a weak opinion, and many *hadith* scholars have criticized this report. Ibn Hibban, though, said that this is the best report.

The people of Kufah narrated that the Prophet, upon whom be peace, did not raise his hands upon bowing or rising. But, in fact, this is a very weak statement, for it contains many defects and is therefore invalid. Even if we accept it, as at-Tirmidhi did, it does not invalidate the authentic and well-known *hadith* mentioned earlier. The author of *at-Tanqih* says that perhaps Ibn Mas'ud forgot that the Prophet, upon whom be peace, raised his hands. Az-Zaila'i writes in *Nasb ar-Rayah*, quoting the author of *at-Tanqih*, "It is not strange that Ibn Mas'ud may have forgotten that. Ibn Mas'ud forgot some things from the Qur'an that the Muslims after him never differed about, and those are the last two *surahs* of the Qur'an. He forgot how two people are to stand behind the *imam*, that the Prophet prayed the morning prayer on the Day of Sacrifice (during the *hajj*) at its proper time, how the Prophet, upon whom be peace, combined his prayers at 'Arafah, the position of the forearms and elbows during the prostration, and how the Prophet, upon whom be peace, recited, 'And Him who created the male and the female.' If it is possible that Ibn Mas'ud forgot all of these things concerning the prayer, is it not possible that he also forgot about raising the hands?"

Nafa' related that when Ibn 'Umar stood for the third *rak'ah*, he would raise his hands, an action which he ascribed to the Prophet. (Related by al-Bukhari, Abu Dawud and an-Nasa'i.) While describing the Prophet's prayer, 'Ali said that when he stood from the two prostrations, he would raise his hands until they reached his shoulders and make the *takbir*.

Women have to do this the same way. Says Ash-Shaukani, "Know that this *sunnah* is to be done by men and women. There is no proof to show that there is any difference between them on this point. There is also no proof to show that they are to raise their hands to different levels."

Placing the Right Hand upon the Left. This is a preferred act of the prayer. There are twenty *hadith* from eighteen companions and their followers on this point. Said Sahl ibn Sa'd, "The people were ordered to place their right hand on their left forearm during prayers." Commenting on this, Abu Hazm says, "I do not know if he ascribed this to the Prophet." This *hadith* is related by al-Bukhari, Ahmad and Malik in his *al-Muwatta*. Al-Hafez maintains, "Its ruling is considered to be from the Prophet, upon whom be peace, as it is implied that the one who ordered them to do so was the Prophet." He also related that the Prophet said, "All prophets have been ordered to hasten the breaking of the fast and to delay the (pre-fast dawn) meal, and to place our right hands on our left during prayer."

There is also a *hadith* from Jabir which says, "The Prophet, upon whom be peace, passed by a man praying with his left hand over his right, and (the Prophet) pulled them away and put his right over his left." This is related by Ahmad and others. Evaluating its chain, an-Nawawi says, "Its chain is *sahih*. Ibn 'Abdul-Barr holds, "Nothing has reached me different from that. It is the opinion of most companions and their followers." Malik mentioned it in his *al-Muwatta* and states, "Malik never stopped doing it until he met Allah."

The Position of the Hands. Al-Kamal ibn al-Hamam is of the opinion, "There is no authentic *hadith* stating that one must place the hands under the chest or below the navel. According to the Hanifiyyah, the hands are to be placed below the navel, and the Shafiyyah say below the chest. Ahmad has two narrations corresponding to these two opinions. The correct position is somewhere in the middle - to be equal." Observes at-Tirmidhi, "Knowledgeable companions, their followers and those that came after them believed that one should put his right hand over the left during prayer, while some say above the navel and others say below the navel..." Nevertheless, there do exist *hadith* that the Propet, upon whom be peace, placed his hands on his chest. Reported Hulb at-Ta'i, "I saw the Prophet, upon whom be peace, praying with his right hand over his left upon his chest above the elbow." This is related by Ahmad and at-Tirmidhi, who grades it as *hassan*.

Reported Wa'il ibn Hajr, "Once when I prayed with the Prophet, upon whom be peace, he placed his right hand over his left upon his chest." The report is recorded by Ibn Khuzaimah, who considers it as *sahih*, and by Abu Dawud and an-Nasa'i with the wording, "Then he put his right hand over the back of his left wrist and forearm."

The Opening Supplication. It is preferred for the person to begin his prayer with one of the supplications that the Prophet, upon whom be peace, used to begin his prayers. This occurs after the opening *takbir* and before the recitation of *al-Fatihah*. Some of the supplications that have been related are:

1) Reported Abu Hurairah, "When the Prophet, upon whom be peace, made the opening *takbir*, he would be quiet for a little while before his recitation. I asked him, 'O Messenger of Allah, may my father and mother be sacrificed for you, why are you quiet between the (opening) *takbir* and your recitation? What do you say (at that time)?' He said, 'I say, O Allah, make the distance between me and my sins as far as you have made the distance between the East and the West. O Allah, cleanse me of my sins as a white garment is cleansed of dirt. O Allah, purify me from my sins by snow, rain and hail." (Related by al-Bukhari, Muslim, Abu Dawud, an-Nasa'i and Ibn Majah.)

2) Reported 'Ali, that when the Prophet stood for prayer, he would make the *takbir* and then say, "I have turned my face to the one who created the heavens and the earth as a sincere submissive (person), and I am not one of the polytheists. My prayers, my sacrifice, my life and my death are all for Allah, the Lord of the Worlds. He has no partner. That is what I have been ordered and I am of those who submit. O Allah, you are the King and there is no Lord besides You. You are my Lord and I am Your slave. I have wronged my soul and You are aware of my sins, so forgive all of my sins. No one forgives sins save You. Guide me to the best character. No one can guide to the best of that save You. Turn me away from its evil, and no one can turn me from its evil save You. At your beck and call, all the good is in Your hands and evil is not to You. And I am for You and to You are the blessings and the exaltedness. I seek your forgiveness and return unto You." (Related by Ahmad, Muslim, at-Tirmidhi, Abu Dawud and others.)

3) It is related that 'Umar used to say, after the beginning *takbir*, "Glory be to You, O Allah, and to You is the praise. Blessed is Your name and most high is Your honor. There is no Lord besides You." This *hadith* is related by Muslim with a broken chain. Ad-Daraqutni traces it back to the Prophet and back to 'Umar.

Commenting on it, Ibn al-Qayyim says, "It has been authenticated that 'Umar began with that in the place (of the preceding prayer) of the Prophet, upon whom be peace. He would recite it aloud and teach it to the people. And owing to that fact, it is considered to have its source with the Prophet, upon whom be peace. For that reason, Imam Ahmad says, "I act by what has been related from 'Umar. If a person begins with something that has been related, it is good."

4) 'Asim ibn Humaid asked 'Aishah how the Prophet, upon whom be peace, began his late-night prayers. She replied, "You have asked me about something that no one before you has asked. When he would stand for prayer, he would make the *takbir* ten times (after the opening *takbir*), and then say '*Al-hamdu lillah*' ten times. He would then ask forgiveness ten times, and then would say, "O Allah, forgive me, guide me, provide for me, sustain me and give me refuge from a constraining place on the Day of Resurrection." (Related by Abu Dawud, an-Nasa'i and Ibn Majah.)

5) 'Abdurahman ibn 'Auf asked 'Aishah how the Prophet, upon whom be peace, began his prayer when he would pray during the night. She said, "When he would get up during the night, he would begin his prayer with, 'O Allah, Lord of Gabriel, Mikhail and Israfil, Creator of the heavens and the earth, Knower of the Unseen and the Seen. You will judge between Your slaves concerning matters wherein they differ. Guide me to the truth in those matters wherein they differ by Your permission, for You guide whom You will to the straight path." (Related by Muslim, Abu Dawud, at-Tirmidhi, an-Nasa'i and Ibn Majah.)

6) Nafa' ibn Jubair ibn Mut'am related from his father who said, "I heard the Messenger of Allah say in his voluntary prayer, '*Allahu akbar kabeera*' three times, '*al-Hamdu lillah katheera*' three times, '*Subhanallahi bukratan wa asila*' three times, and then 'O Allah, I seek refuge in You from Satan the accursed and from his pricking, spittle and puffing.' I said, 'O Messenger of Allah, what are his pricking, spittle and puffing?' He said, 'His pricking is the insanity by which he takes the children of Adam. His spittle is arrogance, and his puffing is (evil) poetry." (Related by Ahmad, Abu Dawud, Ibn Majah and Ibn Hibban.)

7) Ibn 'Abbas related that when the Prophet, upon whom be peace, got up for the night prayer, he would say, "O Allah, to You is the praise. You are the support of the heavens and the earth and whatever is therein. To You is the praise. You are the light of the heavens and the earth and whatever is therein. To You is the praise. You are the Truth. Your promise is true. The meeting with You is true. Your speech is true. Paradise is true. Hell-fire is true. Your prophets are true. Muhammad is true. The hour is true. O Allah, to You have I submitted, and in You have I believed. In You I put my trust, and to You do I come. For You do I dispute, and to You is the judgement. Forgive me my earlier and later sins, and what has been private

and public. You are the predecessor and the successor. There is no god except You. There is no lord other than You. There is no power or might except in Allah." This *hadith* is related by al-Bukhari, Muslim, Abu Dawud, at-Tirmidhi, an-Nasa'i, Ibn Majah and Malik. In Abu Dawud's version, the Prophet, upon whom be peace, said that after the opening *takbir.*

8) It is a preferred act for the one in prayer to seek refuge from Satan between his opening supplication and his Qur'anic recitation. Allah says, "When you recite the Qur'an, seek refuge in Allah from the outcast Satan." In the preceding *hadith* of Nafa' ibn Jubair, the Prophet is reported to have said, "O Allah, I seek refuge in you from Satan, the outcast." Said Ibn al-Mundhir, "It has been related from the Prophet, upon whom be peace, that he would say, 'I seek refuge in Allah from Satan, the outcast' before reciting."

9) It is *sunnah* to say ,"I seek refuge in..." silently. In *al-Mughni,* it states, "One should say the seeking of refuge silently and not aloud, and I do not know of any difference of opinion on that point." But ash-Shaf'i was of the opinion that one may choose between saying it silently or aloud in those prayers recited aloud. It has been related that Abu Hurairah recited aloud, but this report has a weak chain.

10) The seeking of refuge is to be done in the first *rak'ah* only. Reported Abu Hurairah, "When the Prophet, upon whom be peace, would get up for the second *rak'ah,* he would begin with *'al-Hamdu lillahi, rabb ul-'aalimeen',* without having any period of silence." (Related by Muslim.)

Speaking of it, Ibn al-Qayyim says, "The jurists differ over whether or not that is a time to say, 'I seek refuge...' But they agree that it is not a place to make the opening supplication. On the former point, there are two opinions, both of them related from Ahmad. Some of his companions concluded that either the prayer is only one recitation, so it is sufficient just to seek refuge once, or that each recital is a recital by itself that requires the seeking of refuge. They do not dispute the fact that the opening supplication is for the whole prayer. It is sufficient to seek refuge only once, as it is apparent from the authentic *hadith.*" Then he mentions the preceding *hadith* of Abu Hurairah, and says, "It is sufficient just to make one opening supplication, since there is no real break between the recital of the prayer. The only thing that is between them is the remembrance of Allah, and so on. Therefore, it will be considered as one recital. Ash-

Shaukani has the final word, and says, 'It is best just to do what
has been related from the *sunnah*, and that is to seek refuge in the
first *rak'ah* only."

Saying 'Ameen. It is *sunnah* for everyone to say *'ameen* after
reciting *al-Fatihah*. The word *ameen* is not part of *al-Fatihah*, but
rather a supplication meaning, "O Allah, respond (to or answer what
we have said). It should be said aloud in the prayers where the
recital is aloud, and quietly in the prayers where the recital is silent.
Said Na'eem al-Mujamir, "I prayed behind Abu Hurairah and he
said, 'In the name of Allah, the Compassionate, the Merciful,' then
recited *al-Fatihah*, and closed it with *'ameen.* The people also said
'ameen. After the prayer, Abu Hurairah said, 'By the One in whose
Hand is my soul, I have followed the prayer of the Prophet."

Al-Bukhari mentioned this *hadith* in *mu'allaq* from while others,
such as an-Nasa'i, Ibn Khuzaimah, Ibn Hibban and Ibn as-Siraj
related it.[18] Al-Bukhari records that Ibn Shihab (az-Zuhri) said, "The
Messenger of Allah, upon whom be peace, would say, *'ameen."*

Says 'Ata, " *'Ameen* is a supplication." Ibn az-Zubair and those
behind him would say *'ameen* and the mosque would ring with their
voices.

Reported Nafa', "Ibn 'Umar did not encourage the people to say
it aloud, nor did he discourage them. I have heard him report that."
Reporting on this same subject, Abu Hurairah said, "When the
Messenger of Allah, upon whom be peace, would recite, '...Not with
those with whom You are displeased and not of those who have gone
astray,' he would say, *'ameen* such that those close to him could hear
him." (Related by Abu Dawud.) Ibn Majah's version is, "Until the
people in the first row would hear him, and the mosque would ring
with the sound." Al-Hakim also relates this *hadith*, and says that
it is *sahih* according to the criterion of al-Bukhari and Muslim.
Al-Baihaqi calls it *hassan sahih*. Ad-Daraqutni considers it as *hassan*.

A similar report from Wa'il ibn Jubair says, "I heard the Messenger
of Allah, upon whom be peace, recite, '...and not of those who have
gone astray,' and then say *'ameen,* and make it long with his voice."
This was related by Ahmad. Abu Dawud has it with the wording,
"And he would raise his voice with it." At-Tirmidhi classifies it as
hassan and states, "More than one knowledgeable companion and

---

[18]I believe this should be as-Siraj without the "ibn."

those who followed them have said that a person should raise his voice while saying 'ameen and not make it silent." Ibn Hajr holds that the chain of this *hadith* is *sahih*. Reported 'Ata, "I have found two hundred companions of the Prophet, upon whom be peace, in this mosque and when the *imam* recited,'...and not of those who have gone astray,' I heard them say 'ameen." 'Aishah reported that the Prophet, upon whom be peace, said, 'The Jews do not envy you for anything more than they envy you for the salutations and the saying of 'ameen behind the *imam*." (Related by Ahmad and Ibn Majah.)[19]

It is preferred to say 'ameen along with the *imam*, and not before or after him. Abu Hurairah reported that the Prophet, upon whom be peace, said, When the *imam* recites, '... not of those with whom You are angered nor of those who have gone astray,' you should say 'ameen. If this corresponds to when the angels say it, he will have all of his previous sins forgiven." (Related by al-Bukhari.) He also reported that the Prophet said, "When the *imam* recites, '...not of those with whom you are angered nor of those who have gone astray,' then say 'ameen (along with the *imam*), for the angels say 'ameen and the *imam* says 'ameen. If his 'ameen corresponds to the 'ameen of the angels, he will have his previous sins forgiven." (Related by Ahmad, Abu Dawud and an-Nasa'i.)

Qur'anic Recitation After *al-Fatihah*. It is *sunnah* for the person to recite a section of the Qur'an after *al-Fatihah* during the two *rak'ah* of the morning prayer and the Friday prayer, and the first two *rak'ah* of the noon, afternoon, sunset and night prayers, and in all of the *rak'ah* of the superogatory prayers. Abu Qatadah reported that the Prophet, upon whom be peace, would recite *al-Fatihah* and some *surah* in the first two *rak'ah* of the noon prayer, and only *al-Fatihah* in the last two *rak'ah*. Sometimes he would recite some verses. The first *rak'ah's* recital would be longer than the second. That was how it was done in the afternoon and morning prayers. This is related by al-Bukhari, Muslim and by Abu Dawud, who adds,

---

[19]In *Silsilat al-Ahadith adh-Dah'eefah* (numbers 951 and 952), al-Albani has discussed those *hadith* that state that the mosque would ring with all the people saying 'ameen, and so on, and he has declared them all to be weak. For example, he rejects the statement of 'Ata because of its weakness caused by unknown narrators in its chain. And in *al-Umm* by ash-Shafi, who has himself recorded a *hadith* like the above, he states that the followers should only say 'ameen to themselves and not aloud, although the *imam* does say it aloud as confirmed from authentic *hadith*. But it is certain that Abu Hurairah and Ibn az-Zubair raised their voices in saying 'ameen while they were not the *imams*. Allah knows best. - J.Z.

"We think he did that in order to allow people to catch the first *rak'ah*."

Jabir ibn Sumrah reported that the people of Kufah complained about Sa'd to 'Umar, causing 'Umar to dismiss him and replace him with 'Ammar. They had many complaints about Sa'd, even claiming that he did not pray properly. 'Umar sent for him and said, "O Abu Ishaq (Sa'd), these people claim that you do not pray properly." Sa'd replied, "By Allah, I prayed with them in the same manner that the Messenger of Allah, upon whom be peace, prayed with us, and I never shortened it in any way. I would lengthen the first two *rak'ah* of the night prayer and shorten the last two." Said 'Umar, "This is what I expected of you." He sent him back to Kufah with one or two people to ask the people of Kufah about him. All of the people praised him until they went to the mosque of the tribe of 'Abs. A man named Usamah ibn Qatadah, also known as Abu Sa'da, stood and said, "Since I am under oath I must inform you that Sa'd never accompanied the army, did not distribute the booty justly, and was not just in his legal verdicts. Sa'd then said, "I pray to Allah for three things: O Allah, if this slave of Yours is lying and stood only for show, then give him a long life, increase his poverty and put him to trials." Years later, when Usamah was asked how he was doing, he would answer that he was an old man in trial due to Sa'd's supplication. 'Abdul-Malik (one of the narrators) said that he had seen the man afterwards with his eyebrows overhanging his eyes due to old age, and he would tease and assault the young girls along the paths. (Related by al-Bukhari.)

Said Abu Hurairah, "A recitation should be done in every prayer. What we heard from the Prophet, upon whom be peace, we let you hear. What he was silent about, we are silent about with you. If one does not add anything to *al-Fatihah*, it is sufficient. If one does add something, it is good." (Related by al-Bukhari.)

How to Perform the Recital after *al-Fatihah*. This may be done in any of the following manners: Said Al-Hussain, "In the fighting at Khorasan we had three hundred companions with us, and one of them would lead the prayer, recite some verses from the Qur'an and then bow." It is related that Ibn 'Abbas would recite *al-Fatihah* and some verses from *al-Baqarah* in every *rak'ah*. (Related by ad-Daraqutni with a strong chain.) Al-Baihaqi narrates from 'Abdullah ibn as-Sa'ib that the Prophet, upon whom be peace, recited *al-Mu'minun* in the morning prayer, and when he came to the part which refers to Moses, Aaron or Jesus, he would cough and bow." 'Umar read in the first *rak'ah* 120 verses from the seven long surahs (Mathnawi).[20] (Al-Ahnaf read *al-Kahf* in the first *rak'ah* and *Yunus* or *Yusuf* in the second, and said that he prayed the morning prayer with 'Umar (and he recited them). Ibn Mas'ud read forty verses from *al-Anfal* in the first *rak'ah* and a surah from the ten short *surahs* (Mufassil)[21] in the second. Qatadah reported about a person who read one *surah* in two *rak'ah* or repeated the same *surah* twice, and then commented: 'It is all the Book of Allah." 'Ubaidullah ibn Thabit related that Anas said, "One of the helpers (*Ansar*) led the people in prayer at (the mosque) of Quba'. Before he began his recitation he would always recite, 'Say: He is Allah, the One,' until he finished that *surah*, and then he would recite another *surah*. He did that in every *rak'ah*. They said to him, 'You begin with that *surah*, but we don't find it sufficient until you add another *surah* to it?' He said, 'I will not stop doing so. I like to lead you in the prayer with that. If you don't like it, I will leave (leading you in the prayers).' They thought that he was the best among them, so they didn't want someone else to lead them. They referred the matter to the Prophet, upon whom be peace, and he said, 'O so and so, what has kept you from doing what your companions have asked you? Why do you keep reciting that *surah* in every *rak'ah*?' He said, 'I love that *surah*.' The Prophet, upon whom be peace, said, 'Your love for that *surah* will cause you to enter Paradise." A man from the tribe of Juhinah reported that he heard the Prophet, upon whom be peace, recite, "When the earth quakes," in the morning prayer in both *rak'ah*. And the man said, "I do not know if he forgot that he had recited it or if he did it on purpose." This *hadith* is related by Abu Dawud. The chain has nothing in it that can be criticized.

Recitation after al-Fatihah. Here we shall mention what Ibn al-Qayyim learned about the Prophet's recitation following *al-Fatihah* in different prayers. He commented, "When the Prophet finished *al-Fatihah*, he would sometimes make a lengthy recitation, and sometimes a short one if he was travelling or similarly engaged. But most of the time, he made a recitation of intermediate length.

The Recitation in the Morning Prayer. He would read from sixty to one hundred verses during the morning prayer. Sometimes

---

[20]Surahs 36:49.

[21]Surah 50:114.

he would read *surah Qaf, ar-Rum, at-Takwir,* or *az-Zilzal* in the last two *rak'ah.* While travelling, he would sometimes read the last two *surahs* of the Qur'an. Sometimes he would read the first portion of *al-Mu'minun* until he would reach the story of Moses and Aaron in the first *rak'ah,* and then he would cough and bow. On Fridays he would read *Alif, Lam, Mim, Tanzil as-Sajdah,* or *ad-Dahr* in their complete forms. He did not do what many people do today, which is reciting part of this *surah* and part of another. Many ignorant people think that it is best to recite something with a prostration on Friday morning. But this is just plain ignorance. Some scholars dislike that one should read a *surah* with a prostration due to this ignorant thought. The Prophet, upon whom be peace, used to recite these two *surahs* because they contained reminders of man's creation, the return unto Allah, the creation of Adam, the entry into Paradise and Hell-fire, and other matters that did or will specifically occur on a Friday. Therefore, he would recite them on Friday to remind his companions of the events of that day. He would recite *Qaf, al-Qamr, al-A'la* and *al-Ghashiyyah* on days of great importance like Friday, the *'Id* days, and so on.

The Recitation in the Noon Prayers. He would sometimes make this recitation lengthy. Abu Sa'eed even once said, "While he was standing in the noon prayer, one could go to *al-Baqi'e* and take care of some matter, return to his family, make ablution, return, and still find the Prophet, upon whom be peace, in the first *rak'ah* due to the length of his recital." (Related by Muslim.) He would sometimes recite all of *Alif, Lam, Mim, Tanzil,* or *al-A'la,* or *al-Lail,* or sometimes *al-Buruj* or *at-Tariq.*

The Recitation in the Morning Prayer. This would be half the length of the noon prayer recitation if that recitation was long or the same length if it was short.

The Recitation in the Sunset Prayer. The Prophet would recite different *surahs* in the sunset prayer on different days. Sometimes he would recite *al-A'raf* in the two *rak'ahs* and sometimes *at-Tur* or *al-Mursilat.* Says Abu 'Umar ibn 'Abdul-Barr, "It is related that the Prophet, upon whom be peace, recited *al-A'raf* or *as-Saffat* or *Ha-Mim Dukhan* or *al-A'la* or *at-Tin* or the last two *surahs* of *al-Mufassil.* All of that is related through authentic chains." Marwan ibn al-Hakim used to do this, and when Zaid ibn Thabit objected to it he said, "What is wrong with you that you always recite one of the short *surahs* from *al-Mufassil* during the sunset prayer? I have seen the Prophet, upon whom be peace, reciting a long chapter therein." Marwan asked, "And what is a long chapter?" He answered, "*Al-A'raf.*" This *hadith* is *sahih*. Abu Dawud, an-Nasa'i, Ibn Majah and at-Tirmidhi related it. An-Nasa'i records that 'Aishah said, "The Prophet, upon whom be peace, read *al-A'raf* during the sunset prayer and he divided it between the two *rak'ahs.*" To always recite a short *surah* from *al-Mufassil* is an act that differs from the *sunnah*, and this is what Marwan ibn al-Hakim did.

The Recitation in the Night Prayer. In the night prayer, the Prophet would recite *at-Tin*, and he taught Mu'adh to recite *ash-Shams*, *al-A'la*, *al-Lail*, and so on. He objected to Mu'adh reciting *al-Baqarah* at that time. After the prayer, he (Mu'adh) went to the tribe of 'Amr ibn 'Auf, and when part of the night had passed, he repeated his prayer, and recited *al-Baqarah* there. On being informed about him, the Prophet said to him, "Mu'adh, are you one who puts people to hardships?'"

The Recitation in the Friday Prayer. He would recite *al-Jumu'ah*, *al-Munafiqun* or *al-Ghashiyyah*, in their complete forms, or *al-A'la* and *al-Ghashiyyah*. He never recited just the ending of some *surahs* which began with "O you who believe..." *surah al-Jumu'ah).* Those who insist on doing so every Friday are not following the *sunnah.*

The Recitation in the Two 'Ids. He would recite *Qaf* or *al-Qamar* completely, and sometimes *al-A'la* and *al-Ghashiyyah*. The rightly-

---

[1]The next statement that Sabiq quotes from Ibn al-Qayyim is very hard to comprehend without some further explanation. First, stating the entire *hadith* would be helpful. Jabir ibn 'Abdullah reported that Mu'adh ibn Jabal would pray with the Messenger of Allah and then he would lead his people in prayer. One night when a part of it had already passed he led them in prayer and recited *surah al-Baqarah*. When he did this one man said the *tasleem* and prayed by himself and left. Afterwards the people told that man that he had become a hypocrite. The man argued that he had not, and that he would inform the Prophet about what had happened. He told the Prophet that his people had to work all day long, and so on, and Mu'adh started reading *al-Baqarah*, after he had offered the prayer with the Prophet. Then the Prophet told Mu'adh, "O Mu'adh are you one who puts people to hardships?" (You should recite *ash-Shams*, *adh-Dhuhah*, *al-Lail* or *al-A'la*.") (Related by *al-Bukhari* and *Muslim*.) What Ibn al-Qayyim basically said in *Zad al-Ma'ad* is that one must look at the entire context of the *hadith* in which case it would be seen that it is not disliked to read extremely lengthy portions of the Qur'an or to put the people to hardship after part of the night had already passed, and so on. - J.Z.

guided caliphs did the same. Once Abu Bakr read *al-Baqarah* in the morning prayer until the sun was about to rise. They said, "O successor of the Messenger of Allah, the sun is about to rise." He said, "Had it risen, you would not have found us negligent." 'Umar would recite *Yusuf, an-Nahl, Hud, al-Isra'* and similar *surahs*. If reciting long *surahs* was abrogated, it would have been known to the *khalifahs* or to those who may have criticized them. Muslim records from Jabir ibn Sumrah that the Messenger of Allah, upon whom be peace, recited *Qaf* in the morning prayer, and that his subsequent prayers during that day would be shorter. Umm al-Fadhl heard Ibn 'Abbas recite *al-Mursilat* and she told him, "O my son, that recital reminded me of that *surah*. It was the last one that I heard the Prophet, upon whom be peace, recite, and he read it in the sunset prayer." That is one of the latest actions that we have from him.

Given the above, we may now interpret the Prophet's *hadith*, "O you who lead the people in prayer, be easy on them," and Anas' statement, "The Prophet, upon whom be peace, conducted the prayer very lightly, though it was complete." 'Easiness' or 'lightness' is a relative term. We must return to how the Prophet behaved to understand and follow his example correctly. It is not to be determined by the whims and desires of those who are present for prayer. The Prophet, upon whom be peace, did not order the people to differ from his practice, even though he knew that behind him were the aged, weak and people with needs to tend to. He performed his prayer in the same manner that he asked others to pray — 'light' or 'easy'. If his prayers were somewhat long, they were still easy compared to how long he could have made them. The guidance that he came with and practiced is the one that decides our affairs and disputes for us. This is supported by the *hadith* recorded by an-Nasa'i and others in which Ibn 'Umar reported that the Prophet, upon whom be peace, ordered those who lead prayers to be 'easy' by reciting *as-Saffat*. Therefore, a *surah* the length of *as-Saffat*[2] is part of what the Prophet, upon whom be peace, meant when he said that the *imams* should be easy on the people.

Reciting a Specific *Surah*. The Prophet, upon whom be peace,

---

[2]*As-Saffat* is *surah* 37. It contains 182 short verses. This was the Prophet's interpretation of being easy upon the people. Some people maintain that one should only read from the last 30th of the Qur'an in order to be easy on the people. Here, Sabiq (may Allah have mercy on him) has clearly shown the fallacy of their argument. - J.Z.

did not confine his recitation of the Qur'an in prayers to some specific *surahs*, (except for the Friday and *'Id* prayers). Concerning the other prayers, Abu Dawud has recorded a *hadith* from 'Amr ibn Shu'aib from his father on the authority of his grandfather who said, "There is no separate *surah*, large or small, except the ones I heard the Prophet recite while leading the people in one of the obligatory prayers. He used to recite the entire *surah* in two *rak'ahs*, or just the initial part of the *surah*. It has not been recorded from him that he would recite from the middle or the end of the *surah*, nor that he would recite two *surahs* in one *rak'ah* during the obligatory prayers. He would, however, do so during voluntary prayers. Said Ibn Mas'ud, "I know the *surahs* the Prophet used to recite together in one *rak'ah*: *ar-Rahman* and *an-Najm*, *al-Qamar* and *al-Haqqah*, *at-Tur* and *adh-Dhariyat*, *al-Waqi'ah* and *Noon*, and so on." But this *hadith* does not tell us if this was during obligatory or voluntary prayers. The latter is more probable. He rarely recited one *surah* in two (both) *rak'ahs*. Abu Dawud records that a man from the tribe of Juhainah heard the Prophet, upon whom be peace, recite the complete *surah az-Zilzal* twice in both *rak'ahs* of the morning prayer. The man commented, "I do not know if he did this out of forgetfulness or if he recited it twice intentionally."

Lengthening the First *Rak'ah* of the Morning Prayer. The Prophet, upon whom be peace, would make the first *rak'ah* of the morning prayer longer than the second. At times, he would continue to prolong his recitation until he heard no more footsteps (of the people coming to catch the prayer). He made the morning prayer the longest of his (obligatory) prayers. This is because its recitation is witnessed by Allah and the angels. It is also stated that it is witnessed by both the angels who record the daytime deeds and those who record the nighttime deeds. Whether it is Allah and His angels or His angels alone who witness that time, or does it continue until the morning prayer is over or until the sun rises cannot be said with certainty, though both of the statements are correct.

Furthermore, since the morning prayer has the least number of *rak'ah*, the recitation is prolonged to compensate for it. It is prayed right after sleep. As such, people are well rested. Also, it occurs before they have engaged themselves in their livelihood and other worldly affairs. The spirit as well as the body is responsive to the words of Allah. This makes the recital easier to ponder over and comprehend. Also, prayer is the basis and the first of all works. Therefore, it is preferred to prolong the recital of the morning prayer. This would be recognized by one who is familiar with Islamic law and its aim, purpose and wisdom.

How The Prophet Would Recite the Qur'an. He would draw out his voice over the long vowels, pause at the end of every verse, and elongate his voice with the recital. This ends the section that has been taken from the writings of Ibn al-Qayyim.

What Is Preferred to be Done During the Recitation. It is *sunnah* to make one's voice beautiful and nice while reciting the Qur'an. The Prophet, upon whom be peace, said, "Beautify your voices with the Qur'an." He also said, "He is not one of us who does not chant the Qur'an," "The one with the best voice with the Qur'an is the one that when you hear him, you feel that he fears Allah," and "Allah never listened to anything like he listened to his Prophet chanting the Qur'an with a beautiful voice."[3]

Says an-Nawawi, "It is *sunnah* for anyone who is reciting the Qur'an, whether he is praying or not, to ask Allah for His blessings when he comes to a verse of mercy. When he comes to a verse (describing) punishment, he should seek refuge in Allah from Hell-fire, punishment, evil, from what is hated, or he may say, "Allah, I ask You for well-being, etc." When he comes to a verse that glorifies or exalts Allah, he should say, "Glory be to Allah," or "Blessed be Allah, the Lord of the Worlds," and so on. Hudhaifah ibn al-Yaman is reported to have said, "I prayed with the Prophet, upon whom be peace, one night, and he started reading *al-Baqarah*. I said to myself, 'He will bow after one hundred verses,' but he continued. Then I said, 'He will complete it and bow,' but he moved to recite very

---

[3]Sabiq has mentioned these *hadith* without any commentary or explanation that they deserve. First, the wording of the first *hadith* is incorrect. It should read, "Beautify the Qur'an with your voices." Second, we must determine the meanings of chanting or beautifying the Qur'an. As as-Suyuti makes clear in *al-Itqan*, it certainly does not refer to the imaginative innovations that some people have introduced into the reciting of the Qur'an. According to al-Baidawi, the *hadith* means that one should beautify one's voice by the fear of Allah while reciting the Qur'an. This interpretation is supported by the third *hadith* mentioned by Sabiq. Some say that it means to recite the Qur'an with the correct vowel points, and so on. (Cf., *Faidh al-Qadeer*, op. cit., volume 4, p. 68.) Ibn al-Athir points to the fact that it may simply mean to make one's voice nice while reciting the Qur'an in its proper manner. Al-Munawi says that the meaning of "chant" is to recite the Qur'an in a nice voice but without missing a letter or adding a letter, and so on, as that is absolutely forbidden. According to Ibn al-Athir, the meaning of "chant" is to recite the Qur'an aloud. (Cf., *an-Nihayah*, op. cit., volume 3, p. 391.) An-Nawawi, in his commentary to *Sahih Muslim*, concludes that it is to recite the Qur'an aloud with a good voice. - J.Z.

slowly *āl 'Imran* and then *an-Nisa'.* When he came to a verse glorifying Allah, he would glorify Him. If he came to a verse that mentioned
a request, he would request it. If he came to something that (one
should) seek refuge from, he would seek refuge." This was related
by Muslim. Among the Shaf'iyyah, the glorifying, requesting and
seeking refuge should be done during the prayer and at other times.
The *imam*, followers and one praying by himself should all do so,
for they are supplications that one should say, like *'ameen.* It is
preferred that when reading, "Is not Allah the most conclusive of
all judges?" / *at-Tin*:8 / one should say, "Certainly, and I am one of
the witnesses to that. When one reads, "Is not He (who does so) able
to bring the dead to life? / *al-Qiyamah*:40 /, he should say, "Certainly,
and I bear witness (to it)." When one reads, "Glorify the name of
your Lord, the Most High," (*al-A'la: 1*), he should say, "Glory to
my Lord, the Most High." That should be said during prayer and
otherwise.

When The Prayer is to be Aloud or Subdued. It is *sunnah* to
recite aloud in the two *rak'ah* of the morning and the Friday congregational prayer, in the first two *rak'ah* of the evening and the night
prayer, in the two *'id* prayers, the prayer for eclipses, and the prayer
of asking for rain. The recital should be subdued during all of the
noon and the afternoon prayer, during the last *rak'ah* of the evening
prayer, and during the last two *rak'ah* of the night prayer. Concerning voluntary prayers, those made during the days should be subdued, while those made during the night can be either loud or
subdued.

It is best to be moderate in one's recital. One night, the Prophet,
upon whom be peace, passed by Abu Bakr when he was praying in
a very low voice, and he passed by 'Umar who was praying with his
voice raised. (Later), when they were together with him, he said, "O
Abu Bakr, I passed by you and you were praying in a very low voice."
He said, "O Messenger of Allah, the one who I was praying to could
hear me." And he said to 'Umar, "O 'Umar, I passed by you and you
were praying with a raised voice." He said, "O Messenger of Allah,
this was to stop the drowsiness and to drive away Satan." The
Prophet, upon whom be peace, said, "O Abu Bakr, raise your voice
somewhat. And 'Umar, lower your voice somewhat." (Related by
Abu Dawud and Ahmad.) If one forgets and recites aloud when he
should be silent or vice-versa, there is no blame upon him.[4] If one

---

[4] He does not make the two prostrations of forgetfulness.

recalls the correction while he is doing the mistaken act, he may change to the correct way.

Reciting Behind an *Imam*. One's prayer is not accepted unless *al-Fatihah* is recited in every *rak'ah*. But, one who is praying behind an *imam* is to keep quiet while the *imam* is reciting aloud, as Allah says in the Qur'an, "When the Qur'an is recited, listen and remain silent that you may attain mercy." The Prophet, upon whom be peace, also said, "When the *imam* makes the *takbir*, (you too) make the *takbir*. When he recites, be silent." (Related by Muslim.) One *hadith* states, "Whoever is praying behind an *imam*, the *imam's* recital is his recital. If the *imam* reads quietly, then all of the followers must also make their own recital. If one cannot hear the *imam's* recital, he must make his own recital.[5]

Commenting on this subject, Abu Bakr al-'Arabi says, "What we see as the strongest opinion is that one must recite during the prayers in which the *imam's* recital is subdued. But, during the prayers where the *imam* recites aloud, one may not recite. This is based on the following three proofs: a) This was the practice of the people of Madinah,[6] b) it is the ruling of the Qur'an, as Allah says, "When the Qur'an is recited, listen and remain silent," and c) this is supported by two *hadith*: one from 'Imran ibn Hussain states, 'I know that some of you compete with me (in my recital...),' and 'If it is recited, you should listen.' The preceding *hadith* is the weightiest position according to the following argument: If one cannot recite along with the *imam*, then when can one recite? If one says, 'While he is silent,' then we say, 'It is not necessary for him to be silent,'[7] so how can something that is obligatory be dependent on something that is not obligatory? But we have found a way in which the person

---

[5]Some Hanafiyyah are of the opinion that in all the prayers the recital of the *imam* suffices for the followers even when his prayer is silent. Therefore, in all of the prayers that they pray behind an *imam* they do not recite anything. This opinion has been refuted by many. Sabiq is said to be a Hanafi. - J.Z.

[6]Note that Ibn al-'Arabi was a Maliki scholar. According to the Malikiyyah, the practice of the people of Madinah is a strong proof. - J.Z.

[7]It has become quite common nowadays for *imams* to be silent for a period after reciting *al-Fatihah* in order to give those behind them a chance to recite it. In *Silsilat al-Ahadith adh-Dha'eefah* (numbers 546, 547) al-Albani has discussed the *hadith* relevant to the subject. He has found such *hadith* to be weak. Finally, he quotes Ibn Taimiyyah who says that such a long pause to allow others to read *al-Fatihah* is an innovation. - J.Z.

may 'recite' with the *imam*, and that is the recitation of the heart and of concentrating on what is being recited. This is the method of the Qur'an and the *hadith*, and the way the worship has been preserved. It is also part of following the *sunnah*. One is to act by what is the strongest (opinion). This was also the choice of az-Zuhri and Ibn al-Mubarak, and it is a statement from Malik, Ahmad and Ishaq. Ibn Taimiyyah supports it and shows it to be the strongest opinion.

Making the *Takbir* upon Moving from Position to Position. It is *sunnah* to make the *takbir* upon every rising, lowering, standing or sitting, except when one comes up from bowing, in which case one should say, "Allah hears him who praises Him." Reported Ibn Mas'ud, "I saw the Messenger of Allah make the *takbir* upon every lowering, rising, standing and sitting." This is related by Ahmad, an-Nasa'i and at-Tirmidhi, who called it *shaih*.

Says at-Tirmidhi, "The companions of the Prophet, upon whom be peace, including Abu Bakr, 'Umar, 'Uthman, 'Ali and others, acted according to this *hadith*, as did their followers and the majority of the jurists and scholars." Abu Bakr ibn 'Abdurahman ibn al-Harith reported that he heard Abu Hurairah say, "When the Prophet, upon whom be peace, stood for prayer, he would make the *takbir* while standing. Then he made the *takbir* while bowing. When coming up from the bowing, he would say, "*Sami' Allahu liman hamidah* (Allah hears him who praises Him). While standing, he would say, "*Rabbana lakal-hamd* (Our Lord, to You is the praise)." Then he would say, "*Allahu akbar*" when he would go down for the prostration, when he raised his head, and when he stood from his sitting after the two prostrations. He did that in every *rak'ah* until he finished the prayer. He prayed in that manner until he left this world." (Related by Ahmad, al-Bukhari, Muslim and Abu Dawud.)

'Ikrimah said to Ibn 'Abbas, "I prayed the noon prayer in al-Butha behind a foolish old man. He would make twelve *takbirs* by saying it when he prostrated and when he raised his head." Ibn 'Abbas said, "That is the prayer of Abu al-Qasim (the Prophet)." (Related by Ahmad and al-Bukhari.) It is preferrable to start the *takbir* when one begins one's changing of position.

The Manner of Bowing. When one bows, one's hands must reach one's knees. It is *sunnah* to make the height of the head equal to that of the hips. The hands should be supported by the knees and should be apart from one's sides. The hands should be open upon one's knees and thighs, and the palms should be flat. It is reported that 'Uqbah ibn 'Amr would bow with his arms separated, his hands on his knees, and his fingers opened beyond his knees. He said, "This is how I saw the Messenger of Allah pray." (Related by Ahmad, Abu Dawud and an-Nasa'i.)

Abu Humaid reported that when the Prophet, upon whom be peace, bowed, he would be straight, his head neither up nor down (with respect to his hips), and he would place his hands on his knees as if he was holding them." (Related by an-Nasa'i.)

Muslim records 'Aishah reporting that when the Prophet bowed, his head would be neither risen nor lowered, but rather between those two positions. Said 'Ali, "If you put a cup of water on the back of the Prophet, upon whom be peace, while he was bowing, its contents would not spill." This is related by Ahmad. Abu Dawud recorded it in his *Kitab al-Muraseel.*

Said Mus'ab ibn Sa'd, "I prayed next to my father. I joined both of my hands and put them between my thighs (while bowing). He stopped me and said, 'We used to do that, but were later ordered (by the Prophet) to put our hands on our knees.'" (Related by "the group.")

The Remembrance of Allah During the Bowing. It is preferred to remember Allah with the following words, "*Subhana Rabiyy al-'Adheem* (Glory to my Lord, the Great.)" Reported 'Uqbah ibn 'Amr, "When 'Glorify the name of your Lord, the Great,' was revealed, the Prophet told us, 'Do so in your bowings." This is related by Ahmad, Abu Dawud and others with a good chain.

Reported Hudhaifah, "I prayed with the Messenger of Allah, upon whom be peace, and while bowing he would say, '*Subhana Rabiyy al-'Adheem.*" (Related by Muslim, Abu Dawud, an-Nasa'i, at-Tirmidhi and Ibn Majah.)

The phrase *Subhana Rabiyy al-'Adheem wa bihamdihi* has been related through a number of chains, but all of them are weak. Ash-Shaukani maintains, "The different chains support each other. It is perfectly acceptable for one who is praying to limit himself to *Subhana Rabiyy al-'Adheem* or to add one of the following:

a) 'Ali reported that while bowing, the Messenger of Allah, upon whom be peace, would say, "O Allah, for You have I bowed, and it is You that I have believed in and to You have I submitted. You are my Lord. My hearing, sight, marrow, bones and nerves and what is carried by my feet are for Allah, the Lord of the Worlds." (Related by Ahmad, Muslim, Abu Dawud and others.)

b) 'Aishah reported that while bowing and prostrating, the Messenger of Allah, upon whom be peace, would say, "Glorified and Holy are You, Lord of the angels and the souls."

c) Reported 'Auf ibn Malik, "I prayed with the Messenger of Allah one night. He recited *al-Baqarah* and while bowing said, 'Glory be to the One of Omnipotence, the Master of the dominions, of grandeur and of honor.'" (Related by Abu Dawud, at-Tirmidhi and an-Nasa'i.)

d) 'Aishah said that when the Prophet, upon whom be peace, bowed or prostrated, he would often say, "Glory and praise be to You, O Allah, our Lord. O Allah, forgive me." This was how he applied the Qur'an.[8] (Related by Ahmad, al-Bukhari, Muslim and others.)

What Is Said Upon Rising From Bowing and Standing. It is preferred for the one who is praying, whether he be the *imam*, follower or praying by himself, to say, "Allah hears him who praises Him," upon coming up from the bowing. When he is standing straight, he should say, "Our Lord, and to You is the praise," or "O Allah, Our Lord, and to You is the praise." Abu Hurairah reported that when the Prophet, upon whom be peace, rose from bowing he would say, "Allah hears him who praises Him," and while standing (straight) he would say, "Our Lord, and to You is the praise." (Related by Ahmad, al-Bukhari and Muslim.)

Al-Bukhari records in the *hadith* from Anas, "When he says, 'Allah hears him who praises Him,' you say, 'O Allah, our Lord, and to You is the praise." Ahmad and others record a *hadith* from Abu Hurairah in which the Prophet, upon whom be peace, is quoted as saying, "When the *imam* says, 'Allah hears him who praises Him,' you say, 'O Allah, our Lord, and to You is the praise.' If one's statement corresponds to that of the angels, all of his previous sins will be forgiven." The Prophet said, "Pray as you have seen me pray." This applies to all of his glorifying and praise statements, even if the person is following the *imam*. The answer to those who say, 'One should not combine both of these sayings' ('Allah hears him...' and 'O Allah, our Lord...') but only say the one of praise, has been given by an-Nawawi who said, "Our companions say that the mentioning of the command, 'And you should say, O Allah, our Lord...' is in conjunction with 'Allah hears him who praises him.' But the Prophet,

---

[8]He was referring to the verse, "Then hymn the praises of thy Lord and seek forgiveness of Him." - Sabiq's footnote.

upon whom be peace, only mentioned the statement, 'O Allah, Our Lord, to you is the praise,' because they had already heard the statement, 'Allah hears him who praises Him' aloud from him. It was his *sunnah* to say that phrase aloud, but they did not hear him say, 'Our Lord, to You is the praise' because he said it in a subdued voice. They knew the Prophet's words, 'Pray as you have seen me pray,' and knew that it was to be taken in the general sense without any restrictions. They used to say, 'Allah hears him who praises Him,' and therefore there was no need for the Prophet, upon whom be peace, to order them to say it again. But they did not know, 'Our Lord, to You is the praise,' and therefore he ordered them to say it."

The two phrases are the least that one should say while standing. But one may add any of the supplicatory words mentioned in the following *hadith*:

a) Said Raf'ah ibn Rafa', "One day we prayed behind the Messenger of Allah, upon whom be peace. When he raised his head from bowing, he said, 'Allah hears him who praises Him,' and a man behind him said, 'Our Lord, to You is the praise, as much as it can be and as blessed as it can be.' When the Prophet, upon whom be peace, finished the prayer he said, 'Who said that phrase earlier?' A man said, 'I did, O Messenger of Allah.' The Prophet said, 'I saw more than thirty angels chasing after you to see who would record it first.'" (Related by Ahmad, al-Bukhari, Malik and Abu Dawud.)

b) 'Ali reported that when the Prophet raised his head from bowing he would say, "Allah hears him who praises Him, and to You is the praise filling up the heavens and the earth, what is between them and filling up whatever You wish in addition to that." (Related by Ahmad, Muslim, Abu Dawud and at-Tirmidhi.)

c) 'Abdullah ibn Abu 'Aufa reported that when the Prophet raised his head from bowing he would say, "O Allah, to You is the praise filling up the skies and the earth and filling up whatever You wish in addition to that. O Allah, purify me with snow, hail and cold water. O Allah, purify me from sins and cleanse me from them as one cleans a white garment from filth." (Related by Ahmad, Muslim, Abu Dawud and Ibn Majah.)

d) Said Abu Sa'eed al-Khudri, "When the Prophet, upon whom be peace, would say, 'Allah hears him who praises Him,' he would (also) say, 'O Allah, to You is the praise filling up the skies and the earth, and filling up what You wish in addition to that. You are the One who is worthy of praise and glory. This is the most correct statement that a slave could make. And we are all slaves unto You. There is no one who can prevent what You have given. And there is no one who can give what You have prevented. No one can benefit from fortune (in the face of) Your fortune.'" (Related by Muslim, Ahmad and Abu Dawud.)

e) It has also been authentically reported from the Prophet, upon whom be peace, that after saying "Allah hears him who praises Him," he would say, "To my Lord is the praise, to my Lord is the praise," until he would be standing for as long as he was bowing.

How To Prostrate. Most scholars prefer that one place his knees on the floor before his hands. Ibn al-Mundhir related this from 'Umar an-Nakha'i, Muslim ibn Yasar, Sufyan al-Thauri, Ahmad, Ishaq and other jurists including Ibn al-Mundhir himself. Abu at-Tayyeb said that most jurists agree with this. Ibn al-Qayyim said, "When the Prophet, upon whom be peace, prayed, he would place his knees (on the floor) before his hands, then his hands, his forehead and nose. This is what is authentic and has been related by Shuraik from 'Asim ibn Kaleeb on the authority of his father from Wa'il ibn Hajr who said, 'I saw the Messenger of Allah, upon whom be peace, while prostrating, placing his knees (on the floor) before his hands. Upon getting up, he would raise his hands before his knees. I never saw him do otherwise." Malik, al-Auza'i, Ibn Hazm and Ahmad maintain that it is preferred to place the hands down first and then the knees. Says al-Auza'i, "I saw the people placing their hands on the floor before their knees." Ibn Abu Dawud comments, "That is the statement of the people of *hadith*." There is also a difference of opinion concerning how one should stand up from the prostration after the first (or third) *rak'ah*. Some say one should raise the hands from the floor first while others say that one should raise the knees first.

It is preferred for the one who is prostrating to follow the following points:

One should place one's nose, forehead and hands upon the floor, separating them from the sides of the body. Wa'il ibn Hajr reported that when the Messenger of Allah prostrated, he would place his forehead between his palms and separate his arms from the sides of his body. (Related by Abu Dawud.) Abu Humaid reported that when the Prophet, upon whom be peace, prostrated, he would place his nose and forehead upon the floor, keep his arms away from his sides, and place his hands parallel to his shoulders. This is related by Ibn Khuzaimah and at-Tirmidhi, who called it *hassan sahih*.

One should place one's hands parallel to one's ears or shoulders, as both of these acts have been related. Some scholars combine these two acts by placing the ends of the thumbs parallel to the ears and the palms parallel to the shoulders.

One should have one's fingers together and stretched out. Al-Hakim and Ibn Hibban record that when the Prophet, upon whom be peace, bowed he would have his fingers separated and when he prostrated he would keep his fingers together.

One should have one's fingers facing the *qiblah*. Al-Bukhari recorded from Abu Humaid that when the Prophet, upon whom be peace, prostrated, his fingers would be neither spread out nor clasped together, and his toes would be directed toward the *qiblah*.

The Length of Time of the Prostration and What is to be Said Therein. It is preferred for the one who is prostrating to say *Subhana Rabiyy al-A'la* (Glory to my Lord, the Most High). 'Uqbah ibn 'Aamr related that when, "Glorify the name of your Lord, the Most High" was revealed, the Prophet, upon whom be peace, said, "Do so in your prostrations." This is related by Ahmad, Abu Dawud, Ibn Majah and al-Hakim. Its chain is good.

Hudhaifah reported that when the Prophet, upon whom be peace, prostrated, he would say *"Subhana Rabiyy al-A'la."* This is related by Ahmad, Muslim, Abu Dawud, an-Nasa'i, Ibn Majah and at-Tirmidhi, who called it *hassan sahih*. It is a must that one not repeat these sayings less than three times during the bowings and prostrations. Says at-Tirmidhi, "The scholars prefer the one bowing or prostrating to make the glorifications at least three times." According to the majority, the minimum that is sufficient for the prostrations or bowings is one glorification. We have already mentioned that "calmness" is obligatory, and this requires a time of at least one glorification.

According to some scholars, the complete glorification is ten. This is based on the following *hadith:* Sa'eed ibn Jubair related that Anas said, "I have not seen anyone being more similar to the Prophet's prayer than this boy ('Umar ibn 'Abdul-'Aziz). We estimated the number of the glorifications that he made during his bowing to be ten and in his prostrations also to be ten." This is related by Ahmad, Abu Dawud and an-Nasa'i with a good chain.

Commenting on the subject, ash-Shaukani says, "Some hold that this proves that the complete (number of) glorifications is ten. The more sound opinion is that an individual who is praying may offer as many glorifications as he wishes. There are authentic *hadith* that state that the Prophet, upon whom be peace, elongated his glorifications during prostrations. The *imam* may also do so if he knows the followers will not get tired by making it longer."

Says Ibn 'Abdul-Barr, "It is a must that every *imam* should be easy (by not making the prayers too long) as has been ordered by the Prophet, even if he knows that those behind him are strong, because he does not know what may have happened to them and what needs they may have to tend to."

Ibn al-Mubarak maintains, "It is preferred for the *imam* to make five glorifications. Therefore, all the people behind him would be able to make (at least) three. It is preferred that one not limit his remembrance during the prostrations to just the glorifications, but he should add some supplications to it. In an authentic *hadith*, it is recorded that the Prophet said, 'The closest one of you comes to his Lord is while he is prostrating, (therefore) make many supplications therein.' And he also said, 'I have prohibited you from reciting while bowing or prostrating. During the bowing, glorify the Lord. During the prostrations, strive your hardest in making supplications. Most likely, you will be listened to." This was related by Ahmad and Muslim.

Many *hadith* are related on this topic, including:

a) 'Ali reported that when the Prophet prostrated he would say, "O Allah, to You have I prostrated, in You have I believed, and to You have I submitted. I have prostrated my face to the One who created me and formed me in the best of forms. He is the One who gave it hearing and sight. Blessed be Allah, the Best of Creators." (Related by Ahmad and Muslim.)

b) While describing the Prophet's late night prayers, Ibn 'Abbas said, "Then he would go to pray and during his prayer or prostration, he would say, 'O Allah, place light in my heart, in my hearing, in my sight, on my right, on my left, in front of me, behind me, above me, below me, and make me light." Reported Shu'bah, "Or he said, 'And make for me light." (Related by Muslim, Ahmad and others.)

Talking of light, an-Nawawi observes, "The scholars say that asking for light for all organs and sides means (asking) to have the truth and guidance made clear for one's self. He asked for this so that there would be no deviation or misguidance left in him."

c) Reported 'Aishah, "I once noticed the Prophet missing from his place of sleep. I felt over his place with my hand and found him prostrating. He was saying, 'O Lord, give my soul God-consciousness and purify it, for You are the best of those who purify. You are its Guardian and Protector." (Related by Ahmad.)

d) Abu Hurairah reported that the Prophet, upon whom be peace, would say while prostrating, "O Allah, forgive all of my sins, the small and large, the first and last, the public and private." (Related by Muslim, Abu Dawud and al-Hakim.)

e) Reported 'Aishah, "One night I missed the Prophet from his bed. I looked for him and found him praying. He was prostrating, his feet were in an upright position and he was saying, 'O Allah, I seek refuge in Your pleasure from Your anger. I seek refuge in Your granting of well-being from Your punishment. I seek refuge in You from You. The praise cannot encompass You and You are as You have praised Yourself." (Related by Muslim, Abu Dawud and an-Nasa'i.)

f) She also reported that one night he was missing and she suspected that he had gone to another one of his wives. She found him while he was bowing or prostrating, and he was saying, "Glory be to You, O Allah, and to You be praise. There is no god besides You." She said, "May my father and mother be sacrificed for you. I thought you were doing something and you were doing something else." (Related by Muslim, Ahmad and an-Nasa'i.)

g) While prostrating the Prophet, upon whom be peace, would say, "O Allah, forgive me (those things that I have been) mistaken in or ignorant, and the action that I have been extravagant in, for You are more knowledgeable of them than me. O Allah, forgive me my serious mistakes and my joking mistakes, my mistakes (that I was unaware of) and of my intentional mistakes, and everything of that which I have done. O Allah, forgive me my past sins and later sins and what was private and what was public. You are my God, and there is no god except You."

Sitting Between the Two Prostrations. It is *sunnah* to sit "spread out" between the two prostrations (to put the left foot down and to sit upon it and to keep the right foot upright with the toes pointing toward the *qiblah*). 'Aishah reported that the Prophet would lay out his left foot and keep his right foot upright. (Related by al-Bukhari and Muslim.) Ibn 'Umar reported that it is from the *sunnah* to keep the right foot upright, with its toes pointing toward the *qiblah*, and to sit upon the left foot. (Related by an-Nasa'i.) Reported Nafa', "When Ibn 'Umar prayed, he would face the *qiblah*, even his shoes." (Reported by al-Athram.) In the *hadith* of Abu Humaid, in which he described the prayer of the Prophet, he stated, "Then he would lay down his left foot and sit upon it until all of his bones were in place, and then he would go to make the prostration (again)." (Related by Ahmad, Abu Dawud, and at-Tirmidhi who classified it as *sahih*.)

It has also been related that *ifa'a* (laying out both feet and sitting upon one's heels) is a preferred act. Comments Abu 'Ubaidah, "This is the statement of the people of *hadith*." Abu az-Zubair related that he heard Tawus say, "We asked Ibn 'Abbas about *ifa'a*, and he said, 'It is *sunnah* to do so.' We said, 'We think it to be too harsh for the man.' He said, 'It is a *sunnah* of your Prophet, upon whom be peace." (Related by Muslim.)

Ibn 'Umar reported that when the Prophet rose from the first prostration, he would sit upon his toes. He used to say, "That is from the *sunnah*." Reported Tawus, "I saw the 'Abdullahs ('Abdullah ibn 'Abbas, 'Abdullah ibn 'Umar and 'Abdullah ibn az-Zubair) sitting with their feet laid flat." The last two reports were related by al-Baihaqi. Talking of its authenticity, Ibn Hajr says, "Its chain is sound."

Concerning *iqa'a* — sitting with the buttocks on the ground and with the thighs straight on the ground — it is disliked by all scholars. Said Abu Hurairah, "The Prophet prohibited us from three things: pecking like a rooster (making the prostration very quickly), sitting like a dog (*iqa'a*), and not turning one's whole head like a fox."[9] This

---

[9]There is quite a difference of opinion over the meaning of *al-Iqa'a*. Unfortunately, Sabiq (may Allah have mercy on him) did little to alleviate the confusion. In *Faidh al-Qadeer*, al-Manawi writes, "*Al-Iqa'a* is sitting on one's buttocks with the thighs erect." Al-Baihaqi said, "There are two types of *al-Iqa'a*. One (which was just mentioned) and which is prohibited. The second has been confirmed from the Prophet and that is sitting with the tiptoes and knees upon the ground, and with the buttocks upon the heels. And that is the *sunnah* of sitting between the two prostrations." (Cf., *Faidh al-Qadeer*, op. cit., volume 6, p. 303.) From that statement we find two types of *al-Iqa'a*, one is disliked and one is *sunnah*. Ibn al-Athir writes, "*Al-Iqa'a* is for a person to put his buttocks on the ground and to make his shank and thighs erect and to put his arms on the ground in a manner that a dog lies down. Some say it is to sit with the buttocks on the heels between the two prostrations. The first statement (is stronger)." (Cf., *an-Nihayah*, op. cit., volume 4, p. 89.) Ibn Mandhur says that the

is related by Ahmad, al-Baihaqi, at-Tabarani and Abu Tala with a *hassan* chain. It is preferred for the one who is sitting between the two prostrations to put his right hand on his right thigh and his left hand on his left thigh with the fingers stretched out and directed toward the *qiblah*. The fingers should be slightly separated and should not go beyond the knees.

Supplications Between the Two Prostrations. It is preferred to make one of the following supplications between the two prostrations. One may repeat them more than once if one wishes to do so. An-Nasa'i and Ibn Majah recorded that Hudhaifah reported that between the two prostrations, the Prophet would say, "O Lord, forgive me." Abu Dawud recorded from Ibn 'Abbas that while prostrating, the Prophet, upon whom be peace, would say, "O Allah, forgive me, have mercy on me, grant me well-being, guide me and provide for me."

The Sitting of "Rest." This refers to a quick sitting that one makes after the second prostration of the first and third *rak'ah*. The scholars differ over this regulation due to the differing *hadith*. Says Ibn al-Qayyim, "The jurists differ over this act. Is it a *sunnah* of the prayer that one should perform, or is it only done due to some necessity? There are two statements on this question and two narrations from Ahmad. Said al-Khallal, 'Ahmad referred to the *hadith* of Malik ibn al-Huwairith regarding the intermediate position of rest (between the two prostrations). He said, 'Yusuf ibn Musa informed me that Abu Umamah was asked about standing up (in the prayer) and he said, 'It should be done on the tops of the feet according to the *hadith* of Rafa'.' In the *hadith* of Ibn 'Ajlan there is no proof that he would stand on the tips of his feet. Many of the companions and others who described the prayers of the Prophet did not mention this sitting, except in what is related by Abu Humaid and Malik ibn al-Huwairith. If it was part of his guidance, he would always do it, and those who described his prayers would have mentioned it.

---

first definition given by Ibn al-Athir is that of the linguists and the latter definition is that of the jurists. (Cf., *Lisan al-'Arab, Dar Sadr, Beirut*, no date, volume 15, p. 192.) In his commentary to *Sahih Muslim* an-Nawawi also noted the above, and went into greater discussion of what scholars had said. There is another *hadith* on the prostration. The Prophet said, "Observe moderation in prostration and let none of you stretch out his forearms (on the ground) like a dog." (Related by Muslim.) - Allah knows best. - J.Z.

The fact that he may have done so does not necessarily make it one of the *sunnahs* of the prayer, unless he did it as a regular practice for the people to follow. Otherwise, he may have done it out of some need to do so, and this would not prove that it is a *sunnah* of the prayer.[10"]

Sitting for *Tashahud*. One should sit for the *tashahud* and place his hands in the following manner:

a) Ibn 'Umar reported that when the Prophet sat for the *tashahud*, he would place his left hand on his left knee and his right hand upon his right knee, and he would form a ring like (fifty-three) and point with his index finger. In another narration it is reported, "He would close his hand and point with his index finger." (Related by Muslim.)

b) Wa'il ibn Hajr reported that the Prophet would place his left palm on his left thigh and knee. He would place the end of his right elbow upon his right thigh and would then close his right hand, forming a circle. In another narration it states, "He would make a circle with his middle finger and thumb and point with his index finger. Then he would raise his finger, and (Wa'il) saw him moving it to make supplications." (Related by Ahmad.) Explaining the *hadith*, al-Baihaqi says, "The implication of 'he would move it' is that he would point with it, not that he would continue to move it." This would be in agreement with the narration of Ibn az-Zubair who reported, "The Prophet would point with his finger while supplicating, and he would not move it." This is related by Abu Dawud with a *sahih* chain. An-Nawawi also mentioned it.[11]

---

[10]In *Silsilat al-Ahadith adh-Dha'eefah* (volume 2, numbers 967 and 968), al-Albani discussed the stance of those who hold Ibn al-Qayyim's opinion and showed that it is based on weak reports, and that the opposing opinion based on other reports is correct. - J.Z.

[11]In his notes to *Mishkat al-Massabih*, al-Albani has discussed the *hadith* of Wa'il ibn Hajr and of Ibn az-Zubair. He said that the first *hadith* has a *sahih* chain. The narrators of the latter *hadith* are all trustworthy. Muhammad ibn 'Ijlan has some weakness due to his memory, but his memory was not so poor to drop the *hadith* from the rank of *hassan*. Therefore, the statement recorded by Sabiq that the chain is *sahih* is incorrect. The important words in the latter *hadith* are, "and he would not move it." According to al-Albani this addition is irregualr and rejected (*shadh* and *munkar*). The statement is not confirmed from Ibn 'Ijlan, sometimes he would

c) Reported az-Zubair, "When the Prophet sat for *tashahud*, he would place his right hand on his right thigh and his left hand on his left thigh. He would point with his middle finger, and would not look beyond his pointing." (Related by Ahmad, Muslim and an-Nasa'i.) This *hadith* shows that one is to place the right hand on the right thigh without closing the hand (making a fist), and that he is not to look beyond his pointing.

The preceding three *hadith* are all authentic, and one may act by any of them.

One should point with one's right index finger, bending it a little, until one says the *salaams* at the end of the prayer. Reported Numair al-Khaza'i, "I saw the Messenger of Allah sitting in the prayer with his forearm along his right thigh. His index finger was raised, curved (or bent) a little, and he was supplicating." This is related by Ahmad, Abu Dawud, an-Nasa'i, Ibn Majah and Ibn Khuzaimah with a good chain.

Said Anas ibn Malik, "The Messenger of Allah, upon whom be peace, passed by Sa'd while he was making supplications (and using) two fingers. The Prophet said to him, 'Just one, Sa'd'" This is related by Ahmed, Abu Dawud, an-Nasa'i and al-Hakim.

Ibn 'Abbas was asked about a man who pointed with his finger while supplicating, and he said, "This is sincere devotion." Says Anas ibn Malik, "That is imploring." Mujahid maintains "Doing this hinders Satan." According to the Shaf'iyyah, one points with the finger only once, when saying "except Allah" in the statement bearing witness. The Hanifiyyah raise the finger in the denial part of the statement (there is no god) and put it back down during the confirmation part (except Allah). The Malikiyyah move the finger to the left and right until they finish the prayer. The Hanbaliyyah point with the finger every time they mention Allah, as a reflection of the oneness of Allah, and they do not move it.

Sitting for the First and Second *Tashahud*. When Abu Humaid described the prayer of the Prophet, upon whom be peace, he said, "When he sat after two *rak'ah*, he would sit upon his left leg and keep his right foot upright. When he sat for the last *rak'ah*, he would

---

mention it and sometimes he wouldn't. The others who related this *hadith* do not mention this addition. Given the above, it is better not to interpret Wa'il ibn Hajr's *hadith* by this latter *hadith*. - J.Z.

pull over his left foot and put his right foot upright (over the left foot) and sit upon his entire posterior." (Related by al-Bukhari.)

Most scholars say that the first *tashahud* is *sunnah*. This is based on the *hadith* of 'Abdullah ibn Buhainah who reported that once the Prophet stood during the noon prayer when he should have sat (for the first *tashahud*). When he finished the prayer, he made two prostrations. He made a *takbir* for each prostration (and it was) while he was sitting before he made the *tasleem*. He made those two prostrations because he had forgotten to sit (for the first *tashahud*). (Related by "the group.")

In *Subul as-Salaam*, it is stated that this *hadith* proves that one who forgets the first *tashahud* must make the prostrations of forgetfulness. The Prophet is, however, reported to have said, "Pray as you have seen me pray." This would point to the first *tashahud* being obligatory, and one would have to do some act to make up for it. But, this also proves that it is not obligatory, for if one misses an act that is obligatory, the two prostrations of foregetfulness are not sufficient to make up for it. That is what Ibn Hajr says in *Fath al-Bari*.

Says Ibn Batal, "The proof is that the two prostrations due to forgetfulness cannot replace something that is obligatory. If one forgets the opening *takbir*, they will not replace it. In the case of the *tashahud*, it is a remembrance that is not said aloud and it is not obligatory." Some say otherwise, because the Prophet used to perform it and, as such, he let others follow him in performing it after he found out that they were leaving it intentionally. But there is some doubt about this argument. Those who say that it is obligatory include al-Laith Ibn Sa'd, Ishaq, ash-Shaf'i and the Hanafiyyah. At-Tabari argues that it is obligatory because originally only two *rak'ah* and the *tashahud* were obligatory. When they were made longer, the original obligations were not done away with. Therefore, it is still obligatory.

It is preferred to make the first *tashahud* quickly. Reported Ibn Mas'ud, "When the Prophet sat after the first two *rak'ah*, it seemed as if he was (sitting) on hot stones." This is related by Ahmad, Abu Dawud, an-Nasa'i, at-Tirmidhi and Ibn Majah. At-Tirmidhi grades it as *hassan* and says, 'Ubaidah (ibn 'Abdullah ibn Mas'ud) did not hear (*hadith*) from his father. He also says, "The scholars act according to this *hadith*. They prefer that one should not sit too long after the first two *rak'ah*, and that he should not add anything to the *tashahud*."

Says Ibn al-Qayyim, "It is not reported from the Prophet that he

would say prayers upon himself or his family during the first
tashahud. Nor would he seek refuge from the torment of the grave
or the Hell-fire, or from the test of life, death and of the false Messiah.
Those who say such supplications are deducing their arguments
from the general application (of the supplications and the word
tashahud), but the correct position is that their proper place is in
the last *tashahud.*

Prayers upon the Prophet, Upon Whom Be Peace.

In the last *tashahud*, it is preferred for the person to say prayers
upon the Prophet in one of the following manners:

a) Reported Mas'ud al-Badri, "Basheer ibn Sa'd said, 'O Messenger
of Allah, we have been ordered to make prayers upon you. How are
we to do it?' The Prophet was quiet and then said, 'Say, O Allah,
shower blessings upon Muhammad and upon the family of Muhammad as you showered blessings upon the family of Abraham. And
grant favors to Muhammad and to the family of Muhammad as you
granted favors to the family of Abraham in this world. You are the
Praiseworthy and Glorious.' And make the salutations as I have
taught you." (Related by Muslim and Ahmad.)

b) Reported Ka'b ibn 'Ajazah, "We said, 'O Messenger of Allah,
show us how we are to make salutations and prayers upon you.' He
said, 'Say, O Allah, shower blessings upon Muhammad and upon
the family of Muhammad as you have showered blessings upon the
family of Abraham. You are the Praiseworthy, the Glorious. O Allah,
grant favors to Muhammad and the family of Muhammad as you
granted favors to the family of Abraham."[12]

The salutations upon the Prophet, upon whom be peace, is a
preferred act and is not obligatory. This contention is based on a
hadith recorded by at-Tirmidhi (who said it is *sahih*), Ahmad and
Abu Dawud from Fidhalah ibn 'Ubaid who said, "The Messenger of
Allah heard a man supplicating in his prayer and he did not make
the prayers on the Prophet. The Prophet said, 'He has hastened.'

---

[12]The reader should note that some texts, *Islam in Focus*, by 'Abdulati, include the
word *sayyidina* (our leader - Muhammad) in the prayer. As far as I have been able
to determine, this is a later addition and, therefore, one should delete it from one's
prayers. - J.Z.

Then he called him and said, 'When one of you prays, begin with the praise and lauding of Allah. Then make prayers upon the Prophet, and supplicate whatever you wish of Allah." The author of *al-Muntaqi* says, "This is a proof for those who say that the prayers upon the Prophet are not obligatory, because he did not order the one who did not do it to repeat his prayer. This is supported by his statement to Ibn Mas'ud, after mentioning (only) the *tashahud*, 'Then choose whatever you wish to ask (of Allah)." In his comments on this *hadith*, ash-Shaukani observes, "In my opinion, there is no confirmed proof that it is obligatory."

Supplications After the Last *Tashahud* and Before the *Tasleem*.[13] It is preferred for the person to supplicate after the final *tashahud* and before making the final salutations (that end the prayer). The person may ask for whatever he wishes of the good of this life and the hereafter. Ibn Mas'ud reported that the Prophet, upon whom be peace, taught him the *tashahud* and then said, "Then choose whatever you wish to ask (of Allah)." (Related by Muslim.)

Supplications are preferred acts in general, regardless of whether they are reported from the Prophet or not, although supplications authenticated by the *sunnah* are better. Some of these are:

a) Abu Hurairah reported that the Messenger of Allah, upon whom be peace, said, "When one of you finishes the final *tashahud*, he should say, 'O Allah, I seek refuge in You from the torment of the Hell-fire and the grave, from the trials of life and death, and from the trials of the false Messiah." (Related by Muslim.)

b) 'Aishah reported that the Messenger of Allah would supplicate in his prayer, "O Allah, I seek refuge in You from the torment of the grave, from the trials of the anti-Christ, and from the trials of life and death. Allah, I seek refuge in You from sin and debt." (Related by Muslim and al-Bukhari.)

c) 'Ali reported that when the Prophet prayed, the last thing he would say between the *tashahud* and the *tasleem* was, "O Allah, forgive my past and later sins, what was in private and what was in public, and what I have been extravagant in. You are more

---

[13]The original Arabic text says , "Supplications before the last *tashahud*..." but this is obviously a typographical error. - J.Z.

knowledgeable of it than I. You are the Promoter and the Retarder. There is no god except You." (Related by Muslim.)

d) 'Abdullah ibn 'Amr reported that Abu Bakr said to the Messenger of Allah, "Teach me a supplication that I may use in my prayers." He told him, "Say, O Allah, I have wronged my soul a great wrong and no one forgives sins except You, so forgive me with such forgiveness that only comes from You and have mercy on me. Verily, You are the Oft-Forgiving, the Oft-Mercful." (Related by al-Bukhari and Muslim.)

e) Handhalah ibn 'Ali said that Muhjan ibn al-Adra' related to him that the Prophet entered the mosque while a man was just about to finish his prayer. The latter made the *tashahud* and said, "O Allah, I am asking You, O Allah, the One, the Only, the Absolute, who begets nor is begotten, nor is anyone like Him, to forgive my sins, for You are the Forgiving, the Merciful." The Prophet then said three times, "He has been forgiven." (Related by Ahmad and Abu Dawud.)

f) Shaddad ibn Aus reported that during his prayer, the Prophet would say, "O Allah, I ask You to confirm me in the affairs, to keep me on the correct path, to make me thankful for your blessings and excellent in Your worship. O Allah, I ask You for a tranquil heart and truthful tongue. O Allah, I ask You for the good of what You know, and I seek refuge in You from the evil of which you are aware, and I ask Your forgiveness from what You know." (Related by an-Nasa'i.)

g) Said Abu Mijlaz, " 'Ammar ibn Yasar led us in the prayer and he made it very short. The people blamed him for that and he told them, 'Did I not complete my bowings and prostrations ... and did I not supplicate therein what the Prophet used to supplicate, saying, 'O Allah by Your knowledge of the unseen and Your power over the creation, let me live if You know that living is best for me, and let me die if You know that dying is better for me. I ask You (to forgive me) for fear of You in what is not seen and what is seen, to make my speech truthful while angry or pleased, and to have the same aim in poverty and riches. Grant me the pleasure of looking to Your face and of the longing to meet You. I seek refuge in You from a harmful loss and from the trials of a misguider. O Allah, embellish me with the beauty of faith, and make us of the guided of the guiders." This is related by Ahmad and an-Nasa'i with a good chain.

h) Abu Saleh related from one of the companions that the Prophet said to a man, "What do you say in your prayer?" He said, "I say the *tashahud* and then I say, 'O Allah, I ask of you Paradise and seek refuge in You from Hell-fire.' But I cannot murmer as good as you or Mu'adh (as eloquent as you are)." The Prophet said, "We ask concerning Paradise and the Hell-fire." (Related by Ahmad and Abu Dawud.)

i) Ibn Mas'ud reported that the Prophet taught him to say this supplication: "O Allah, bring our hearts together and make our relations good. Guide us to the paths of peace and bring us out of the darkness and into the light. Keep us away from lewdness, both hidden and open. O Allah, bless us in our hearing and our sight, in our hearts, our wives and our offspring. Turn unto us, for You are the Oft-Turning, the Oft-Merciful. Make us thankful for Your blessings and complete it upon us." (Related by Ahmad and Abu Dawud.)

j) Said Anas, "We were sitting with the Prophet and a man stood up and prayed. When he bowed and made the *tashahud*, he would supplicate, 'O Allah, I ask of You, for to You is the praise. There is no god except You, the Giver without question, the Creator of the heavens and the earth. O Sublime and Honorable One, O Living and Sustaining One, I ask of You.' The Prophet said to his companions, 'Do you know who he made his supplication with?' They said, 'Allah and His Messenger know best.' He said, 'By the One in whose hand is the soul of Muhammad, he supplicated Allah by His greatest name. If one supplicates by that name, it will be listened to. If he asks by it, it will be given." (Related by an-Nasa'i.)

k) 'Umair ibn Sa'd said, "Ibn Mas'ud used to teach us the *tashahud* of the prayer and then he would say, 'When one of you finishes the *tashahud*, he should say: O Allah, I ask you for all good, that which I am aware of and that which I am not. I seek refuge in You from all evil, that which I am aware of and that which I am not. O Allah, I ask you for the good that your devoted servants asked for. I seek refuge in You from all evil, that which I am aware of and that which I am not. O Allah, I ask you for the good that your devoted servants asked for. I seek refuge in You from the evil that your devoted servants sought refuge for. Our Lord, give us the good of this life and the good of the Hereafter.' He said, 'No prophet or righteous

person supplicated for anything except that it is contained therein."
(Related by Ibn Abu Shaibah and Sa'eed ibn Mansur.)

Words of Remembrance and Supplications After the *Tasleem*. It is *sunnah* for the person to use a number of words of remembrance and supplications which have been related from the Prophet. The many reports include the following:

a) Reported Thauban, "When the Prophet would finish his prayer, he would seek Allah's forgiveness three times and then say, 'O Allah, You are the peace, and from You is peace. You are filled with good, O Sublime and Honorable One." This is related by "the group," except for al-Bukhari. Muslim has the addition, "Waleed said, 'I asked al-Auza'i, 'How did he seek Allah's forgiveness?' He said, 'By saying, 'I seek Allah's forgiveness, I seek Allah's forgiveness, I seek Allah's forgiveness."

b) One day the Prophet took Mu'adh ibn Jabal's hand and said to him, "O Mu'adh, I love you." Mu'adh responded, "May my father and mother be sacrificed for you, O Messenger of Allah, I love you." Then the Prophet said, "I advise you, O Mu'adh, say at the end of every prayer,[14] 'O Allah, aid me in Your remembrance, Your thanks, and in perfecting Your worship." This is related by Ahmad, Abu Dawud, an-Nasa'i, Ibn Khuzaimah, Ibn Hibban and al-Hakim, who said it is *sahih* according to al-Bukhari's and Muslim's criterion.
Abu Hurairah reported that the Messenger of Allah, upon whom be peace, said, "Do you strive your utmost in making a supplication? Then say, 'O Allah, aid us in making Your remembrance, in giving You thanks and in perfecting Your worship."

c) Reported 'Abdullah ibn Zubair, "When the Prophet made the *tasleem* at the end of the prayer, he would say, 'There is no god but Allah the One. There is no partner with Him, to Him belongs the sovereignty and to Him is the praise. He has power over all things.

---

[14] In many of Ibn Taimiyyah's legal verdicts he states that "the end of the prayer" refers to the end of the prayer before the *tasleem* and not to something after the end of the prayer unless it explicitly says so. His interpretation may or may not be correct. Allah knows best. He also states that the *hadith* which state that one should read "the verse of the throne" after every prayer are not confirmed. On this point he seems to be mistaken as scholars of *hadith* such as Ibn Katheer (Ibn Taimiyyah's student) and al-Albani have stated that such *hadith* are acceptable. - J.Z.

There is no might or power save with Allah. We do not worship any but Him. To Him belongs the fortune, the grace and the best praise. There is no god except Allah, and religion is sincerely for Him even if the disbelievers abhor it." (Related by Ahmad, al-Bukhari and Muslim.)

d) Al-Mughirah ibn Shu'bah reported that the Prophet would say at the end of every obligatory prayer, "There is no god except Allah, the One. There is no partner with Him. To Him is the dominion and the praise. He has power over all things. O Allah, none can withhold what You have conferred, nor can one confer what You have withheld. A fortune does not benefit its owner against You." (Related by Ahmad, al-Bukhari and Muslim.)

e) Abu Umamah reported that the Prophet said, "For whoever recites the verse of the throne / *al-Baqarah*:244 / at the end of every prayer, nothing will prevent him from entering Paradise except that (he must) die (first)." (Related by an-Nasa'i and at-Tabarani.)

'Ali reported that the Prophet, upon whom be peace, said, "Whoever recites the verse of the throne at the end (after) of every obligatory prayer will be in Allah's protection until the next prayer." This is related by at-Tabarani with a *hassan* chain.

f) Abu Hurairah related that the Prophet said, "Whoever glorifies Allah after every prayer thirty-three times, and praises Allah thirty-three times and extols Allah's greatness thirty-three times and then says, 'There is no god except Allah, the One. There is no partner with Him. His is the dominion and His is the praise, and He has power over all things,' is forgiven, even if his sins are as abundant as the foam of the sea." (Related by Ahmad, al-Bukhari, Muslim and Abu Dawud.)[15]

g) Ka'b ibn 'Ajrah related that the Prophet said, "There are certain statements which, if one were to utter or observe them at the end of every obligatory prayer, one would not be dismayed. (They are) glorifying Allah thirty-three times, praising Allah thirty-three times and extolling His greatness thirty-four times." (Related by Muslim.)

h) Sumayy reported from Abu Saleh on the authority of Abu

---

[15]This is a mistake. This *hadith* was only related by Muslim, Ahmad, Abu 'Awana and al-Baihaqi.

Hurairah that the poor emigrants went to the Messenger of Allah, upon whom be peace, and said, "The wealthy have gotten the high ranks and everlasting bounties." The Prophet said, "Why is that?" They said, "They pray as we pray and they fast as we fast. (But) they give in charity and we do not give in charity. They free the slaves and we do not free the slaves." The Messenger of Allah told them, "Shall I teach you something by which you may overtake those who surpass you, by which you will surpass those who will come after you, and none will then be better than you except if he does what you do?" They said, "Certainly, O Messenger of Allah." He told them, "Glorify Allah thirty-three times, praise Him thirty-three times, and extol His greatness thirty-four times." So I returned to Abu Saleh and told him what they had said. He took my hand and said, "*Allahu akbar, subhaan Allah, al-hamdu lillah, Allahu akbar, subhaan Allah, al-hamdu lillah...*" until all of them reached thirty-three." (Related by al-Bukhari and Muslim.)

i) The Prophet would say each of the following twenty-five times: *Subhaan Allah, al-hamdu lillah, Allahu akbar* and *La ilaha illa Allah, wa ashadu anna la shareeka lahu. Lahu al-mulk wa lahu al-hamd wa huwa 'ala kulli shaian qadeer* (There is no god except Allah, the One. He has no partner. His is the dominion, His is the praise, and He has power over all things.)

j) 'Abdullah ibn 'Amr reported that the Prophet, upon whom be peace, said, "There are two characteristics which, if one observes them, will cause him to enter Paradise. They are very easy actions, but very few perform them." The people said, "What are they, O Messenger of Allah?" He said, "To praise Allah, extol His greatness and glorify Him at the end of every obligatory prayer ten times each. When one goes to bed, he should glorify Allah, praise Him and extol His greatness one hundred times each. Those are, in total, only 250 actions of the tongue, yet they are equal to 2500 on the scale. Does any of you commit 2500 sins during one day and night?" They asked, "How come those easy actions are performed by so few?" He said, "Satan comes to one during his prayer and reminds him of such and such need, and he fails to say the (above). He comes to him in his bed and makes him sleep so that he can not say them." 'Abdullah said, "I have seen the Messenger of Allah counting them on his fingers." This is related by Abu Dawud and at-Tirmidhi, who called it *hassan sahih*.)

k) It is related from 'Ali that he and Fatimah were seeking a servant to make their work easier. The Prophet refused and said to her, "Shall I tell you of something better than what you have asked for?" They said, "Certainly." He said, "These are words that were taught to me by Gabriel, peace be upon him. Glorify Allah at the end of every prayer ten times, praise Him ten times and extol His greatness ten times. When you go to bed, glorify Allah thirty-three times, praise Him thirty-three times and extol His greatness thirty-four times." Said 'Ali, "By Allah, I never neglected to do what the Messenger of Allah taught us."

l) 'Abdurahman ibn Ghanim reported that the Messenger of Allah said, "Whoever says, 'There is no god but Allah, the One. There is no partner with Him. His is the dominon and His is the praise. In his hand is all the good. He gives life and death, and He has power over all things,' ten times after the sunrise and dawn prayer, before turning away and lifting his leg, will have written for him for each repetition ten good deeds, and will have erased for him ten evil deeds. He will also be raised ten degress, will be protected from every plot, and he will be protected from the outcast Satan. No sin will lead to his destruction except idolatry, and he will be the person with the best deeds, surpassed only by the one who does more and says more than what he has said." This is related by Ahmad and at-Tirmidhi, but without "In His hand is all the good."

m) Muslim ibn al-Harith reported that his father said, "The Messenger of Allah said to me, 'When you pray the morning prayer, before you talk to anyone say, 'O Allah, I seek your protection from the Hell-fire' seven times. If you should die on that day, Allah will record for you protection from the Hell-fire. When you pray the sunset prayer, say before you speak to anyone, 'O Allah, I ask Paradise of You. O Allah, I seek Your protection from the Hell-fire' seven times. If you die during that night, Allah will record for you protection from the Hell-fire." (Related by Ahmad and Abu Dawud.)

n) Al-Bukhari and at-Tirmidhi related that Sa'd ibn Abu Waqqas used to teach the following words to his children, "The Messenger of Allah would seek refuge at the end of every prayer (by saying), 'O Allah, I seek refuge in you from cowardice. I seek refuge in You from miserliness, I seek refuge in You from senility, and I seek refuge in You from the trials of this world, and I seek refuge in You from the torment of the grave."

o) Abu Hatim related that the Prophet would say, upon finishing his prayers, "O Allah, make my religion, which encompasses all of my affairs, good. O Allah, make this world of mine in which I live good. O Allah, I seek refuge in Your pleasure from Your anger. I seek refuge in Your pardoning from your vengeance. I seek refuge in You from You. None can withhold what You have conferred, no one can confer what You have withheld. No possesser of fortune can benefit from his fortune against you."

p) Abu Dawud and al-Hakim recorded that at the end of every prayer the Prophet would say, "O Allah, give me well-being in my body. O Allah, give me well-being in my hearing. O Allah, give me well-being in my seeing. O Allah, I seek refuge in You from disbelief and poverty. O Allah, I seek refuge in You from the torment of the grave. There is no god but You."

q) Ahmad, Abu Dawud and an-Nasa'i recorded, with a chain containing Dawud at-Tafawi who is a weak narrator, from Zaid ibn Arqam that the Prophet would say at the end of his prayers, "O Allah, our Lord, Lord of everything. I bear witness that You are the Lord, You are One, You have no partner. O Allah, Our Lord, Lord of everything. I bear witness that Muhammad is Your servant and Messenger. O Allah, our Lord, the Lord of everything. I bear witness that all of your worshippers are brethren. O Allah, our Lord, Lord of everything. Make me and my family sincere to you during every moment of this life and the Hereafter. O Sublime and Honorable One, listen and respond. Allah is the greatest of the greatest, the light of the heavens and the earth. Allah is the greatest of the greatest, Allah is sufficient for me and He is the most blessed guardian. Allah is the greatest of the greatest.[16]"

r) Ahmad, Ibn Shaibah and Ibn Majah recorded, with a chain that contains an unknown narrator, from Umm Salamah, that the Prophet would say after the *tasleem* of the morning prayer, "O Allah, I ask of You beneficial knowledge, sufficient provisions, and acceptable deeds."[17]

---

[16]I believe this should be Ibn Abu Shaibah. - J.Z.

[17]It is obvious that Sabiq (may Allah have mercy on him) himself was aware of the fact that *hadith* in (q) and (r) are weak. Therefore, it would have been best for him to have deleted these *hadith*, especially considering the fact that so many authentic *hadith* exist and suffice for this topic. - J.Z.

Appendix I

SUPPLICATIONS (DU'A)

‏«غفرانك» (p. 20)

‏«الحمد لله الذى أذهب عنى الأذى وعافانى» ، «الحمد لله الذى أذاقنى لذته ، وأبقى فى قوته ، وأذهب عنى أذاه» (p. 21)

‏«اللهم اغفر لى ذنبى ، ووسع لى فى دارى ، و بارك لى فى رزقى» (p. 33)

‏«اللهم إنى أعوذ برضاك من سخطك ، وأعوذ بمعافاتك من عقوبتك ، وأعوذ بك منك لا أحصى ثناء عليك أنت كما أثنيت على نفسك» (p. 38)

‏«اللهم أسلمت نفسى إليك ، ووجهت وجهى إليك ، وفوضت أمرى إليك ، وألجأت ظهرى إليك ، رغبة ورهبة إليك ، لا ملجأ ولا منجى منك إلا إليك ، اللهم آمنت بكتابك الذى أنزلت ، ونبيك الذى أرسلت» (p. 41)

‏«اللهم رب هذه الدعوة التامة ، والصلاة القائمة ، آت محمداً الوسيلة والفضيلة وابعثه مقاماً محموداً الذى وعدته» (p. 97)

‏«اللهم إن هذا إقبال ليلك ، وإدبار نهارك ، وأصوات دعاتك فاغفر لى» (p. 97)

‏«أقامها الله وأدامها» (p. 98)

‏«التحيات لله ، والصلوات ، والطيبات ، السلام عليك أيها النبى ورحمة الله و بركاته ، السلام

«علينا وعلى عباد الله الصالحين ، أشهد أن لا إله إلا الله ، وأشهد أن محمداً عبده ورسوله» (121 .p)

«التحيات المباركات ، الصلوات الطيبات لله ، السلام عليك أيها النبي ورحمة الله و بركاته ، السلام علينا وعلى عباد الله الصالحين ، أشهد أن لا إله إلا الله ، وأشهد أن محمداً عبده ورسوله» (p. 121)

«اللهم باعد بيني و بين خطاياي كما باعدت بين المشرق والمغرب ، اللهم نقني من خطاياي كما ينقى الثوب الأبيض من الدنس ، اللهم اغسلني من خطاياي بالثلج والماء والبرد» (128 .p)

«وجهت وجهي للذي فطر السموات والأرض حنيفاً مسلماً وما أنا من المشركين ، إن صلاتي ونسكي ومحياي ومماتي لله رب العالمين ، لا شريك له ، و بذلك أمرت وأنا من المسلمين: اللهم أنت الملك لا إله إلا أنت ، أنت ربي وأنا عبدك ، ظلمت نفسي واعترفت بذنبي فاغفر لي ذنوبي جميعاً ، إنه لا يغفر الذنوب إلا أنت ، واهدني لأحسن الأخلاق ، لا يهدي لأحسنها إلا أنت ، واصرف عني سيئها لا يصرف عني سيئها إلا أنت ، لبيك وسعديك ، والخير كله في يديك ، والشر ليس إليك ، وأنا بك وإليك تباركت وتعاليت ؛ أستغفرك وأتوب إليك» (p. 128)

«اللهم رب جبريل وميكائيل وإسرافيل ، فاطر السموات والأرض عالم الغيب والشهادة ، أنت تحكم بين عبادك فيما كانوا فيه يختلفون ، اهدني لما اختلف فيه من الحق بإذنك: إنك تهدي من تشاء إلى صراط مستقيم» (p. 129)

«اللهم لك ركعت ، و بك آمنت ، ولك أسلمت ، أنت ربي خشع سمعي و بصري ومخي وعظمي وعصبي وما استقلت به قدمي لله رب العالمين» (p. 143)

«سبوح قدوس رب الملائكة والروح» (p. 144)

«سبحان ذي الجبروت والملكوت والكبرياء والعظمة» (p. 144)

«سبحانك اللهم ربنا وبحمدك ، اللهم اغفر لي» (p. 144)

«ربنا لك الحمد حمداً كثيراً طيباً مباركاً فيه» (p. 145)

«سمع الله لمن حمده ربنا ولك الحمد ملء السموات والأرض وما بينهما ، وملء ما شئت من شيء بعد» (p. 145)

«اللهم لك الحمد ملء السماء وملء الأرض وملء ما شئت من شيء بعد: اللهم طهرني بالثلج والبرد والماء البارد. اللهم طهرني من الذنوب ونقني منها كما ينقى الثوب الأبيض من الوسخ» (p. 145)

«اللهم ربنا لك الحمد ملء السموات وملء الأرض وملء ما شئت من شيء بعد أهل الثناء والمجد أحق ما قال العبد ، وكلنا لك عبد: لا مانع لما أعطيت ، ولا معطى لما منعت ، ولا ينفع ذا الجد منك الجد» (p. 145)

«اللهم لك سجدت ، وبك آمنت ، ولك أسلمت ، سجد وجهى للذى خلقه فصوره فأحسن صوره ، فشق سمعه وبصره ، فتبارك الله أحسن الخالقين» (p. 148)

«اللهم اجعل فى قلبى نوراً ، وفى سمعى نوراً ، وفى بصرى نوراً ، وعن يمينى نوراً ، وعن يسارى نوراً ، وأمامى نوراً ، وخلفى نوراً ، وفوقى نوراً ، وتحتى نوراً ، واجعلنى نوراً» (p. 148)

«رب اعط نفسى تقواها ، وزكها ، أنت خير من زكاها ، أنت وليها ومولاها» (p. 149)

«اللهم اغفر لى ذنبى كله ، دقه وجله ، وأوله وآخره ، وعلانيته وسره» (p. 149)

«اللهم إنى أعوذ برضاك من سخطك ، وأعوذ بمعافاتك من عقوبتك ، وأعوذ بك منك لا أحصى ثناء عليك أنت كما أثنيت على نفسك» (p. 149)

«سبحانك اللهم وبحمدك ، لا إله إلا أنت» (p. 149)

«اللهم اغفر لى خطيئتى وجهلى ، وإسرافى فى أمرى ، وما أنت أعلم به منى. اللهم اغفر لى جدى وهزلى ، وخطئى ، وعمدى ، وكل ذلك عندى. اللهم اغفر لى ما قدمت وما أخرت ، وما أسررت وما أعلنت. أنت إلهى لا إله إلا أنت» (p. 149)

«اللهم صل على محمد وعلى آل محمد كما صليت على آل ابراهيم إنك حميد مجيد: اللهم بارك على محمد وعلى آل محمد كما باركت على آل ابراهيم إنك حميد مجيد» (p. 155)

«اللهم إنى أعوذ بك من عذاب جهنم ، ومن عذاب القبر ، ومن فتنة المحيا والممات ، ومن شر فتنة المسيخ الدجال» (p. 156)

«اللهم إنى أعوذ بك من عذاب القبر ، وأعوذ بك من فتنة الدجال ، وأعوذ بك من فتنة المحيا والممات: اللهم إنى أعوذ بك من المأثم والمغرم» (p. 156)

«اللهم اغفر لى ما قدمت وما أخرت ، وما أسررت وما أعلنت ، وما أسرفت وما أنت أعلم به منى ، أنت المقدم وأنت المؤخر: لا إله إلا أنت» (p. 156)

«اللهم إنى ظلمت نفسى ظلماً كثيراً ولا يغفر الذنوب إلا أنت فاغفر لى مغفرة من عندك وارحمنى إنك أنت الغفور الرحيم» (p.157)

«اللهم إنى أسألك يا الله الواحد الأحد الصمد الذى لم يلد ولم يولد ولم يكن له كفواً أحد ، أن تغفر لى ذنوبى إنك أنت الغفور الرحيم» (p. 157)

«اللـهم إنى أسألك الـثبـات فى الأمر، والعزيمة على الرشد، وأسألك شكر نعمتك، وحسن عبـادتك، وأسألك قلباً سليماً، ولساناً صادقاً، وأسألك من خيرما تعلم، وأعوذ بك من شرما تعلم، وأستغفرك لما تعلم» (p. 157)

«اللـهم ألف بين قلوبنا، وأصلح ذات بيننا، واهدنا سبل السلام ونجنا من الظلمات إلى النور، وجنبنا الـفـواحش ما ظهر منها وما بطن، و بارك لنا فى أسماعنا وأبصارنا وقلوبنا وأزواجنا وذريـاتـنـا وتب علينا إنك أنت التواب الرحيم، واجعلنا شاكرين لنعمتك، مثنين بها وقابليها وأتمها علينا» (p. 158)

«اللـهم إنى أسألك بأن لك الحمد لا إله إلا أنت المنان؛ بديع السموات والأرض يا ذا الجلال والإكرام يا حى يا قيوم إنى أسألك» (p. 158)

«اللـهم إنى أسألك من الخير كله ما علمت منه وما لم أعلم، وأعوذ بك من الشر كله ما علمت منه وما لم أعلم، اللهم إنى أسألك من خيرما سألك منه عبادك الصالحون، وأعوذ بك من شرما استعاذك منه عبادك الصالحون، ربنا آتنا فى الدنيا حسنة وفى الآخرة حسنة وقنا عذاب النار» (p. 158)

«لا إله إلا الله وحده لا شريك له، له الملك وله الحمد، وهوعلى كل شىء قدير، لا حول ولا قـوة إلا بـالله، ولا نعبد إلا إياه، أهل النعمة والفضل والثناء الحسن، لا إله إلا الله مخلصين له الدين ولو كره الكافرون» (p. 159)

«لا إله إلا الله وحده لا شريك له، له الملك وله الحمد وهوعلى كل شىء قدير» (p. 161)

«اللـهم أجرنى من النار، سبع مرات، فإنك إن مت من يومك كتب الله عز وجل لك جواراً من النـار، وإذا صليت المغرب فقل قبل أن تكلم أحداً من الناس: اللهم إنى أسألك الجنة: اللهم أجرنى من النار، سبع مرات، فإنك إن مت من ليلتك كتب الله عز وجل لك جواراً من النار» (p. 162)

«اللـهم إنى أعوذ بك من البخل، وأعوذ بك من الجبن، وأعوذ بك أن أرد إلى أرذل العمر، وأعوذ بك من فتنة الدنيا، وأعوذ بك من عذاب القبر» (p. 162)

«اللـهم أصلح لى دينى الذى هوعصمة أمرى، وأصلح دنياى التى جعلت فيها معاشى: اللهم إنى أعوذ برضاك من سخطك، وأعوذ بعفوك من نقمتك. وأعوذ بك منك، لا مانع لما أعطيت، ولا معطى لما منعت، ولا ينفع ذا الجد، منك الجد» (p. 163)

«اللـهم عافـنى فى بدنى، اللهم عافنى فى سمعى، اللهم عافنى فى بصرى. اللهم إنى أعوذ بك من الكفر والفقر، اللهم إنى أعوذ بك من عذاب القبر، لا إله إلا أنت» (p. 163)

«اللـهم ربنا ورب كل شىء أنا شهيد أنك الرب وحدك لا شريك لك، اللهم ربنا ورب كل شىء، أنا شهيد أن محمداً عبدك ورسولك: اللهم ربنا ورب كل شىء، أنا شهيد أن العباد

كلـهـم إخـوة: اللهـم ربنـا ورب كل شيء ، اجعلنى مخلصاً لك وأهلي فى كل ساعة من الدنيا والآخرة ، يـا ذا الجلال والإكرام ، اسـمـع واسـتـجـب ؛ الله الأكـبـر الأكبر ، نور السموات والأرض ، الله الأكبر الأكبر ، حسبى الله ونعم الوكيل. الله الأكبر الأكبر» (p. 163)

Appendix II

GLOSSARY

Mutawatir. This is a report of a large number of a narrators whose agreement upon a lie is inconceivable. This condition must be met in the entire chain from the origins of the report to the very end.

According to Muslim scholars, any *hadith* which has been transmitted by *tawatur* and whose reporters based their reports on direct, unambiguous, perception unmixed with rationalization would produce knowledge with certainty.

However, there is a difference of opinion about the required number of narrators for *mutawātir hadith*, ranging from four to several hundreds.

Mutawatir has been divided in two groups:

Mutawatir by words,

Mutawatir by meaning.

Only a few *ahadith* have been mentioned as *mutawātir* by words, meaning all the narrators used the same expression. However, *mutawātir* in the sense and meanings are numerous.

'Ahad. This is a report whose narrators do not reach anywhere near the number for *mutawātir*. It has been divided into many sub-divisions. Some of them are as under:

Al-Mashhur (well-known). This is a *hadith* transmitted by three or more transmitters in every stage.

Al-'Aziz. This is a *hadith* transmitted at least by two narrators in every generation.

Al-Gharib. This is a *hadith* with a single narrator either throughout its *isnād*—after the Companion—or in any stage.

Al-Fard is divided into two kinds:

Fard Mutlaq. This is a report transmitted by a single person.

Fard Nisbi has several meanings:

> i) None of the trustworthy transmitters narrated that particular *hadith* except that particular person (narrator); or others narrated it as well but they were not trustworthy.
>
> ii) None of the people of other regions transmitted that particular *hadith* except the scholars of that particular region.

Marfu'. This is a report consisting of a chain *(isnad)* that goes back to the Prophet, though it might be broken somewhere.

Musnad. In such reports the chain *(isnad)* of the *hadith* is uninterrupted and goes back to the Prophet.

Muttasil. This is a report whose chain is unbroken.

Mauquf. This is a report whose chain goes back to the Companion only.

Maqtu'. This is a report going back to the Successor only.

Mursal. This is a report of the Successor directly from the Prophet, upon whom be peace, without any other Companion in between.

Mu'allaq. This is a report in which one or more authorities from the beginning (from the author or book) is omitted.

Munqati'. This is a report with a single link missing somewhere in the middle, in one place or more.

Mu'dal. In this kind of report two continuous links are missing at one or more than one places.

Mu'an'an. In this kind of report while transmitting the material the term *'an* has been used, which is not explicit in describing the method of receiving the *hadith*.

Musalsal. This is a *hadith* in which all the narrators had a similar situation. For example, all of them used same terminology in narration such as *sami'tu.* Or all of them belong to one region or one occupation. Or they narrated the *hadith* with the same action, for example, all the narrators smiled while narrating a *hadith* because the Prophet had smiled while saying it.

Al-Hadith al-Qudsi. Some of the *hadith* are narrated by the Prophet, saying that Almighty Allah says so and so. These *hadith* are called *Hadith Qudsi.* The meaning of these *hadith* was revealed to the Prophet but he put them in his own expression. The Qur'an is the real word of Almighty Allah and the Prophet had only to receive it and then to teach it to the people, explain it and act accordingly. However, other *hadith* which are not called *Qudsi* cannot be said to be totally uninspired by Allah. The Prophet was never left unguided by Allah. Even his *ijtihadat* were sanctioned by Allah and in case of any lack of clarity it was corrected by Him. Therefore a good deal of *hadith* are *Qudsi* in a sense, but cannot be distinguished from the ones which belong to *ijtihadat of the Prophet.*

INDEX

Going To The Bathroom   16-20

www.ingramcontent.com/pod-product-compliance
Lightning Source LLC
Chambersburg PA
CBHW020853090426
42736CB00008B/352